ROUTLEDGE LIBRARY EDITIONS: GERMAN LITERATURE

Volume 29

GERMAN SONG AND ITS POETRY 1740–1900

GERMAN SONG AND ITS POETRY
1740–1900

J. W. SMEED

LONDON AND NEW YORK

First published in 1987 by Croom Helm Ltd

This edition first published in 2020
by Routledge
2 Park Square, Milton Park, Abingdon, Oxon OX14 4RN

and by Routledge
52 Vanderbilt Avenue, New York, NY 10017

Routledge is an imprint of the Taylor & Francis Group, an informa business

© 1987 J. W. Smeed

All rights reserved. No part of this book may be reprinted or reproduced or utilised in any form or by any electronic, mechanical, or other means, now known or hereafter invented, including photocopying and recording, or in any information storage or retrieval system, without permission in writing from the publishers.

Trademark notice: Product or corporate names may be trademarks or registered trademarks, and are used only for identification and explanation without intent to infringe.

British Library Cataloguing in Publication Data
A catalogue record for this book is available from the British Library

ISBN: 978-0-367-41588-4 (Set)
ISBN: 978-1-00-301460-7 (Set) (ebk)
ISBN: 978-0-367-85696-0 (Volume 29) (hbk)
ISBN: 978-0-367-85702-8 (Volume 29) (pbk)
ISBN: 978-1-00-301443-0 (Volume 29) (ebk)

Publisher's Note
The publisher has gone to great lengths to ensure the quality of this reprint but points out that some imperfections in the original copies may be apparent.

Disclaimer
The publisher has made every effort to trace copyright holders and would welcome correspondence from those they have been unable to trace.

German Song and its Poetry 1740-1900

J. W. Smeed

CROOM HELM
London • New York • Sydney

© 1987 J.W. Smeed
Croom Helm Ltd, Provident House, Burrell Row,
Beckenham, Kent BR3 1AT

Croom Helm Australia, 44-50 Waterloo Road,
North Ryde, 2113, New South Wales

Published in the USA by
Croom Helm
in association with Methuen, Inc.
29 West 35th Street
New York, NY 10001

British Library Cataloguing in Publication Data
Smeed, J.W.
   German song and its poetry, 1740-1900.
   1. Songs, German — History and criticism
   I. Title
   784.3′00943   ML2529
   ISBN 0-7099-4407-1

Library of Congress Cataloging-in-Publication Data
Smeed, J.W. (John William)
   German song and its poetry, 1740-1900.

   Bibliography: p.
   Includes index.
   1. Songs, German — 18th century — History and criticism.
2. Songs, German — 19th century — History and criticism.
3. German poetry — 18th century — History and criticism.
4. German poetry — 19th century — History and criticism.
5. Music and literature. I. Title.
ML2829.S55 1987   784.3′00943   87-6786
ISBN 0-7099-4407-1

Filmset by Mayhew Typesetting, Bristol, England
Printed and bound in Great Britain
by Billings & Sons Limited, Worcester.

Contents

Preface	vii
Abbreviations	ix
Introduction	xi
1. The Beginnings: 1740–80	1
2. 'Im Volkston'	20
3. Switzerland and Austria	38
4. Song-texts in the Latter Part of the Eighteenth Century	49
5. Composers and Performers	60
6. Simplicity as an Ideal	66
7. The New Adventurousness in the Late Eighteenth Century	82
8. The Eighteenth Century — A Summing-up	99
9. From the Turn of the Century to Schumann, Mendelssohn and Franz	103
10. The Development Towards Greater Complexity	128
11. Theories of Song and the Ideal of 'Hausmusik'	143
12. The Importance of Folksong	156
13. A General Assessment	173
14. Paths into the Twentieth Century	204
Select Bibliography	210
Original Versions of Passages Quoted in Translation	237
Index	239

Preface

My reasons for attempting a history of the *Lied* which pays more attention to the minor composers of the eighteenth and nineteenth centuries than has been customary are explained in the Introduction and, I hope, justified in the chapters that follow. In the case of major composers, I have assumed that to sketch briefly their contributions to the genre will be sufficient here, and that any reader who so desires can easily find more detailed treatments. By the same token, I have not quoted extensively from songs which are readily available in collected editions or modern reprints, but have used the available space to give as many extracts as possible from the works of forgotten composers. For the benefit of readers with little or no German, I quote in translation, giving the originals in an appendix, except where the meaning is self-explanatory in the context or where the point to be made is a stylistic one.

As will be seen, the relationship of German poets and composers to their native folk-tradition is an important theme. The Germans are fortunate in having a whole scale of words to express the nuances reaching from genuine folk art to sentimental pastiche. English seems less well equipped. To designate styles in music and poetry which resemble those of folk melody and folk poetry, which are free from archness or false sentiment and which achieved a measure of wide popularity akin to that of folksong proper, I have used the word 'folkish', in order to avoid the derogatory overtones of 'folksy'.

A book which deals with poetry and song will always be in danger of leaving one category of reader unsatisfied or puzzled. I have tried to handle the literary and cultural background in a way that will give musicians the essentials without boring students of literature unduly. Conversely, I felt it necessary to say something about the musical technicalities involved in song, but have tried to do so in such a way that the main point will be conveyed to non-specialists too. For the ultimate test of a song is what it reveals to the ear, not how much it yields on formal musical analysis. This applies particularly to harmony, where the effect of a progression may be electrifying, but would need a whole paragraph to explain it fully.

The need to cover so much ground in a medium-sized book

Preface

inevitably meant severe compression. I am acutely aware that more could profitably have been said on such topics as the early period of Berlin song (Gräfe, Ramler/Krause, etc.: what the Germans call the 'First Berlin School'), the *Singspiel* and its effect on song, Goethe's views on song and his relations with his early composers up to Reichardt and Zelter, and so on. Since all these topics have been competently dealt with elsewhere by greater experts than myself, I felt it sensible to make more space available for a fairly detailed discussion of the less familiar aspects of nineteenth-century song.

I would like to thank the Research Fund Committee of the University of Durham and particularly the Leverhulme Trust for generous grants which enabled me to hunt out material here and abroad, also the Publications Board of the University of Durham for a subvention. To the librarians and staff of the various institutions mentioned in the preamble to the Bibliography I owe a debt of gratitude for much help and advice. My warmest thanks are due to Dr Gudrun Busch and Dr Robert Provine for reading the manuscript and making many helpful suggestions, and to Waltraud Linder-Beroud of the *Deutsches Volksliedarchiv* in Freiburg for expert guidance on the subject of folk poetry.

J.W.S.
Durham

Abbreviations

AMZ = *Allgemeine Musikalische Zeitung* (All references are to columns, not pages.)

DDT = *Denkmäler deutscher Tonkunst*

DTÖ = *Denkmäler der Tonkunst in Österreich*

NrMZ = *Niederrheinische Musik-Zeitung*

NZfM = *Neue Zeitschrift für Musik*

Introduction

There is no doubt that words, when sung to a skilfully devised melody, have a much stronger effect upon us.
(Gottsched)

What is lyric poetry, if it is not sung?
(Wieland)

The *Lied*, as the term is generally used in England to designate a solo song with written-out keyboard accompaniment as opposed to a figured bass which the player was expected to realise,[1] began about the middle of the eighteenth century and quickly became very popular. As early as 1752, J.V. Görner could note proudly that song had become as fashionable in Germany as in other European countries,[2] and five years later Leyding talked in the Preface to his *Oden und Lieder* of an age rich in song ('die itzo liederreichen Zeiten'). As the vogue grew and spread, professionals and amateurs alike composed songs, which appeared in volumes by a single composer, in vocal anthologies or collections where they were combined with piano solos, as separate items in the musical journals and poetic almanacs of the day, and so on. One of these, the *Göttinger Musenalmanach* (1770–1804), is hugely important in any consideration of the joint development of German poetry and music, since most leading poets of the day contributed to it, and many of their poems appeared there in print for the first time together with a musical setting by a popular contemporary composer: C.P.E. Bach, Benda, F.W. Weis, Gluck or Reichardt.

Max Friedlaender, whose check-list in volume 1 of *Das deutsche Lied im 18. Jahrhundert* was first published in 1902, gives nearly eight hundred items appearing between 1736, when Sperontes brought out his *Singende Muse an der Pleisse*, and 1799. Fifty published collections are listed for 1799 alone (and Friedlaender, although tireless in his zeal as hunter and collector, is not exhaustive). By the first half of the nineteenth century, the torrent becomes a deluge: the editors of the *Allgemeine Musikalische Zeitung* declare themselves unable to review anything but a tiny proportion of the masses of newly composed songs which land on their desks (103 items in the space of two months during 1839). 'Has there ever been an age more prolific in song?' G.W. Fink asks in

Introduction

1826. Twenty-two years later, an anonymous contributor reiterates the point, again seeing in the proliferation of song a cause for national pride ('Es ist etwas Schönes um die Begabung des deutschen Volkes für das Lied').[3]

The eighteenth century must have been an exciting time for the music-lover. Where the twentieth-century singer or accompanist finds much of his or her satisfaction in the discovery of works from the past, their eighteenth-century counterparts would have been eagerly seeking out the latest settings of contemporary poetry or awaiting the next issue of their favourite almanac in the confident expectation that it would include songs to brand-new poems by Klopstock, Voß or Stolberg. For the German middle classes of the eighteenth century, says L.L. Albertsen, the Lied was the most important element of daily cultural life.[4] The reasons for the sudden flourishing of song at this time are not far to seek. Leading German poets from Hagedorn on had consistently written large numbers of simple, eminently singable poems (simple in general structure, that is, however subtle in other respects). Such poems were often called *Lieder*, thus signalling that the poet expected them to be set to music. Hence titles like *Lieder mit Melodien*, common in eighteenth-century song-books, are not tautological: the composer is saying that he has supplied melodies to the Lieder written by the poet. The point is well illustrated by one of Goethe's letters to Tomasek, a composer whose songs he admired, in which he says that his 'Lieder' become complete only when realised in song by the composer.[5] The usage will persist through the nineteenth century, with Heine's *Buch der Lieder* (first published in 1827) as the most famous example. In fact, one can say that most great German poets, from the middle of the eighteenth century up to Mörike a century later, wrote at least a significant minority of poems in a formally uncomplicated, 'songlike' style, inviting the composer to step in and set them to music. If we examine the poetry of the Lied, we find an unexpectedly high proportion of good or very good texts. There is a marked contrast with English song from Purcell on, where good composers often squandered their talents on — not to put too fine a point on it — trash. The process in Germany came to resemble a game of leap-frog, with poets encouraged by composers and being encouraged by them in turn, both satisfying and strengthening a demand for domestic song among amateur music-lovers, whose taste in poetry and music was thereby further refined, so that the demand for good songs grew.

Introduction

To study the Lied is to discover vast quantities of virtually unknown material. Even in Germany, the majority of eighteenth-century song-composers are unknown except to a few specialists. Many hundreds of minor nineteenth-century composers are not even names today. In German-speaking countries and America some attention has been paid to at least a few of the minor figures, but in English song-criticism one sometimes looks in vain for any indication that there *were* minor figures. Thus M.J.E. Brown, writing on Mozart's songs, sees the German Lied as created by Schubert and its history as summed up by the four names: Schubert, Schumann, Brahms and Wolf. Arthur Hutchings regards Schubert as the 'father' of the Lied, virtually without predecessors.[6] This is not only an historical oversimplification, but unfair to many forgotten composers who wrote extremely beautiful songs. It is the thought of these neglected masterpieces, as well as a desire to set the historical record straight, that prompts me to attempt this account. If I have concentrated on settings of famous poems — especially when discussing the period from 1800 onwards, this is because I have discovered that it is with the best poetic material that minor composers are most likely to transcend their technical and imaginative limitations. On the whole, it takes a great composer to make much of a trivial text.

Most of the songs to which I shall be referring are difficult to obtain, unless one searches in the big libraries and archives. There are twentieth-century editions of some older composers (including C.P.E. Bach, Gluck, Görner, Reichardt, Schulz, Telemann and Zelter), a facsimile edition or two (Zumsteeg) and a handful of modern anthologies (see Bibliography). But this is a drop in the ocean, and even here the editor will sometimes falsify the original by thickening the piano part, by altering the texts or in some other way. As far as famous composers are concerned, there are of course readily available modern editions of the songs, and shelves of critical and analytical studies devoted to them. Since I cannot hope to add anything substantial to what has already been written on, say, Schubert or Schumann, I have contented myself with placing them and the other leading song-composers in their historical context, defining as briefly as possible their particular contributions to the development of the genre.

Many composers enjoyed exaggerated fame in their day: Annaliese Landau recalls Conradin Kreutzer's high reputation during his lifetime and for a few decades after his death[7]; in the tenth edition of his *Musikalisches Conversations-Lexicon*, published in

Introduction

Leipzig in 1877, Julius Schuberth applies adjectives like 'great' and 'significant' to Anton Rubinstein, devoting approximately twice as much space to him as to Chopin! But who performs Rubinstein and Kreutzer today? If they were to receive due respect as workmanlike *petits maîtres* and their best songs given an airing from time to time, justice would be done; as it is, they have had the misfortune to plummet from undeserved adulation to equally undeserved neglect.

Since any song is in some way or other an interpretation of the poem, I have tried to give equal weight to the poetry and the music. And since the Germans seem more given to theorising than other peoples, it has seemed necessary to summarise the main theories of song, in order to show the links — and, in some areas, the lack of accord — between theory and practice. In addition, I have endeavoured to give some idea of how the Lied, at the various stages of its development, relates to German culture in general.

Titles of songs are often confusing. Hölty's 'Dein Silber schien/durch Eichengrün' appears variously as 'Klage' and 'An den Mond'; Mignon's songs may be given under their first line, or simply be entitled 'Mignon' or 'Aus Wilhelm Meisters Lehrjahren'; Mörike's beautiful and much set 'Das verlassene Mägdlein' is headed 'Am Feuer' in Ehlert's setting. One and the same song may be called 'Klärchens Lied', 'Freudvoll und leidvoll' or 'Die Liebe' in different song-books. To avoid confusion, I have given both the title and the first line wherever doubt could arise.

Notes

1. German usage is much broader.
2. *Sammlung Neuer Oden und Lieder*, iii, Hamburg, 1752, Vorrede. He is thinking particularly of the *chanson* in France.
3. *AMZ*, xxviii, 56 and 1, 778f.
4. 'Goethes Lieder und andere Lieder', in *Deutsche Literatur zur Zeit der Klassik*, edited by K.O. Conrady, Reclam, 1977, p. 175.
5. Letter of 18 July 1820: 'als der Tonkünstler [die Lieder] auch in die Einheit seines Gefühls nochmals [hat] aufnehmen wollen.'
6. Brown, 'Mozart's songs for voice and piano', in *The Music Review*, xvii (1956), 19; Hutchings, *Schubert*, London, 1964, p. 156.
7. *Das einstimmige Kunstlied Conradin Kreutzers*, Leipzig, 1930, pp. 24f. As examples of composers lavishly praised in their day and quite neglected since, one could mention Carl Banck (1804–89) and J. Dessauer (1794–1876).

1
The Beginnings: 1740–80

As I have said, it seems reasonable to date the beginnings of the Lied as we know it from about the 1740s although continuo-song had flourished in Germany for a full century before that. These continuo-songs consisted of the vocal melody plus a bass-line, usually figured, which the player was expected to realise on his instrument (harpsichord, organ, lute and so on: the title-pages and prefaces often give a wide choice of possibilities). The songs were usually strophic and often very simple, direct and fresh in style,[1] so that it is tempting to see them as the natural forerunners of the Lied. But a more elaborate virtuoso style, more commonly associated with cantata and opera, also occasionally invaded these songs, sometimes in such a way that works of a single composer may vary between the utterly simple and the very ornate. Here is part of Heinrich Albert's setting of Simon Dach's 'Herbstlied' (Autumn Song):[2]

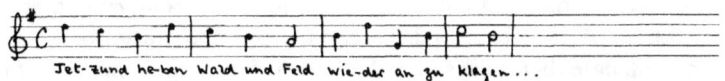

That tune points back to the simple folk-melodies woven by sixteenth-century composers into their polyphonic works, and is at the same time an oddly exact anticipation of the tone to be adopted by J.A.P. Schulz and his imitators when, over a century after Albert, they attempted to reintroduce the style of such folk melodies into their songs. But here is an extract from another piece in the same collection by Albert (iii, 14):

The Beginnings: 1740-80

If we look at the poems it seems no coincidence that Dach's unaffected 'Herbstlied' has a close affinity with the many German folk poems which bewail the passing of summer, while the text of the second extract quoted (also by Dach) is wholly in thrall to the Baroque style, being full of hyperbole, metaphor, apostrophisation and all the tricks of rhetoric. That is to say, the simpler melodic style is most often to be found in combination with a type of verse recognisably close to the German folk tradition, while florid Italianate vocal writing is more likely in settings of mannered Baroque texts which clearly show the invasion of German poetry by classical, Italian and French influences. Study of the texts of seventeenth and early eighteenth-century continuo-song shows the coexistence of simple and homely native strains (pseudo-folksong, versified proverbial wisdom) and Baroque extravaganzas in which half the pantheon is invoked to support the lover's pleas. It is the simple songs drawing on a native poetic tradition which we may justifiably regard as the true predecessors of the Lied.

Sperontes's collection *Singende Muse an der Pleisse* (4 parts, 1736-45)[3] was to prove, if not precisely a forerunner, at least something of a challenge to later song-composers. For Sperontes (J.S. Scholze) did not, as we today would automatically expect, start with the texts and devise suitable melodies for them; in the great majority of cases he took existing instrumental dances and other pieces and fitted poems to these readymade tunes. (This process is called *Liedparodie* by the Germans.) The texts are mainly Sperontes's own, with a minority by the Silesian poet, J.C. Günther. Delightful as the *music* often is, Sperontes's shortcomings as a maker of songs (one can hardly say 'song-composer') are obvious: the words take second place and must somehow accommodate themselves to melodies which owe their existence to musical logic and (often) the exigencies of dance. The matching of words and music has the character of a lottery. Here are two extracts, both involving odes to peace and solitude. The first happens to fit the elegant slow aria very well; the second is at odds with its jaunty polonaise tune (Sperontes had a fatal liking for this particular dance-form):

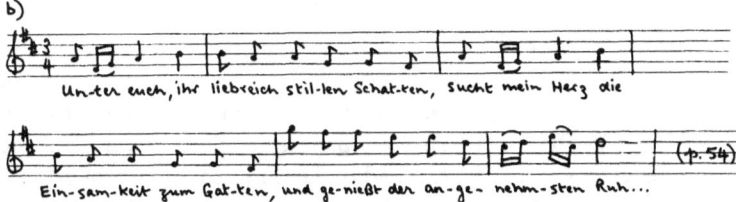

(Note how the phrase 'and enjoys the most pleasant peace' is approached via an upwards leap of a minor ninth!)

Whether musical and poetic declamation accord with each other seems purely accidental. In the following passage, 'schmal' and 'Brücke' fit the accents of the tune well, but impossible weight is laid (twice!) on the indefinite article. A composer who took the text as his starting point would never, if he knew his job, be guilty of such resoundingly false accentuation:

The popularity of the *Singende Muse* is, however, well attested and not difficult to understand. It offered fairly simple songs well suited to domestic music-making in a period when most composers were cultivating the florid style of opera and cantata, a period in which the technically less demanding type of continuo-song was falling out of fashion. But it does not need much historical hindsight to perceive that Sperontes's method of 'parody' was a false start as far as the Lied was concerned. So it comes as no surprise to find song-composers of the 1740s and 50s reacting vigorously against this method and insisting that they, unlike Sperontes, had not put the cart before the horse. 'I have suited my tunes to the poems, according to their titles and contents', says Görner in 1752. Similarly, C.G. Krause a year later sees song as a collaboration between poet and composer in which, however, the poet leads and the composer must follow. C.F. Endter, writing in 1757, is yet more emphatic: 'I regard it as an inviolable law that the musical expression should agree as completely as possible with the sentiments of the poem which is to be set to music.'[4]

No account of any aspect of life in eighteenth-century Germany can afford to underrate the importance of middle-class values and culture. The growing prosperity of the middle classes, especially the merchants in the important trading cities, led to a new confidence and self-assertiveness. This found its expression in the countless imitations of *The Tatler* and *The Spectator* which began to appear, from the second decade of the century onwards, in Hamburg and other cities. Called *moralische Wochenschriften* (moral weeklies) by the Germans, these papers extolled the values of the middle-class way of life, claimed that the merchant or professional man was at least as worthy and useful to society as the aristocrat and propounded a somewhat utilitarian philosophy of life, which praised reasonableness, virtue, moderation, a pious and philanthropic existence within a framework of solid but unpretentious prosperity, etc. In this rather comfortable view, professional or business success, the approbation of one's fellow-men and of God, moral integrity and a judicious pursuit of pleasure all coexisted happily. Music-making was very much a part of the innocent and convivial domestic culture of the prosperous middle classes, so that a demand for printed music, both instrumental and vocal, grew rapidly. Side by side with the collections of easy keyboard music, we find increasing numbers of songs: settings of German texts, predominantly secular and light in tone, well within the technical compass of the amateur performers. (The precise way in which the poetry of these songs reflected the values of the largely middle-class consumers will be discussed later.)

Opposition to the florid and often Italianate style of opera and cantata was strong. J.G. Gottsched, the most influential writer on aesthetics in the mid-eighteenth century, made merry at the ornate and 'unnatural' style reigning in the operas and cantatas of his day (*Versuch einer Critischen Dichtkunst*, ii, 3–4). He and his sympathisers disliked virtuoso display with its trills and scales, and rejected the melismatic attitude towards word-setting that could devote twenty bars of music to a single phrase. They detested the sort of mannerist lingering on key words ('rise', 'fall', 'sigh', etc.) which had played such an important part in Western European vocal music from the late Renaissance on. Attacks on the florid manner are common in theoretical works, in the prefaces to collections of song and, to a lesser extent, in the moral weeklies. If such complaints continue to be made into the early 1780s, this merely shows that some German song-composers were slow to learn this particular lesson, especially in regard to ornamentation (see below).

The opposition was not merely on aesthetic grounds; it was undoubtedly coloured by patriotic resentment, dislike of the many foreign virtuosi hired by the courts, part of a general distrust of foreign affectations and fashions. To mock a fashionable castrato

The Beginnings: 1740–80

who buried the vocal line under trills and conceits (and sang in a language incomprehensible to most Germans anyhow) was part and parcel of a more general attack, closely linked to all the polemical contrasts made in the moral weeklies between a solid and unpretentious *German* way of life and the posturings of courtiers and dandies who preferred French to German and prided themselves on following the latest French and Italian fashions.

Hence, the new school of song, together with the *Singspiel* (ballad-opera) with its catchy songs to German texts, was in one important way Germany's answer to foreign vogues. We have already heard Görner taking pride in the fact that Germany was belatedly catching up on other countries in the matter of song. Similarly, Löwen's ode 'An die Deutschen', set to music by Marpurg and included by him in volume ii of the *Berlinische Oden und Lieder* (1759), urges the Germans to prize their own poets and composers and not to over-praise 'welsche Triller' (*welsch* = Italian). The anonymous compiler of the *Musikalisches Handbuch* of 1782, a sort of critical lexicon of contemporary musicians, virtually takes 'German' as a yardstick of worth, stressing the 'German-ness' of C.P.E. Bach's melodies and praising Gluck for having purified music from foreign dross. The parallel with some of the moral weeklies, where it is axiomatically assumed that 'German' = good, while 'foreign' = showy, untrustworthy, immoral, etc., is quite clear; the general point has simply been applied to the musical sphere. Those who think of the nineteenth century as the heyday of nationalistic fervour in music may find this surprising, but to the student of eighteenth-century Germany who finds evidence of the Germans' resentment of foreign cultural domination at every turn, it will seem natural enough.

As we listen to 'Die Forelle' or Schumann's 'Nußbaum', we might be tempted to think of the Lied as something natural and spontaneous, needing no theoretical underpinning. But in the eighteenth century, treatises and essays which sought to explain the function, possibilities and limits of song seem almost as common as the songs themselves. If we find this puzzling, says Gudrun Busch, we should bear in mind the strong Rationalistic and speculative tendencies of the German Enlightenment together with the fact that the Lied was still a comparative novelty.[5] In the middle of the century there gradually grew up around the genre a system of what Busch calls 'musical rhetoric'. To discuss this in detail would call for a book of its own; in the following few pages I will try to sum up eighteenth-century theories of music as they affect song, and show how they influenced at least the general attitude of song-composers to their craft.

At the root of these theories is a constant appeal to 'nature'. Unfortunately, *Natur* was one of the most used but vaguest words in eighteenth-century Germany. To begin with, it was used to suggest that the basic elements of music did not need to be invented by man, but already existed in nature, so that a capacity to respond to music was something innate. Song, particularly, was seen as natural: a primitive and instinctive mode of expression, more direct in its appeal than instrumental music. Hence, composers and performers alike must cultivate 'natural' strains and not obscure or destroy them by 'art'. We have already encountered one form taken by this view: the opposition to florid (= 'unnatural') styles of vocal writing. E.C. Dressler (1774) distinguishes between virtuosity, which merely amazes the hearer, and a natural style, which moves him. Examples of this sort of distinction could be multiplied almost indefinitely. The danger is, of course, that 'nature' comes to be used as a blanket term of approval; once you have praised a composer for being natural or condemned him for being the opposite, you need elaborate no further. (The anonymous compiler of the 1782 *Musikalisches Handbuch* is much given to this practice in his critical judgements.) Many composers seem confident that a reference to 'die Natur' or 'das Natürliche' in the title or preface to a book of songs will automatically commend it to the public. The terms 'nature' and 'art' are bandied about everywhere, as when Johann Mattheson notes that too much art obscures the beauty of nature, or F.G. Fleischer says that his aim was to combine art with nature in his songs.[6] Although modern commentators on eighteenth-century aesthetics (musical and otherwise) agree that 'nature' was a very woolly concept, one can perhaps summarise eighteenth-century notions roughly as follows: song proceeded from a natural impulse and was able to speak to us directly and forcefully. The composer's task was to discipline and give form to this primitive gift through his art, without ever allowing melodic freshness and directness to be eclipsed by artificiality.

In addition, we find the concept of nature applied to song in a more specific way: through an appeal to man's 'natural' feelings.[7] According to this line of reasoning, nature in its broadest sense necessarily includes all human thoughts, impulses, passions, etc. Music can 'imitate' these: that is, translate them into sound in such a way that the listener will recognise and share the emotions which the composer set out to express. So music is imitation of nature ('Nachahmung der Natur' and similar phrases constantly figure in these discussions), not in the naïve sense of echoing bird-song or conjuring up storms and rustling winds, but by virtue of its power to excite, calm, evoke, recall or otherwise communicate emotions. (This is a sphere in which many slight differences can be found among the various theorists; some see the role of music as mainly emotional, others stress its power to inspire or improve, yet others ascribe a cathartic role to it.) Over and above all this, Scheibe, Mizler and others insist on the pleasurable aspect of music.

Since the word most generally current in eighteenth-century formal usage to designate human passions and emotions was *Affekte*, the theory of music just hinted at was nearly always referred to as *die Affektenlehre* ('theory of the passions'). Although some French writings on music (notably by J.-J. Rousseau and Batteux) became well known in Germany, these did no more than reinforce theories already current; the Germans had already arrived at the notion of the Affektenlehre as a natural consequence and extension of the view that all art is essentially mimetic. Again, slight differences are to be found as between one theory and another, but all agree on the fundamental way in which music 'imitates nature'. The ultimate aim of music is to excite our emotions through tones and rhythms, says Johann Mattheson in 1739. Three years later, Mizler adds his aesthetic point: music must move and calm our passions while delighting the ear. Mizler goes on to say that the best compositions are those which most exactly express, or provide a parallel in sound to, human emotions.[8] J.J. Quantz, in his famous treaty on flute-playing (*Versuch einer Anweisung die flûte traversière zu spielen*, 1752), likens the effect of music to that produced by a skilful speaker; here Busch's point about musical rhetoric is exactly illustrated:

> Both in putting together what is to be presented and in presenting it, the speaker and the musician share the same basic intention: namely, to master the listener's hearts, to arouse or calm their passions and transport them now into this emotional state, now into that. (*Versuch*, xi, 1)

Quantz goes on to argue that the performer must not only perceive what the mood of the piece is, he must also partake of it during performance if he is to pass it on to his listeners (xi, 15). This view, which is certainly an oversimplification of what goes on in the musician's head and heart during performance, was widely accepted in the eighteenth century. The other main point of interest here is that Quantz goes on to warn against embellishments which interfere with the realisation of the mood. This is a point which many eighteenth-century song-composers, as well as instrumentalists, could profitably have taken to heart.

It is manifest that this general theory of music as mirror of the passions could easily be tailored for song. Any poem at all suitable for musical setting (philosophical poetry and certain other categories were ruled out) was thought of as expressing, or being permeated by, a ruling mood (*Hauptaffekt*).

The song-composer must express and communicate this mood, says C.G. Krause, making use of the limited means at his disposal. (The context makes it perfectly clear that Krause is not thinking of the limited possibilities of voice plus solo accompaniment as opposed to more elaborate combinations; he has the technical shortcomings of amateur performers in mind.) J.N. Forkel, in his *Musikalisch-kritische Bibliothek* (1778–9), goes into a little more detail:

> Music, as a language of the passions and feelings, has the duty to excite those feelings and sensations which accord with the notions and feelings sketched in the poem. Thereby music puts the listener into a state of mind which prepares him for the impressions which the poet wishes to urge on him, with the end of making the listener receptive to the poet's ideas.[9]

Statements-of-intent by eighteenth-century song-composers, in the prefaces to their published collections and elsewhere, constantly assure us that this was, indeed, their prime aim. Endter (1757) tells us that he has tried to reproduce as clearly as possible the ruling mood which can be sensed in each poem — 'der Hauptaffekt, der in jedem Liede vorzüglich gespüret wird'. The same point is made in very similar terms by J.G. Müthel (1759). F.A. Beck (1775) gives us a glimpse of the actual process of composition as governed by the Affektenlehre:

> I always strove to transport myself to the best of my ability into the mood required by the poet's imagination. I

The Beginnings: 1740–80

summoned up my modest knowledge of music, to unite the thoughts of the poet with pleasing and sympathetic music and never tired of correcting my work, until it seemed to me that the musical tones expressed the mood of the poetry.

The emotional chain linking the poet, through the composer, to the performer is made complete when J.F. Reichardt assures us that his mood had to match that expressed in the poem before he could set about putting it to music and that the singer will always do well to choose songs which accord with his or her mood at any given time. S.F. Brede, too, assumes an emotional rapport between performer and songs.[10] In both cases, that too easy assumption that you have to *feel* sad in order to sing a sad song well, similar to the notion put forward by Quantz regarding instrumental music, is evident. This idea gains force as the century progresses and as a mood of gentle melancholy and sensibility (*Empfindsamkeit*) comes more and more to dominate not only poetry, but artistic endeavour in general.

The Affektenlehre obviously has some validity and has equally obvious shortcomings. Above all, it assumes general agreement as to what the Hauptaffekt of any poem actually is. But a poem of any subtlety will draw quite widely differing responses from different people. Nevertheless, song-composers *must* proceed on the assumption that it is possible to devise musical correlatives to a given mood or emotion and that those who hear the music will respond accordingly. (Whether the musical device is in itself an expression of the emotion — as eighteenth-century theorists seemed to think — or whether the two things become associated and thus gradually equated with each other is, no doubt, a fascinating aesthetic and philosophical problem, but is of secondary importance in the present discussion.) Even where different settings of the one poem hint at somewhat different reactions to the text on the part of different composers, there usually turn out to be boundaries beyond which the composer strays only at the risk of alienating his hearers; one cannot readily imagine anyone much later than Sperontes matching an ode in praise of solitude to a cheerful polonaise tune.

As the foregoing summary will have shown, German musicologists were indefatigable theorists, and composers were quick to take up these theories, claiming in preface after preface, dedication after dedication, to have been guided by them, especially by the quest for 'nature' and the Affektenlehre. Many other aspects of the relationship between words and music were discussed in the eighteenth century: correct declamation and accentuation, correspondences between musical rhythms and poetic metres, problems bound up with strophic composition, the question of what kinds of poems could or could not be made into songs, and so on. Some of these matters will be returned to in due course; it is sufficient for the moment to note that they all flow from, and in some way depend on, the notion of the Affektenlehre. It will have emerged that theoretical and practical considerations are inextricably entwined. Acceptance of the Affektenlehre inevitably influenced the composer in his setting of a poem and also coloured the performance of the song that resulted. Evidence of how songs were performed in domestic music-making is naturally scanty and inconclusive. But there is abundant evidence which enables us to compare the composers' theory and practice. As we shall see presently when we come to examine some of the songs, theory and practice do not always coincide. But it must be remembered that it is a good deal easier to make phrases about the happy marriage of words and music, or of art and nature, about correct declamation or flowing, 'natural' melodies than it is to compose songs that consistently realise these ideals.

The first two decades in the history of the Lied saw the publication of several important collections, often bringing together the works of a dozen or so composers. One of the most celebrated and influential compilations was F.W. Marpurg's *Berlinische Oden und Lieder* (three parts, 1756–63), which included songs by Marpurg himself, Agricola, C.P.E. Bach, Graun, Kirnberger, Quantz and others. In addition of course, there were numerous smaller collections by individual composers. At first the texts were mainly light and playful: *Scherzlieder* and *scherzhafte Lieder* are labels commonly encountered. Marpurg's advance notice of the *Berlinische Oden und Lieder* talks of a light style of song, which fits the character of the poetry ('ein leichter und dem Charakter der Poesie zukommender Gesang'); Görner, in the Preface to Part iii of his *Sammlung neuer Oden und Lieder* (1752) says that he has aimed at a pleasing, charming, jesting, amorous, merry tone ('das Gefällige, das Reizende, das Scherzende, das Tändelnde, das Verliebte, das Lustige'). Titles throughout the 1750s constantly sound a note of innocent merriment and playfulness:

A.C. Kuntzen, *Lieder zum unschuldigen Zeitvertreib* (1748–56)
J.J.C. Bode, *Zärtliche und scherzhaffte Lieder* (1754)

The Beginnings: 1740–80

C.F. Endter, *Lieder zum Scherz and Zeitvertreib* (1757)
A.B.V. Herbing, *Musicalische Belustigungen* (1758)

The songs included in Marpurg's *Historisch-kritische Beiträge* (1754 ff) are *all* headed 'Scherzlieder' and are evidently intended as lollipops in an otherwise serious journal. More earnest texts are not wholly lacking in these early decades, but tend to appear as independent, specialised collections under such titles as *Geistliche Lieder, Moralische Lieder* or *Freymaurer-Lieder*. However, the lighter and more playful poems easily predominate.

The poet most often set to music in this period was Friedrich von Hagedorn (1708–54), a writer of great elegance and lightness of touch, whose graceful verse was strongly influenced by Classical and French models. He cites the authority of Horace in claiming his right to sing of the pleasures of wine and youth and, in fact, was widely alluded to in his day as 'our German Horace'.

The type of poems written by Hagedorn and his many imitators are very much in the Arcadian/bucolic strain which has played so large a part in Western European poetry (and music) from the age of the Renaissance. Shepherds and shepherdesses, called Amintas, Belinda, Phyllis, Damon and so on, dance and flirt their way through an Arcadian never-never-land where the sun always shines and gentle zephyrs rustle the leaves of the spreading elm. There is open and constant indebtedness to Anacreon and Horace. The atmosphere is one of fairly harmless hedonism with many exhortations to enjoy life before it slips away. As in the madrigals of a century and a half earlier, the humble rural idyll is always represented as superior to the care-ridden life of the rich and powerful. Some texts suggest clearly that these collections were aimed not only at a domestic bourgeois public, but also at student circles. One song in Ramler/Krause's *Lieder der Deutschen* (ii, 1767, no. 23) contains a jocose reference to Leibniz's doctrine of monads; another (iii, 1768, no. 19) praises the life of idleness specifically from a student's point of view: leave poring over your dusty books. ('Bruder, laß das Buch voll Staub!/Willst du länger mit ihm wachen?') The *Berlinische Oden und Lieder* contain, in addition to the types of text already mentioned, a number of satirical songs, often with a refrain pointing the moral. These usually attack some fairly harmless type of folly or pretentiousness, often the 'folly' of not accepting and enjoying life. Although the poems themselves are always light in tone, there is some link here with more serious notions currently being

The Beginnings: 1740–80

expressed in the moral weeklies and works of popular and 'practical' philosophy, namely that it is perfectly right and proper to embrace a moderate degree of hedonism, provided that you neither damage your own constitution or moral well-being nor threaten the interests of others. This link[11] helps to explain the otherwise odd phenomenon that so many eminently respectable men, often occupying high professional positions, extolled kissing on grassy banks and urged their readers to drink deep while there was still time, that equally respectable composers eagerly set these mildly amoral texts to music and that the resultant songs were then sung in middle-class households of, no doubt, impeccable rectitude.

As far as the music is concerned, nearly all these early songs are set strophically — a logical consequence of the Affektenlehre, which encouraged the composer to search out the dominating mood of the poem, devise a melody to fit this and stick to it throughout all the stanzas. The songs are written in two staves, the upper one nearly always carrying the old soprano clef, then still in common usage. Not only were there only two staves; there were nearly always just two lines of music, a bass and an upper part in which the right hand of the accompaniment doubled the vocal line. This simple texture was so widespread and persistent that, even as late as 1782, J.W. Haßler finds it necessary to stipulate that the pianist should not double the voice part, but play only the *obbligato* line given in smaller type (*Clavier- und Singstücke*, i). To revert to the 1750s and 60s, however: where composers abandon the strict two-part form, it is usually to add a simple inner line, usually moving parallel to the voice at an interval of a third or a sixth.

Figured basses soon disappear almost entirely (except in Switzerland, where practically all aspects of song-writing remained profoundly conservative throughout the eighteenth century). The reasons can be surmised. It is probable that amateur accompanists were no longer thought of as able to cope technically. For, although the realisation of a figured bass was still an indispensable part of learning a keyboard instrument, it is, like transposition, a skill which quickly withers if not regularly practised. J.W. Hertel, in the Preface to his *Vier und zwanzig neue Oden und Lieder* of 1760, is explicit: he has written out some accompaniments more fully for the benefit of those who cannot realise a figured bass for themselves. Players with the necessary ability would, of course, have added inner parts to the accompaniment, even where no figures were given. A more interesting reason for

The Beginnings: 1740–80

not giving figured basses, and certainly one which we can now see as being of greater historical significance, is given by C.P.E. Bach in the Preface to his Gellert-settings (1758): 'I have added the necessary harmonies and ornaments to my melodies. In this way, I have not had to abandon them to the arbitrary whims of a pedantic figured bass-player.' Bach, that is, writes out his accompaniments in full because he fears insensitive realisation, not because he imagines that players will be technically unequal to the task. It is highly significant that this spirited opposition to the vestigial traces of the continuo-song comes from one of the first German song-composers to have seen the potential of an independent keyboard accompaniment.[12]

But in general, despite the decline of the figured bass, the general manner of writing among many of the less able composers remained in thrall to the near-defunct continuo style. In many songs, the left hand of the accompaniment is still virtually a figured bass without the figures. This persisted even into the late 1770s:

(G.W. Burmann, in *Monatliche Clavier-Unterhaltungen*, Berlin, 1779, p. 21)

Only very slowly, partly perhaps as a side-effect of the rise to popularity of the early pianos, did a freer style of keyboard writing in the song-accompaniments become widespread. Certainly up to 1770, the accompaniment, usually performed on a harpsichord or clavichord, played a minor role: not only did it double the vocal line, there were comparatively few solo preludes, interludes or postludes. (The move towards greater independence, obviously of incalculable importance in the history of the Lied, will be discussed below.) In the decades under discussion, the singer and player will most often have been one and the same person; the historical development, by which the keyboard part became both more independent of the voice and gradually more technically demanding must have been the main factor that turned song into a team effort.

Composers of the mid-eighteenth century constantly insist that their songs are intended to be easily singable for amateurs. Telemann, on the title-page of his *Oden* (1741), promises that they will place no strain on anyone's vocal cords; C.P.E. Bach tells the purchasers of his Cramer-settings (1774) that the melodies are tailored for the needs of musical amateurs ('Liebhaber, die in der Ausführung noch nicht stark sind'). One could multiply examples at will from the three decades that separate those two assurances. In certain obvious ways, the composers are speaking no more than plain truth. We no longer find scales and arpeggios which demand great technical expertise from the singer, nor extended phrases which test his or her breath-control, nor yet, except in a few isolated instances, the constant use of difficult leaps. But the statements quoted above should not lead one to expect an unproblematically lyrical style of vocal writing. All too many songs of the period are ungrateful for the voice in a variety of ways.

To begin with, despite the reaction against Sperontes's habit of tacking words on to ready-made instrumental pieces, many songs still seem more suited to instrumental performance than for singing. Even in the 1750s some composers still headed their songs with the name of the dance to which the piece was related: 'als Menuet', 'als Pollnisch', etc. Even where the composer does not give the game away in this manner, links with instrumental dance-music are often clear. (Marpurg's *Berlinische Oden und Lieder* offer many illustrations.)

To say that the vocal writing is instrumental in character does not necessarily imply a link with dance-forms, however: some songs exactly resemble slow airs from the keyboard suites of the day and would probably sound better as keyboard solos. From Fleischer's setting of Gleim's 'An den Schlaf':

A song by Graun, printed in Marpurg's *Historisch-kritische Beiträge* (i, 1755, p. 6) is like a brisk movement from a sonata for flute or oboe:

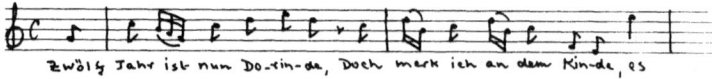

The Beginnings: 1740–80

(At the same time, the setting of 'schön' is not far from what Telemann had condemned as the 'ha-ha-ha, he-he-he' of operatic style!)

The most interesting collections, seen as a stage in the early history of the Lied, are those in which markedly instrumental writing coexists with a more truly songlike style. Telemann's *Oden* contains dance-forms not much different in their effect from similar pieces in Sperontes, however different Telemann's *procedure* as a composer might have been (see nos. 2, 17 and 20). But the collection also contains little gems written in an eminently singable style (see 'An den Schlaf': below, p. 35). Görner too veers between the instrumental and the songlike, with the stress on the latter. Since Görner is one of the liveliest and most individual of the early song-composers, a word on him might not come amiss. We have already heard of his preference for light and playful texts. In setting these, he offers few surprises in terms of harmony or modulation, but compensates through his liking for unexpected (irregular or asymmetrical) phrase-lengths, which give many of his songs a piquancy lacking in the more regular eight or sixteen-bar constructions of most of his contemporaries:

Another 'instrumental' feature in many of the early songs was the use of snap-rhythms, never easy to sing and often hopelessly at odds with the words. Yet other songs are over-ornamented, despite constant insistence from theorists and composers that too much embellishment makes it more difficult to communicate the mood of the poem. This is not to say that decoration as such was condemned, only excessive indulgence. (C.P.E. Bach makes a comparison with the use of spices.) The situation is complicated by the fact that the singer was not necessarily expected to perform all the ornaments which the keyboard player would put in as a matter of course. There are many songs which would certainly benefit from the omission of a mordant here and an *appoggiatura*

there, and there is no reason to doubt that singers used their discretion. But there are plenty of cases where the flourishes are inseparable from the song, where no minor simplification would be possible. Of the following examples from J.E. Bach's *Sammlung auserlesener Fabeln* (1749), the first sounds like an extract from one of J.S. Bach's cantatas, the second like a piece of operatic showmanship:

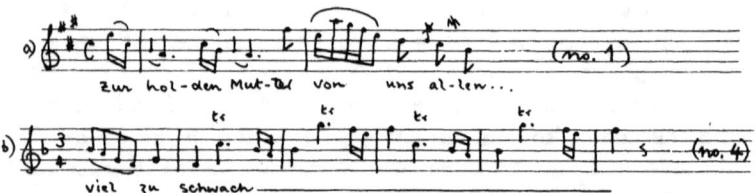

I do not wish to exaggerate the prominence of these 'unvocal' characteristics, but merely to state the incontrovertible fact that an era in which song-composers constantly insisted on the need for naturalness, ease and simplicity produced numbers of songs which were markedly instrumental in character or which contained ornaments and rhythmic figures which are very difficult to sing convincingly. How is one to account for the paradox that C.E. Rosenbaum (1760), who believed that song should be a 'copy of nature', was guilty of one affront against the true spirit of song after another: displeasingly jerky phrasing, to name just one? One cannot always put such things down to the composers' lack of ability, for some of the extracts just cited are by very able composers. The explanation may in part be bound up with the Affektenlehre. Contemporary theory insisted that the composer should express the general mood of the poem without bothering too much about details: 'Überhaupt, ich habe auf den ganzen, und nicht auf den einzeln [sic!] Ausdruck jeder Ode gesehen', says Görner in the Preface to Part iii of his *Sammlung* and many echoed this point. What was meant, of course, was that the Lied had no place for the mannered emphasis of individual words or for elaborate melisma. But an almost inevitable consequence was that composers devised tunes which were attractive in themselves, which corresponded to the Hauptaffekt of the poem, but which were neither particularly songlike nor particularly apt settings in terms of stress, declamation, *tessitura*, etc. Here is part of an anonymous setting (*Lieder, mit neuen Melodien*, Anspach, 1756, no. 11) of J.F.W. Zachariae's 'Du Echo meiner Klagen', in which the piano is praised for its ability to sympathise with the singer and

The Beginnings: 1740–80

echo his plaints. The elegaic tune (marked 'traurig' by the composer) fits the general mood well:

But there is an awful leap of an octave on to '*mei*ner', and to compound the situation a further wrongheaded emphasis on 'mein' two bars later. Zachariae's rapt testimony to the curative powers of the piano has come to sound rather testy, as if the singer were defending his claim on the instrument's sympathy against all comers ('*my* plaints, *my* strings'). Where theorists of song had made the obligatory point about the Hauptaffekt of the poem and had gone on to stress the need for scrupulously careful word-setting, many composers remembered the first and forgot the second, always to the detriment of the song.

There may be a more general reason for the shortcomings of many of these early songs: they are *early* songs. The genre was still in its infancy; moreover, many of the composers were active and eminent in other fields and wrote songs as a minor sideline. The emphasis placed on 'scherzhaft' may even have given the impression that composing songs was relaxation from more testing activities and may thus have led to a slightly slipshod set of operating criteria, however exacting the theories might sound. In addition, of course, many of the early song-composers were amateurs (see below, pp. 60f). Whatever the reasons, the fact remains that, apart from C.P.E. Bach, few seemed to be aware that a song, to be wholly successful, must represent at all points a musically *and* poetically satisfying realisation of the text. The theorists may have put the general notion of the Lied on a pedestal, but one does not always have the impression that the many composers of the *Sammlungen scherzhafter Lieder* practised what was preached.

A comparison with England may be instructive. Here there was an unbroken line of fresh and genuinely melodious song reaching from Tudor times to the ballad-operas of the eighteenth century. Art-song constantly refreshed and invigorated itself from folksong and other popular sources. The constrast with Germany where, for a century and a half, folksong and other forms of native popular music were looked down on by 'respectable' composers, is manifest. If one can make a general criticism regarding this first stage of the Lied, it would be that a spontaneous, genuinely songlike note is comparatively rare. The 1780s saw the first systematic and determined attempt to remedy this deficiency and to introduce the general style of German folksong into the Lied: the songs that resulted came to be known as 'Lieder im Volkston'.

Notes

1. For accounts of seventeenth-century German song, see W. Vetter, *Das frühdeutsche Lied*, 2 vols., Münster, 1928 and Richard Hinton Thomas, *Poetry and song in the German Baroque* . . ., Oxford, 1963.

2. Heinrich Albert, *Arien oder Melodeyen etlicher . . . Lieder*, 8 parts, Königsberg, 1640, iv, 13. Modern edition: *DDT*, i, 12-13.

3. Modern edition: *DDT*, i, 35-6. I am indebted to Edward Buhle's Introduction.

4. J.V. Görner, in the Preface to his *Sammlung neuer Oden and Lieder*, iii (1752); C.G. Krause, *Von der musikalischen Poesie*, 1753, iii, 48; C.F. Endter, in the Preface to his *Lieder zum Scherz und Zeitvertreib*, 1757.

5. Gudrun Busch, *C.Ph.E. Bach und seine Lieder*, Regensburg, 1957 (= *Kölner Beiträge zur Musikforschung*, xii), p. 257. Busch gives much information on eighteenth-century theories of music. Other accounts which I have found useful are: J. Birke, *Christian Wolffs Metaphysik und die zeitgenössische Literatur- und Musiktheorie* . . ., Berlin, 1966; Hugo Goldschmidt, *Die Musikästhetik des 18. Jahrhunderts*, Zurich and Leipzig, 1915; Walter Serauky, *Die musikalische Nachahmungsästhetik im Zeitraum von 1700 bis 1850*, Münster, 1929.

6. For Mattheson, see *Der Vollkommene Capellmeister*, Hamburg, 1739 (facsimile reprint, Bärenreiter, 1954), p. 135; for Fleischer, see the Preface to his *Oden und Lieder mit Melodien*, Brunswick and Hildesheim, 1756.

7. See particularly J.A. Scheibe, *Critischer Musikus*, Hamburg, 1737/40, *passim* and Lorenz Mizler, *Musikalische Bibliothek*, Leipzig, 1739/54, ii, 63f. Works by J.A. Hiller, C.G. Krause, F.W. Marpurg, J. Mattheson and C.D.F. Schubart have also been consulted.

8. Mattheson, *Capellmeister*, p. 127; Mizler, iii, 158.

9. For Krause, see his letter to Marpurg, printed in the latter's *Kritische Briefe über die Tonkunst*, i(Berlin), 1759, 169; for Forkel, see his *Musikalisch-kritische Bibliothek*, i (1778), 108 — facsimile reprint, Hildesheim, 1964. I have given a free translation of Forkel's pedantic and woolly German: original in the Appendix. The metaphor that music was the language of the passions had been a common trope in German musical theory for decades: cf Ramler/Krause, *Oden und Melodien*, i(1753), *Vorbericht*.

10. See Reichardt's 'Good advice instead of a preface' in Part 1 of his *Oden und Lieder* (1779) and the Preface to Brede's *Lieder und Gesänge*, 1786.

11. For more on this, see below, p. 56.

12. Busch (*C.Ph.E. Bach*, p. 312) sees this as one of his greatest contributions to the development of song. In this discussion, I have used

'figured bass' rather than 'continuo' advisedly. Where much eighteenth-century music with keyboard continuo dispensed with figures, the song-books, where still in the tradition of continuo-song, are nearly always still figured; this again suggests that the composers had little trust in the performers.

2
'Im Volkston'

Here, the most famous and influential work is J.A.P. Schulz's *Lieder im Volkston* (3 parts, 1782–90). It is not, of course, entirely without predecessors; even as early as Görner we can find a handful of songs possessing something of the directness and immediacy of folksong, although any pastiche of the strains of folksong was certainly far from Görner's mind. But, as we have seen, too many songs by Görner's contemporaries and immediate successors smacked of the study rather than of the open fields or even the informal drawing-room.

Before we examine what was meant by the 'Volkston', it is necessary to say something about the way in which the general notion of folk art suddenly became respectable a decade before Schulz published his songs, to show how musical and poetic styles and enthusiasms are interdependent. At the time when the early song-composers were busily setting Arcadian ditties, folk music and folk poetry — although undoubtedly enjoying a vigorous but largely unrecorded life — were ignored by most composers and poets. (Hagedorn was an honourable exception among the poets, but his admiration of English and Scottish folk balladry did not colour his own poetry.) The sudden ambition to aim at a Volkston in music must have been greatly stimulated and encouraged, if not exactly provoked, by the popularity enjoyed by folk poetry from about 1770 onwards.

The prime mover as far as poetry was concerned was J.G. Herder, whose essay 'Auszug aus einem Briefwechsel über Ossian und die Lieder alter Völker'[1] appeared in the collection *Von deutscher Art und Kunst* in 1773 and whose anthology of *Volkslieder*, later more emotively rechristened *Stimmen der Völker in Liedern*, first came out in 1778–9. On the basis of these two works, it is possible to sum up Herder's views on the nature of folk poetry and its relevance for contemporary poets.

For Herder, reacting against what he saw as the over-civilised and over-polished poetry of the day, 'cultivated', 'artifice' (*Künstelei*), 'reflection' and 'rules' are words of abuse; 'strong', 'wild' and even 'disjointed' (*abgebrochen*) words of praise. A Rousseauesque antithesis of 'nature' and 'civilisation' is applied to poetry: the more regular, correct and learned it is, the further it has removed itself from its true (primitive) sources. Hence, Herder mocks those who despise folk poetry because it is unpolished and technically 'incorrect', and instead prizes it for its spontaneity, its closeness to the daily reality of shared experiences, its concrete and dramatic terseness and its immediate rhythmic and melodic appeal (Herder uses *melodisch* to designate the musical values residing in the verse, not the tune to which it was sung.) He casts his net wide, drawing on and quoting folk poems and folk ballads from many different cultures — plus a good deal that has little in common with what we would today label folk poetry. If a poem seemed direct and unpolished, if it appeared to arise out of a fount of experience and feelings common to a whole people, if it was intriguingly old, if it gave the impression of long survival through popular acceptance — this was enough.

But it is not the scholarly correctness of Herder's views that concerns us here; it is their inspirational effect. It could even be argued that a more objective and sober account would have been less dynamic in its impact. Herder's work falls into three clearly defined, interrelated parts: his own activity as collector and champion of folk poetry, his advice to fellow-Germans to go into the field and seek out surviving examples of folksong for themselves and — most important in the long run — his insistence that contemporary poetry should draw sustenance and inspiration from the general style of folk poetry. Who will have the courage to collect and publish these old poems in defiance of conservatively minded critics? he asks in the 'Ossian' essay. The task must be carried out, for poets ignore this common source and common heritage at their peril; folk poems are 'material for poetry' (*Volkslieder*, part ii, Introduction). Goethe, while still a student in Strasbourg, was attracted to Herder's ideas, went out to hunt for surviving examples of folk poetry in Alsace, and imitated the strains of folk poems and folk ballads in his early poetry in all manner of ways. If Herder's work had had no other impact, this would be sufficient to ensure it immortality.

'Im Volkston'

G.A. Bürger shared Herder's views; the essay 'Herzensausguss über Volks-Poesie' of 1776 (Outpourings of the heart concerning folk poetry) is both a criticism of the contemporary literary scene, which Bürger saw as pedantic and dominated by foreign models, and a call on German poets to return for inspiration to their native folk poetry. A curious compartmentalisation will have been noted; Herder and Bürger rhapsodise over folk poetry *as poetry*, for its intrinsic vigour and beauty and for its potential as a practical stimulus for young poets. But — although Herder constantly refers to these poems as being *sung* by the people — he gives no melodies and does not really communicate the impression that a folk poem truly exists only in the singing. Hence, like Arnim and Brentano forty years later (see Chapter 12), he cites no melodies. In the decade which separates the Ossian essay from Schulz's *Lieder im Volkston*, it was left to C.F.D. Schubart to pay due attention to the tunes of Volkslieder. Schubart (1739–91) was one of the comparatively rare figures in the history of German song who were poet and composer in one. He was thus more qualified to see the interdependence of text and melody than was Herder. In an article — ostensibly a review of Johann André's *Scherzhafte und zärtliche Lieder* — published in the *Deutsche Chronik* of 9 January 1775,[2] he maintains that all too many songs of the last twenty years have been laboured and pedantic, and singles out Marpurg and Kirnberger for stricture. Yet 'we still have folksongs which are over a hundred years old — but how natural and light [in tone] they are! The notes seem to have come from the heart' (p. 23). Like Herder, Schubart uses 'naïve', 'simple' and 'unaffected' (*ungekünstelt*) as terms of praise. He complements Herder in that — where Herder had recommended the texts as source of inspiration for poets — he implies that composers might profitably be guided by the melodies. Later, in his *Ideen zu einer Ästhetik der Tonkunst*, Schubart makes this perfectly explicit, adding that it is very difficult to touch this particular chord and that copying external features of existing folk melodies is not enough.[3]

This is not the place for a detailed account of Schubart's role in the history of the Lied and in the literary movement known as the *Sturm und Drang*;[4] suffice it to say that in him the poet who admired folk poetry and the composer who advocated and cultivated the Volkston are combined. But in general, the pursuit and reclamation of the Volkslied proceeded in two related but fundamentally independent ways. Only in the nineteenth century were collections of folk poems with melodies to become commonplace, so that poets, musicians and scholars could see at a glance the fusion of words and music in the popular tradition. But for thirty years after Herder and twenty years after Schulz, champions of the poetry and composers who sought inspiration in the music tended to go their own ways. This undoubtedly helps to explain the curious fact that, for at least two decades after 'Lieder im Volkston' became the rage, there are very few settings of German folksong texts to be found, even among avowed followers of Schulz.

But there is a vitally important *indirect* link between the newly awakened interest in the Volkslied and the development of German song. Goethe is only the most famous among many poets who found inspiration in the style of folk poetry. This means that many hundreds of poems were written more or less in emulation of folksong: love-songs, nature poems (especially those in which the seasons are linked to stages in man's emotional life), narrative ballads, etc. The form, style and imagery were, on the whole, direct and homely: the typical German folksong stanza of four lines of three or four beats with a simple rhyme-pattern (usually ABAB) was much cultivated. The poetry of Goethe, Bürger, Hölty, Claudius, Voß, Stolberg and others offers countless examples. Such poems positively invite composers to set them in a simple and direct style — 'im Volkston', in fact, even before Schulz had popularised the phrase. For examples, one could take the many songs to texts by Hölty and Voß in the *Göttinger Musenalmanach* throughout the 1770s or the earliest settings of such Goethe lyrics as 'Heidenröslein', 'Mailied' and 'Jägers Abendlied'. But the main direct influence which led to a more 'folkish' style in German song undoubtedly came from Schulz. Since he and his immediate successors took many of their texts from Hölty, Bürger, Voß and the rest, the two lines of development merge.

Schulz, who lived from 1747 to 1800, discovered his style before the publication of the *Lieder im Volkston* and continued to compose in very similar vein until his death. But the *Lieder im Volkston*[5] make up his most important contribution to German song — and also contain a revealing theoretical statement in the Preface (*Vorbericht*) to the second edition of Part i (1785). I have chosen texts from the best poets, says Schulz, but only such as are suitable for the kind of song which I wish to write. Unlike many eighteenth-century composers who refer to the 'best German poets' in their prefaces, Schulz can make his claim with justification.

'Im Volkston'

His collection contains a large proportion of very good short lyrics by Voß, Stolberg, Claudius, Hölty and Bürger. There is a balance between serious and lighthearted texts, with many unaffected and extremely charming songs of love and nature and a pronounced Pietistic note in the more earnest poems. However intense some of the poems may be in emotional content, they nearly all have the structural and stylistic simplicity to which I referred above; this is what Schulz meant by saying that he chose only texts which were suited to his musical purposes. Turning to his music, Schulz says that he laboured to make his songs simple, unforced, easy to memorise. At this point, he uses a phrase which was to become famous: he has striven for 'the appearance of familiarity' ('der Schein des Bekannten'). What he means by this is that his tunes are meant to have the general characteristics of folk melodies without actually *being* folk melodies.[6] That his notion of 'familiarity' is related to the style of folksong is further stressed by his use, in the *Vorbericht*, of words like *Volkslied, Volkston* and *volksmäßig*. The last of these is very significant in its context: the composer says that his songs are intended to be 'mehr volksmäßig als kunstmäßig', near the 'natural' strains of popular melody, owing little to 'art'. With this statement-of-intent in mind, let us look at the songs with a view to seeing how the 'Schein des Bekannten' manifests itself.

The songs are, almost without exception, strophic, printed in two systems, with vocal line and bass, filled out from time to time with an inner part moving parallel to the voice in thirds or sixths, less often with a full chordal texture. There are few solo passages for the keyboard; the accompaniment is, on the whole, given an austerely subsidiary role. Schulz displays hardly any of the defects that had so often marred earlier German songs: there is no 'instrumental' writing, no trace of virtuosity, little in the way of embellishment at all. The *Vorbericht* had condemned 'useless ornaments' (unnütze Zierereyen) — and Schulz, unlike some composers, practised what he preached in this respect. The word-setting in the *Lieder im Volkston* can hardly be faulted. Harmonically, there are few surprises: chromatic passages or touches of minor colouring within a song in the major mode. And such unexpected passages are strictly reserved by the composer for points of emotional tension or drama. The majority of the songs are in a regular rhythm with symmetrical phrase-lengths, matching a similar regularity in the poetry. Schulz has a pronounced liking for 6/8 rhythms, so that the *Lieder im Volkston* contain many

'Im Volkston'

wistful little songs in a slow siciliano style:

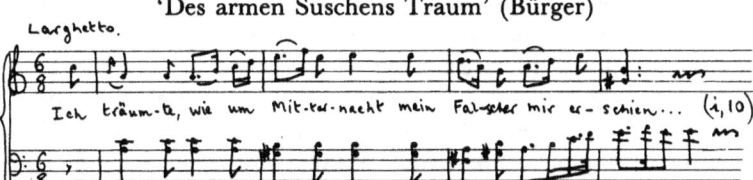

Within the chosen regular patterns, the slightest rhythmic variations are extraordinarily effective:

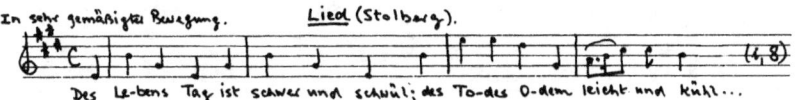

Schulz's characteristic melodies are deceptively simple, often moving stepwise or up and down a major or minor triad — music is here truly 'celebrating its elements', as Thomas Mann was to say much later and in a rather different context. Melismatic writing is on the whole confined to pairs of slurred notes. Vocal leaps of more than a third are used sparingly. Where they occur, they are usually at the beginning of a phrase: conventional leaps from the upbeat. More unexpected and expressive intervals occur only when the emotional intensity of the text demands it; the same restraint and judgement which we have already noted with regard to Schulz's rare departures from conventional harmonies applies here too. Bürger's 'Schwanenlied' (Swansong) is a good example. Schulz's setting of this expression of utterly hopeless love depends for its poignant effect very largely on falling intervals of the diminished fifth and the seventh, otherwise rare in Schulz:

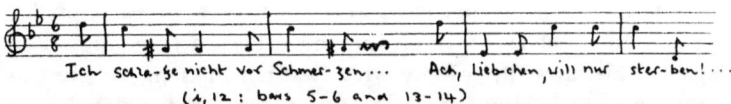

Equally uncharacteristic and equally effective is the slurred rise of a diminished seventh on the word 'arm' in Stolberg's 'Lied eines Unglücklichen' (i, 30) at the emotive phrase 'break, break, poor heart!' (Not so appropriate in the subsequent stanzas, however!)

It may be noted that, apart from these few exceptions which always owe their existence to the need for a particular effect, all the characteristics listed could equally well relate to actual German folk melodies. When one bears in mind Schubart's warning that it is difficult to achieve the Volkston without descending to mere copying and when one sees how fatally easy it was for some of Schulz's followers to slip into triviality (see below), one's respect for Schulz can only be heightened. His melodic instinct and sure taste allowed him to walk the tightrope between being inspired by popular melody and aping it, between the simple and the trivial, with barely a falter:

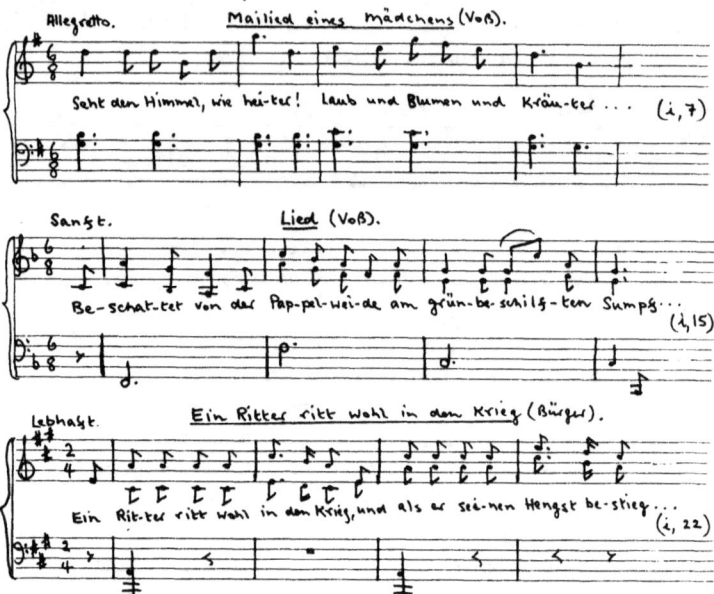

One's slightly uncertain first reaction to such songs — is that a real folksong or a very skilful imitation? — is in itself a justification of the phrase 'der Schein des Bekannten'. As in the third extract quoted, the bass line is often kept to an irreducible minimum and the upper parts move in parallel thirds or sixths, lending themselves to unaccompanied two-part singing. This again underlines the affinity with German folksong, where this practice was common, and many tunes seem either tailored to or owe their lasting popularity to the fact that they lend themselves to such primitive 'a capella' textures.

The distinction between 'der Schein des Bekannten' and 'das Bekannte' obviously implies a desire on Schulz's part to distance himself from certain aspects of folk music, presumably its occasional banalities and sentimentalities and the witless high

'Im Volkston'

spirits of the 'Hollahiaho' or 'Juchheisa' type of song. Even the most ardent champions of folk art distinguished between 'the people' and 'the mob' (*Pöbel*) and between folksongs and street songs (*Gassenmelodien*). In addition, no doubt, Schulz would have thought it beneath his dignity as a composer merely to tailor existing tunes to fit new poems. He would have seen in the best of German folk melodies lively and sometimes deeply emotive musical ideas expressed in quite simple and symmetrical musical structures admirably suited to the type of poem which most attracted him as composer. In his work we find a process of metamorphosis, whereby popular folk melodies or types of folk melody reappear in new guises, mysteriously transformed into the composer's private property, yet retaining echoes or distant memories of their popular source. This is truly 'der Schein des Bekannten'. We cannot, of course, say *exactly* which folk melodies inspired Schulz or in what precise form he would have known the traditional tunes. Very few folk melodies were recorded in the eighteenth century, so that our knowledge has to be based on older records (arrangements by sixteenth-century composers, etc.) or those made by nineteenth-century collectors. The tentative demonstration of the 'metamorphosis' of folk melodies which follows is based on comparison of Schulz tunes with folk melodies going back to the sixteenth century or earlier or with others which, while recorded in the early part of the nineteenth century, must have enjoyed wide circulation in the eighteenth. Despite the inevitable uncertainties and the rather conjectural nature of the exercise, such specific comparisons will, I believe, indicate the heritage of the *Lieder im Volkston* better than a verbal account of the German folksong idiom ever could.

My first example shows Schulz's indebtedness to a type of elegaic melody in 6/8 which is common in the German folk tradition:

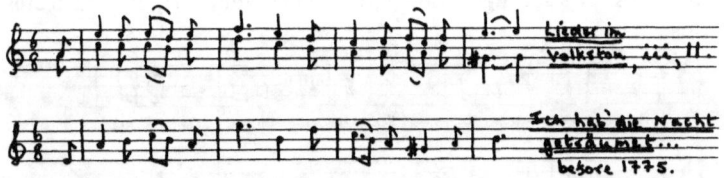

In the following song, an affinity to a folk melody popular since the sixteenth century becomes apparent if Schulz's tune is pruned of its modest melismatic touches:

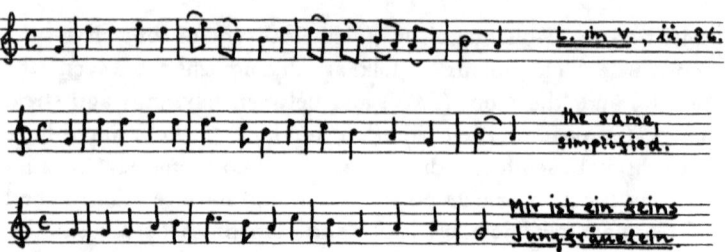

There are a number of similar cases in Schulz, slight elaborations of common folksong patterns (see, for instance, *Lieder im Volkston*, ii, 11 and the *Göttinger Musenalmanach*, 1802, p. 210). Finally, in Schulz's setting of Stolberg's 'Rundgesang', it may not be fanciful to postulate a recollection of an old and much loved spring song, which guided the composer's pen, if only unconsciously:

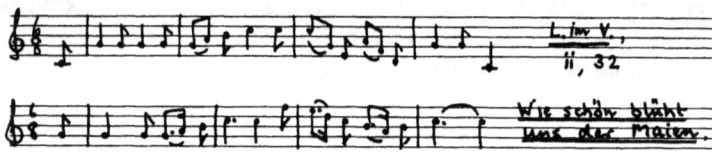

These examples will have shown, among other things, how the fundamentally regular and diatonic nature of so many German folk melodies made Schulz's task easier and helped to ensure the popularity of his songs. Everyone who sang or listened to the *Lieder im Volkston* will have known folk tunes similar to those just cited; hence Schulz's desire to create the 'Schein des Bekannten' will undoubtedly have been fulfilled.

We must return briefly to Schulz's careful distinction between a song which gives the illusion of familiarity and a familiar song ('Schein des Bekannten . . . das Bekannte'). His songs may be an affectionate and skilful pastiche of folk melody, but he is never straitjacketed by the technical and stylistic limitations of such melodies. His setting of Bürger's 'Liebeszauber' (i, 20) illustrates this:

An actual folk melody would hardly break into triplets in that fashion. But, having achieved the 'Schein des Bekannten' in the body of his song, Schulz feels free to indulge himself in that witty closing phrase.

The *Lieder im Volkston* became instantly popular and were much imitated. Reichardt praises Schulz in the essay 'An junge Künstler' (*Deutsches Kunstmagazin*, 1782); G.B. Flaschner (1789) talks of his 'excellent folksongs'. F.L.A. Kunzen, in the Preface to his *Weisen und lyrische Gesänge* of 1788, couples his tribute to Schulz with an appeal to 'mother Nature' and a distinction between 'der Schein des Bekannten' and 'das Bekannte' which exactly echoes Schulz. Typical of the 1780s is this extract from the Preface to J.G. Naumann's collection (1784): 'The times in which dazzling and forced styles found approval are past. Men who had a deeper feeling for the simple tones of nature quickly recognised those errors and took care to avoid the rocks of false taste.' (The opposition of 'false taste' to natural simplicity recalls Schubart and has its parallel in Herder's views on poetry.)

German song had, from the 1740s, been intended for amateurs although, as we have seen, earlier composers had not always been conspicuously successful in producing works that were easily singable and direct in their appeal. After Schulz, the notion of easily memorable and technically undemanding song became linked with that of the Volkston. Here is Flaschner again:

> In general I believe that so-called folksong [it is clear from the context that he means simple poetry written in a folkish style] must be set to music in a melodious way, for the very name shows that it is not intended for those with a knowledge of music as much as for people who, while not knowing music, like to sing . . .

It seems evident that Flaschner's ideal was a type of song which could be easily sung to its accompaniment in the drawing-room, but which could also be taken up for unaccompanied singing in the streets and fields, for he talks with evident pride of a song of his, 'Der Traum', which was rendered 'with fair correctness' by the common people ('das bald von den gemeinsten Leuten ziemlich richtig gesungen [wurde]'). Examination of the song shows that it is truly in the style of Schulz and would, indeed, have lent itself to unaccompanied singing, either solo or in two parts:

'Im Volkston'

The similarity to Schulz's setting of Bürger's *Ein Ritter ritt wohl* is very marked (see p. 26).

Having noted that it is a difficult thing to hit off, Schubart went on to equate the genuinely popular style with 'nature': the common people wanted 'Naturlaute', not elaborate melodies.[7] But Schulz and the other composers of 'Lieder im Volkston' were not trying to compose artificial folk tunes which could be released into the streets like balloons. Their aim was to seek inspiration in the 'Naturlaute' of folksong in the hope of producing a genuinely popular domestic song which might also find a wider, less musically educated public into the bargain. Flaschner's testimony, plus the broad and lasting popularity of some of Schulz's songs, show that their ambition was, to some extent at least, realised. Songs like Stolberg's 'An die Natur', Voß's 'Des Jahres letzte Stunde' and Claudius's 'Täglich zu singen' (all set by Schulz and included in the *Lieder im Volkston*) were reprinted in countless popular anthologies of song in the late eighteenth century and throughout the nineteenth, gradually achieving the status of honorary folksongs. (The Germans use the term *volkstümliches Lied*, to distinguish between, say, a Claudius poem as set by Schulz and an old folksong — *Volkslied* — where both poet and composer are unknown, although these pieces may well appear side by side in an anthology of song, both labelled 'Volkslied'.) The popularity of the three songs just mentioned depends equally on the poetry and the music. 'An die Natur' expresses the poet's veneration for nature simply but movingly in terms of mother-love; in 'Des Jahres letzte Stunde', the mixture of conviviality and solemnity would commend itself to the rather sentimental and ambivalent mood of a New Year's Eve gathering; 'Täglich zu singen' is a hymn of thanks, in which the poet expresses his joy in the natural universe and his contentment with a humble sufficiency. Meanwhile, Schulz's melodies almost add up to an implied definition of the Volkston:

'Im Volkston'

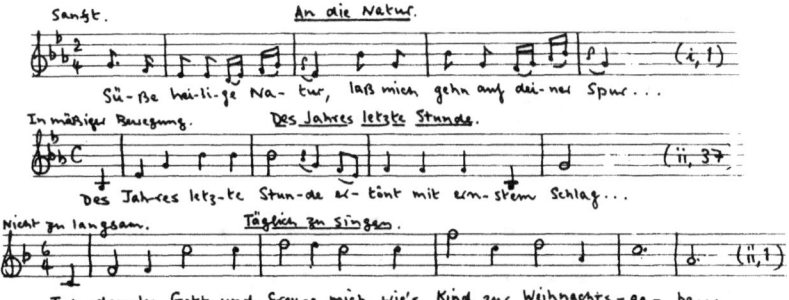

Examination of the works of Schulz's disciples and imitators confirms that — as Schubart warned — simplicity is difficult to achieve. It may be that imitation is the sincerest form of flattery, but lame copying of external features is the most pointless. The most imitable aspects of a man's style are often the least appealing. In his setting of G.K. Pfeffel's 'Der freie Mann' (which the poet himself styled 'ein Volkslied'), Kallenbach combines Schulz's liking for extrovert but rather vapid unison textures with a sequence of hackneyed block chords in a vein also encountered in the *Lieder im Volkston*. J.A. Hiller's setting of 'Urians Reise um die Welt' (*Letztes Opfer*, 1790, p. 2) is similar, the unison passages here suggesting the brash cheerfulness of a corporal exhorting the troops to sing and swing their arms as they march.

Even where the composer does not descend to the mere borrowing of formulae, we can see that the Volkston can easily degenerate into triviality in hands less able than Schulz's. Here is J.R. Berls, in his *Neue Volkslieder fürs Klavier* of 1797 (no. 4):

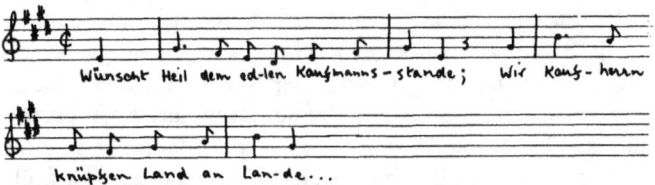

The title is interesting. Berls, a schoolmaster in Thüringen, was very active in the encouragement of music-making in the school where he taught. His collection contains poems newly written by himself and others, intended to be sung by the local people for their amusement and edification. The texts comprise a sort of miniature Book of Estates, praising the ruler and the merchant and describing the social usefulness of various trades and crafts, together with the practitioners' pride and self-respect. The notion of poetry for the people (Volks*lied*) is thus allied to that of music in the style of the people (Volks*ton*), however feeble the execution may be in both fields.

But many composers found genuine inspiration in Schulz. The following extracts[8] will speak for themselves:

Other composers who, in my opinion, successfully emulated Schulz include J.G. Keller (1782), Witthauer (1785), F.L.A. Kunzen (1788) and Andreas Romberg (1793). Romberg is one of a long line of composers to use 'Volkston' at the head of a song, where we might normally expect an indication of tempo or mood. The word, which started as the composer's definition of his ideal, has become an injunction (a rather vague one, it must be confessed) to the singer. Significantly, Goethe's 'Heidenröslein' and 'Der Fischer', two poems very obviously inspired by folk poem and folk ballad respectively, are given this heading by Romberg. A simple and direct style of song-writing, faintly reminiscent of folksong and sometimes still labelled 'im Volkston', will persist through the nineteenth century; we will encounter it in some of Schubert's settings of Hölty and Claudius, in his wonderful pastiche of a folk ballad, 'Der König in Thule', and in new compositions of folksong texts by hordes of minor composers.

It will have been noticed that the musical style implied by the label 'Volkston' did not by any means quickly and automatically come to be applied to actual folk poetry, although it usually went with a preference for poems which were structurally and metrically uncomplicated and which expressed a simple mood or told a simple story. Goethe, Bürger, Hölty, Claudius and Voß could all quite justifiably have echoed Schulz and said that their lyrics too had the 'Schein des Bekannten' which he strove for in music. But the true folk poems which appeared in song-collections up to the end of the century can almost be counted on the fingers.

'Im Volkston'

Following C.P.E. Bach, Christoph Rheineck set the 'Nonnenlied' ('S' ist kein verdrießlicher Lebe') and C.G. Hausius has a couple of folksong texts in his collection of 1794.[9] Why this paucity? Corona Schröter's choice of texts for her *Fünf und Zwanzig Lieder* (1786) may give a clue. Twelve of these are headed 'aus den Volcksliedern', meaning that they are taken from Herder's anthology. But only four are original German poems, and even here just one could qualify as a folk poem in any normally accepted sense of the word. The other eight texts are translations, mainly from the English and Scottish. The same thing can be said of the Herder-texts set by the early Viennese song-composers. The reasons are, I believe, twofold. Native folksong, where not simply dredged up out of childhood memories, would still, for most educated people, have been associated with peasants, wandering apprentices, craftsmen and manual workers (hence Dressler's derogatory 'Gassen-Melodien').[10] There had been no lack of opposition to the praise bestowed on the 'rough' songs of 'unlettered' people by Herder and Bürger. Reliable printed sources for genuine old German folk poetry were to remain very rare until the turn of the century. On the other hand, Herder's translation of poems and ballads from foreign cultures had an exotic fascination and had, moreover, acquired something of a literary stamp by virtue of *being* translations. Scottish and border ballads, particularly, were surrounded by a misty romantic aura and attracted many German and Austrian composers. The flood of songs based on *German* folk poetry came later, as a result of the second, more nationalistic stage in the rehabilitation of German folk poetry initiated by the Romantics after the turn of the century.

If folksong — directly and indirectly — was one potent influence on the development of the Lied, the chorale was another. Indeed, the sacred character of church music and the cheerfulness of folk melodies are, according to Goethe,[11] the two pivots around which all true music revolves. Whether or not this is true in general, it certainly applies to German culture, where the chorale enjoyed an unbroken tradition and affected all classes of people. One might expect the style of the chorale to influence settings of sacred texts only, and at first this is broadly true. Side by side with the collections of *Scherzhafte Lieder*, we find books of *Geistliche Lieder*, often intended for solo domestic singing, but in a marked hymnlike style. Some are written in a foursquare, block-chord manner and are virtually indistinguishable from hymns.

Other collections combine chordal pieces with what are more obviously solo songs. Yet other composers (especially in Switzerland) print a solo version with accompaniment on the left-hand page and extra vocal parts opposite. A collection that seems equally fitted to church and domestic use is Quantz's *Neue Kirchen-Melodien* of 1760. Here Quantz takes issue with composers who make impossible demands on the congregation and adds that he has wanted to set sacred texts (they are all by Gellert, in fact) in such a way that they could easily be sung by the whole congregation. The songs are all in two parts, vocal line and figured bass. While they certainly could be used in church services, it is just as easy to imagine them as domestic music for solo voice:

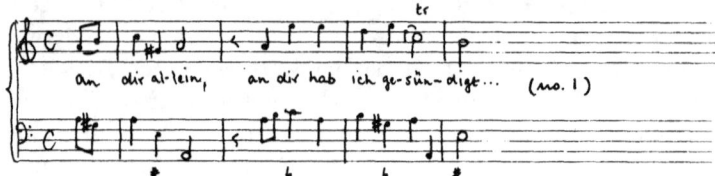

C.P.E. Bach's sacred songs range from quite straightforward choral textures to very elaborate, expressive and even daring short works. In the last quarter of the century we find several collections of sacred texts in which two types of piece (solo and choral) coexist and are intended to serve different purposes.[12] At the same time, we increasingly find a mixture of secular and sacred poems in the one song-book, with the latter inclining towards the musical style of the choral. F.G. Fleischer's *Sammlung größerer und kleinerer Singstücke* of 1788 is such a collection in which, it may be said, the setting of a meditation on death (Sturm's 'Betrachtung des Todes'), composed unmistakably in the style of a chorale, provides the only pleasing touch in an otherwise stiff and pedantic volume:

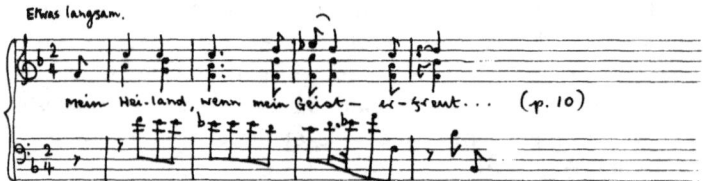

So, by about the third quarter of the century the chorale had established itself firmly within the growing tradition of the Lied as one of a number of models or possibilities. It gradually came to

'Im Volkston'

be used not only for sacred texts but for the more solemn type of secular or semi-secular poem: odes to friendship or the more exalted forms of love, to peace, nature, the fatherland, etc. Here are two representative examples:

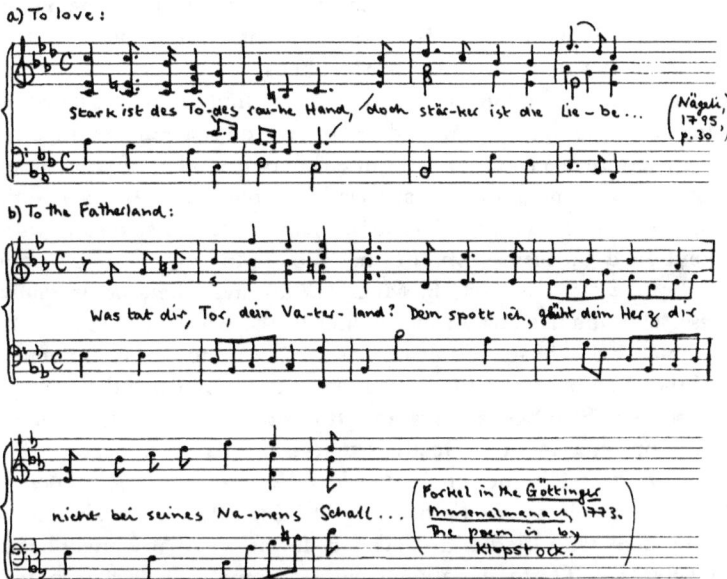

The following song by Telemann, to a poem of Hagedorn's celebrating sleep ('An den Schlaf'), is stylistically very close to the chorale settings with figured bass included by Krebs in his *Klavierübung* of the same decade:[13]

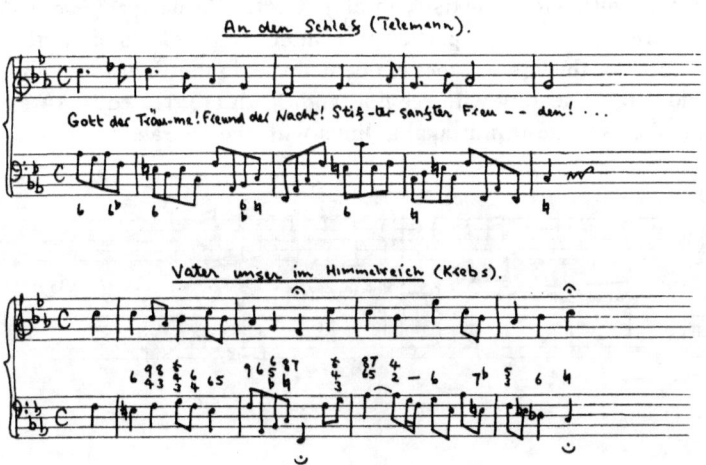

'Im Volkston'

The only essential *musical* difference is that Krebs makes greater demands on the player's ability to realise a figured bass; the contrast with Telemann's quite basic figuration affords yet another illustration of the way in which song-composers went out of their way to keep things simple. But in other respects the pieces are virtually interchangeable — except that the deity addressed in Telemann's song is 'gracious Morpheus'.

In one and the same collection we may find the composer passing from the lighter tone and texture of the scherzhaftes Lied or the Lied im Volkston to this quite different model, often with an accompaniment more or less strictly in four parts. But it is not, functionally speaking, a chorale any more; it is a solo song with keyboard accompaniment in the manner of a chorale ('choral*mäßig*'). In fact, F. Muck (1793) and others occasionally use 'choralmäßig' as an instruction to the performer, exactly as Romberg had headed some of *his* songs 'Volkston'. The influence of the chorale on the Lied continues into the nineteenth century: in some of Schubert's songs, in settings of patriotic texts, in more than one treatment of Goethe's marvellous hymn to peace, 'Der du von dem Himmel bist' (*Wandrers Nachtlied, ii*). The influence of the chorale seems particularly striking when it coexists in a song-book with Lieder im Volkston, for here two absolutely basic elements in German national culture come together: a shared realm of mainly secular experience, often concerning love, nature, the seasons, daily life, etc. (folksong) and a more elevated set of associations which, as we have seen, can be evoked for particular areas of secular experience but are more likely to be found in harness with sacred texts (chorale). G.H. Warneke's *Lieder mit Melodien* of 1780 is a particularly interesting collection in this context, for the lighter types of poem are set in the Volkston, while serious texts dealing with religion and death are treated in a way that shows quite unmistakable links with the chorale:

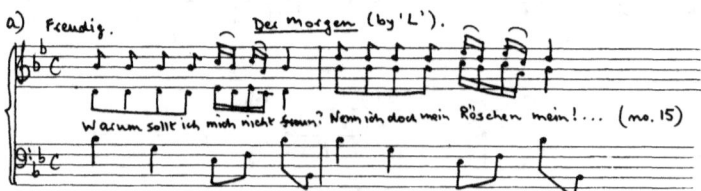

'Im Volkston'

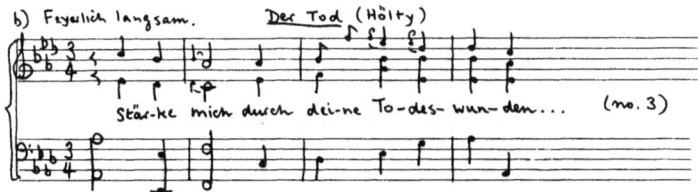

Notes

1. The coupling in the title seems strange today, but in those days *Ossian* was still widely accepted as a collection of fragments of ancient bardic poetry. Another source of the vogue for folk poetry leads, to some extent independently of Herder, from the poets of the *Göttinger Hainbund* direct to Schulz (see pp. 23f and 50).
2. *Deutsche Chronik auf das Jahr 1775*, Ulm, 1775, no. 3. For Reichardt on folk poetry, see *Musikalisches Kunstmagazin*, i (1782), 3/5, 99f and 154f.
3. 'Vom Kammerstyle' — pp. 354f in the 1806 edition.
4. For more, see R. Hammerstein, 'Christian Friedrich Daniel Schubart . . .', Diss. (Freiburg) 1943. Schubart's influence on song was more limited than that of Schulz, being virtually confined to southern Germany.
5. Published in three volumes: i(1782), ii(1785), iii(1790).
6. This distinction had been anticipated by E.C. Dressler in 1774: in order to appeal to us, songs must be natural but should not fall into the tones of vulgar street-melodies (*Gassen-Melodien*).
7. *Ideen zu einer Ästhetik der Tonkunst*, p. 354 in the 1806 edition.
8. C.G. Tag, *Lieder beim Klavier*, 1783, i,3; F. Preu, *Lieder fürs Clavier*, ii(1785), p. 18; Eicken, *Lieder für das Klavier*, 1793, p. 25.
9. Rheineck, *Dritte Lieder-Sammlung*, 1784, p. 9; Hausius, *Frohe und gesellige Lieder*, 1794, pp. 17 and 27. Dalberg sets the *Nonnelied* too, in his *Lieder mit Clavierbegleitung* of 1780. It is noteworthy that another song in his collection — that is, before he could have seen Schulz's work — carries the heading 'Im Volkston'.
10. See above, note 6. For an account of attempts to distinguish between 'music for the people' and 'music for the mob', see Schwab, *Sangbarkeit, Popularität und Kunstlied*, Regensburg, 1969, p. 94.
11. Goethe, *Werke (Festausgabe)*, Leipzig, 1926, xiv, 300.
12. See Schulz, *Johann Peter Uzens lyrische Gedichte religiösen Innhalts*, 1784, and his *Religiöse Oden und Lieder*, 1786, also Reichardt, *Cäcilie*, 1795.
13. Telemann, *Oden*, no. 5; Krebs, *Klavierübung*, edited by Kurt Soldan, Edition Peters 4178, p. 23. The extract from Krebs has been transposed to facilitate comparison.

3
Switzerland and Austria

The foregoing account has dealt almost exclusively with Germany. The songs written in Switzerland and Austria during this period, for all that they shared certain characteristics with songs being composed in Berlin, Leipzig and Stuttgart, followed slightly different paths and merit a separate discussion.

Switzerland

One immediately noticeable feature of Swiss song is its intense patriotism. Patriotism had not been lacking in German song, of course, as we see from the popularity of Klopstock's (to us) embarrassing 'Vaterlandslied', with its ideal of a blue-eyed German maiden: 'Ich bin ein deutsches Mädchen!/Mein Aug' ist blau, und sanft mein Blick'. But a patriotic or nationalistic tone was not as common in Germany as in Switzerland, if only because it was impossible for Germany, divided as it was into a host of independent states, to have any well-developed sense of nationhood. Hence, *Schweizerlieder* on the title-page of a song-book means much more than the equally common *Deutsche Lieder*; the Swiss composer is proclaiming his patriotism, while the German, as often as not, is merely signalling that the *texts* of his songs are in German rather than French or Italian.

Johannes Schmidlin's *Schweizerlieder* of 1769 may serve us as a starting-point. In the thirty-seventh song in this collection, Lavater's 'Lied eines Schweizerischen Geistlichen', the singer raises his voice in praise of the homeland which gave him his life and his freedom:

Auch ich will meine Stimm erheben,
Fürs Vaterland, das mir mein Leben
Und mit dem Leben Freyheit gab!

In J.H. Egli's similarly entitled collection of 1787, the praise of the fatherland extends to all areas of experience; the nature-poems are hymns in praise of identified landscapes or places, the wanderer is greeted by the sun as he returns, rejoicing, to his Swiss home, the harvest song celebrates a Swiss harvest gathered in by Swiss peasants. A song (no. xxxiv) glorifying republican freedom sets off this happy state against the slave-like existence of the subject in a monarchy. The antithesis is exactly similar to that constantly made in the Swiss moral weeklies from the early part of the eighteenth century onwards.[1]

After the patriotism, the most striking characteristic of the Swiss collections is their highminded moralising tone. Titles like *Auserlesene moralische Lieder* abound. Schmidlin publishes his *Singendes und spielendes Vergnügen* of 1752 in order to encourage feelings of ardent religiosity ('zur Erweckung des innern Christenthums'). There are, to be true, more lighthearted texts in some of the collections, but they never descend to the even mildly salacious or improper. The unnamed composer of the *Musikalischwöchentliche Belustigungen* (1775) stresses that his aim has been to give innocent pleasure which will offend no one but 'misanthropic hypochondriacs'. The secular texts in the somewhat surprisingly named *Fortsetzung Auserlesener moralischer Lieder* (1780) certainly include a sprinkling of Arcadian love-songs, but of the most innocuous kind. But moral and religious texts usually predominate. The editor of the *Auserlesene moralische Lieder* of 1776 assures his public that there is plenty of room for his collection, since the demand for this type of music grows daily. The combination of highminded patriotism, religious feeling and moral uplift gives Swiss song a different flavour from that of the works being produced in Germany in these decades. It has led some critics to sound faintly patronising: Schmidlin shows 'a sincere appreciation of something genuinely Swiss', while Egli is 'healthy, clean and uplifting'.[2] This makes it all sound like a plateful of muesli washed down by milk straight from the cow, which is perhaps a little unfair. For pride in republican freedom and scorn of those lands where ministers with golden chains lay iron chains on the common people (as a satirist in one of the Swiss moral weeklies has it) is no bad thing. And at least Swiss song is relatively free from

Switzerland and Austria

the artificialities of Arcadian dalliance.

When we turn to the musical styles in eighteenth-century Swiss song, it must be admitted that these are conservative, if not downright old fashioned. In the earlier collections, the layout probably make the songs *look* more archaic than they really are: Schmidlin's *Singendes und spielendes Vergnügen* has a cramped underlay which reminds one of seventeenth-century song-books, while the notes resemble the fossilised tadpoles of sixteenth-century music printing. But even if one allows for this, the music undoubtedly lags behind Germany. The question of figured bass provides a good yardstick. As we have seen, the figured bass disappeared quickly from German song as part of a general desire to escape from the legacy of the continuo-song. But we find figured basses persisting in Swiss song through the latter decades of the century and even slightly beyond 1800.

A surprisingly high proportion of Swiss song-books combine solos and partsongs, often printing the songs in a way that leaves the choice to the performer(s). It is very common to find the top voice and figured bass on the left-hand side of the page, with additional voice or voices opposite. Here is the layout as in Egli (1787), an arrangement typical of many collections of the 1770s and 80s:

Left-hand page	Right-hand page
cantus i plus figured bass	cantus ii
	sung bass part
additional stanzas of text	the remaining stanzas of text

This type of general-purpose composition must have hindered the development of an idiomatic style of solo song and this, when it did come about, was undoubtedly encouraged by a growing familiarity with German song. In addition to internal (stylistic) hints in collections of the 80s, there is the direct evidence of anthologies like Egli's *Musicalische Blumenlese* of 1786, which contains songs by C.P.E. Bach, Reichardt, Schulz and others. It is, then, in this period of Swiss song that a more fluent vocal style and an approach to the 'Volkston' can be found. True, Schmidlin had praised 'naturalness and simplicity' in the Preface to his *Schweizerlieder* of 1769, but there is little of artless simplicity about the songs; they are rather rigid and pedantic melodies with figured bass. The Volkston enters as part of the general awareness of developments in Germany. The affinity with Schulz is perfectly evident in J.J. Walder's setting of Stolberg's 'Lied' ('Des Lebens Tag ist schwer und schwül' — included in Egli's collection of 1785-6) — and lives on, notably in the songs of Egli himself and in those of H.G. Nägeli, up to the turn of the century and for a decade or so thereafter.

From about 1780 onwards, Swiss composers rapidly make up for lost time. The anonymous collection, *Fortsetzung Auserlesener moralischer Lieder* (1780), seems to stand at the crossroads. Some of its songs are stiff and old-fashioned, with the vocal line in thrall to what is in effect still a continuo-bass. Other pieces, however, are much more flowing and lyrical and have idiomatic accompaniments clearly conceived for the fortepiano. It is a decade later, in the works of Ernst Häußler and H.G. Nägeli, that the enrichment of Swiss song through German (and, perhaps, Austrian) influences is most marked, however.

Häußler published four collections in the 1790s (see Bibliography). His songs show a skilful marriage of voice and accompaniment, with independent and varied writing for the fortepiano. (It is safe to use this term; the dynamic markings leave us in no doubt.) Häußler's idiom is not unlike Zumsteeg's, although his use of wistful little keyboard figures to link vocal phrases can remind us of Mozart:

His songs, although seldom unconventional, possess great charm.

Nägeli continued to compose well into the nineteenth century and is also important for his theoretical writings in the *AMZ* and elsewhere, but it is generally agreed that his most important contribution to song-writing came with the publication, in three parts between 1795 and 1799, of the *Lieder in Musik gesezt*. We have already heard of his indebtedness to Schulz; his liking for German sources is also reflected in his choice of texts, which are mostly from German poets, including Klopstock and Goethe. He has been described as a Romantic (Cox, p. 400); if this means that he grafts Romantic elements on to a musical idiom learnt from Schulz, I would agree. His is a modest, but very engaging talent, at its best when he does not try to overreach himself (as he certainly does in the through-composed setting of Goethe's 'Auf dem See' in part 3). As an example of Nägeli at his best, one could cite his version of Stolberg's 'An die Natur' (ii, 4–5). The simple, hymnlike tune is reminiscent of Schulz, although there is just enough of the unexpected to hold our interest without disturbing the peaceful atmosphere of the whole. Unusually, Nägeli sets this poem in ternary form instead of using the more common strophic method.[3] This is, however, justified by the slight increase in emotional urgency in the middle stanza and the verbal recapitulations in the third.

Austria

The *Klavierlied*[4] established itself here rather later than in Germany, the main reason being, no doubt, the great popularity of opera, oratorio, *Singspiel* and all manner of stage pieces containing songs or simple arias. The prime mover in the creation of a Viennese style of song was Josef Anton Steffan, who published the first two parts of his *Sammlung deutscher Lieder* in 1778 and 1779. Haydn and Mozart published German songs in the 1780s and there was a host of minor composers active throughout the decade.[5] Although Vienna was a meeting-place of cultures and highly cosmopolitan in atmosphere, there seems no doubt that the sudden flowering of German song was in large part a reaction against French and Italian fashions in vocal music. 'Those who often look in vain for a German song among the flood of Italian and French pieces to be found in all homes are here offered a collection of German songs', says Steffan in the Preface to the first part of his *Sammlung*.

But the example of Italian *bel canto* and French *chanson* must have helped to bring about a graceful and flowing vocal style in these early songs. As we shall see, Viennese song has its shortcomings, but the pedantry often encountered among the composers of the first Berlin school (Marpurg *et al.*) is not among them. Coming comparatively late on the scene, the Viennese found it easy to write idiomatically for the fortepiano, no longer such a novelty as it had been when the German composers became aware of it in the late 1750s and 60s. In fact, three composers specify this instrument on their title-pages (Holzer: 'Fortepiano', 1779; Ruprecht: 'Pianoforte', *c.* 1785; Grünwald: 'Fortepiano', 1785). The accompaniment plays a role of great importance and independence in these Viennese collections; the texture is varied and preludes, interludes and postludes abound. Steffan, particularly, shows great skill in integrating these into his songs, so that vocal passages and solo piano phrases and interludes merge with one another, answer each other or likewise form a unity.[5]

If there is a criticism to be made of this late eighteenth-century Viennese school of song, it is perhaps on the grounds of poetic sensibility rather than technical accomplishment. Comparison of two songs by Steffan will illustrate this. His setting of 'Das Veilchen'[6] is reasonably successful, provided that one concedes the possibility of taking Goethe's text in a lighthearted spirit throughout, regarding the 'sterb' ich doch durch sie' as mock-passion and mock-tragedy. But Steffan's setting of Klopstock's 'Im Frühlingsschatten fand ich sie',[7] with its snap rhythms and little flourishes in the keyboard part is quite wrong for this rapt poem. Both songs are competently written; the limitations are poetic and imaginative ones. (In German song, especially in the earlier decades, the situation was often reversed.) In fact, it is difficult to think of a Viennese song which is badly written — but the response to the text often seems a hit-or-miss affair. This leads us to the vexed question of the choice of poems.

There is no better way of illustrating the point I wish to make than by taking F.J. Freystädter's *Sechs Lieder der besten deutschen Dichter* of 1795. If the title is to be taken seriously, the best German poets of the day were Blumauer, Ratschky, Halem, Cronegk and Koller! It is no exaggeration to say that the huge majority of poems set by the Viennese composers from the late 1770s to the end of the century were trivial. Simple love lyrics and Arcadian ditties are all too common, although some composers, among them Ruprecht and Maria Theresia Paradis, showed a preference for the poetry of 'sensibility'. One finds a few songs to texts by Goethe, Klopstock, Bürger and Herder, but for the rest it is impossible to disagree with Norbert Tschulik when he says that musical considerations, not poetic ones, were what counted.[8]

Switzerland and Austria

The contrast with Germany, where Goethe, Klopstock, Claudius, Voß, Stolberg, Hölty, Bürger and many others were tirelessly set to music, could hardly be greater. It is small wonder that Reichardt criticised both Haydn and Mozart for their choice of texts.

The larger and more important part of Haydn's contribution to solo song consists of settings of English and Scottish texts; his taste in German poetry was uneven, to put it mildly.[9] Mozart, if only because he was one of the greatest geniuses ever to write for the human voice, presents us with an even more extreme case, for he wrote about thirty songs to German texts, only a handful of which have much virtue as poems. When one compares him to infinitely less talented composers who, nevertheless, nearly always picked on the best available poems (Reichardt, Zelter, Zumsteeg), the contrast cannot but sadden. A glance at his only Goethe-setting ('Das Veilchen', K476) shows us what might have been. Unlike Steffan, Mozart seems to have responded instinctively to the nuances of this graceful little poem. Goethe sets the scene (the meadow in which a modest violet grows) in a style that clearly evokes the world of folk poetry:

Ein Veilchen auf der Wiese stand
Gebückt in sich und unbekannt;
Es war ein herzigs Veilchen . . .

— but the atmosphere at once becomes Rococo as the shepherdess trips on to the scene:

Da kam eine junge Schäferin
Mit leichtem Schritt und munterm Sinn
Daher, daher,
Die Wiese her und sang.

Mozart echoes this change with the utmost precision in his music. When Goethe presently strikes a note of hopeless longing, the composer again responds, this time with a modulation into the tonic minor and a highly expressive portamento through a diminished seventh. Song and poem are too familiar to need further description: suffice it to say that Mozart has followed each turn of the narrative and each change of mood unerringly, to produce an unsurpassed realisation of this deceptively simple text. My point is not only that it is a matter of regret that he never set other texts by Goethe; it is that a certain sort of Goethe poem, in which a traditional rococo vein was taken up, exploited with the utmost skill and elegance and imbued with a depth and spontaneity of feeling usually lacking in such texts, would have been uniquely suited to Mozart's genius. What would we not give for a Mozart setting of, say, 'Mit einem gemalten Band'?

To return to the general situation in Vienna during these decades: at a time when the German song-composers really were setting 'the best German poets', Viennese composers — although writing with grace and skill — showed no awareness of the fact that the aesthetic experience afforded by a song could be heightened by the choice of an outstandingly good text. 'Kleine Schöne, küsse mich' or 'Siehe, mein Röschen, der Frühling ist da' seemed quite adequate as raw material. The indifference to poetic values seems to have been compounded after Mozart's death by a mixture of pusillanimity and a misguided notion of what was acceptable in drawing-room song. For if we look at the 1799 Breitkopf & Härtel edition of Mozart's collected songs, we find quite drastic reworkings by Daniel Jäger of several poems.[10]

The original text of 'Sei du mein Trost' (K391), by J.T. Hermes, is a cheerless ode to solitude, depicting a wanderer weighed down by cares and longing only for peace in death. Jäger's version, 'An die Einsamkeit', softens this into a desire for death, unless lost love and friendship are restored. Here is Hermes's final stanza:

O daß dein Reiz, geliebte Einsamkeit,
Mir oft das Bild des Grabes brächte!
So lockt des Abends Dunkelheit
Zur tiefen Ruhe schöner Nächte.

(Oh that your charms, beloved solitude, might often evoke the image of the grave! So it is that the darkness of evening entices us to the deep peace of blessed nights.) And here is what Jäger put in its place:

Ach! einmal nur noch höre mich, Geschick,
Vollend' und drück' ins Grab mich nieder!
Nimm mir dies Leben, oder gib
Mir, was du raubtest, Liebe, wieder!

(Oh destiny, hear me just once more: make an end and lower me into my grave! Take my life or restore what you stole from me: love!) Hermes's original is almost a precursor of the Harper's songs in *Wilhelm Meisters Lehrjahre*: Jäger's version is a poetic aspirin by comparison.

More than the avoidance of uncomfortable emotion is at the root of Jäger's reworking of the 'Lied zur Gesellenreise' (K468). This Masonic song was composed in 1785, during a short period in which Freemasonry was enjoying the protection and sympathy of Joseph II. The poem has obvious affinities with the Masonic sections of *Die Zauberflöte*, seeing life as an apprenticeship leading to wisdom:

Die ihr einem neuen Grade
Der Erkenntnis nun euch naht,
Wandert fest auf eurem Pfade,
Wißt, es ist der Weisheit Pfad.
Nur der unverdroßne Mann
Mag dem Quell des Lichts sich nahn.

But — oases of comparative tolerance apart — Freemasonry was regarded with suspicion in Austria, as in other Catholic countries, for being cosmopolitan, anticlerical and latitudinarian. Jäger obviously felt it tactful to recast the text, draining it of all Masonic implications while preserving the anonymous poet's central image. His version, now entitled 'Lebensreise', is concerned with the notion that the journey through life, if unaccompanied by friends, would be intolerable.

Another example of political cowardice (or, to be polite, prudence) can be seen in the reworking of Hermes's 'Verdankt sei es dem Glanz der Großen' (K392), from which Jäger excised all hints of social criticism (see below, p. 57). But even the slightest intrusion of social realities into a song was enough to alarm him. The anonymous text, 'Die kleine Spinnerin' (K531), had explained the girl's reluctance to leave her spinning wheel and join in the merrymaking thus:

Für meiner kleinen Schwestern Paar
Spinn' ich zu Hemdchen Linnen:
Die Teurung wächst ja jedes Jahr,
Und ich, sollt' ich nicht spinnen?

(I am spinning linen to make shifts for my two little sisters. Things

Switzerland and Austria

get dearer year by year — and I'm supposed to stop spinning?) Jäger turns the song into a girl-sees-through-masculine-wiles ditty of the most trivial kind:

Was hätt' ich auch von euch, ihr Herrn?
Man kennt ja eure Weise!
Ihr neckt und scherzt und dreht euch gern
Mit Mädchen um im Kreise . . .

(What else could I expect from you men? We know your ways! You tease and joke and like to whirl the girls round in the dance.) No one would suspect that, in the original, the girl had turned away from the boy's advances out of hard financial necessity!

Jäger's and the publishers' intention was clearly to make the texts as inoffensive as possible.[11] The implication is that drawing-room song has nothing to do with uncomfortable realities, a proposition that would have surprised the German song-composers of the day, many of whom set Hermes's texts unaltered. Yet Jäger was so successful that his versions were sung for more than a century. This has certainly harmed Mozart's reputation as a song-composer by turning some of the few interesting and hardhitting texts that he set into trivialities. Since most of the poems chosen by Mozart's Viennese contemporaries were, as we have seen, poetic trifles, this bowdlerisation is doubly to be regretted.

Notes

1. See J.W. Smeed, *The Theophrastan Character*, Oxford, 1985, pp. 82f.
2. David Cox, 'Switzerland', in *A History of Song*, ed. Stevens, London, 1960, p. 399.
3. Nägeli is here following Neubauer's example (1788, no. 5). But the strophic form was preferred — by André (three versions), Reichardt, Schulz and, later, Schubert and Loewe.
4. See Bibliography, section 3, under Friberth and Hofmann, Holzer, Pohl, Ruprecht, Grünwald, Paradis and Hackel. Volume 54 of *DTÖ*, ed. M. Ansion and I. Schaffenberg, Graz, 1960, gives a good selection.
5. For representative examples, see i(1778), no. 1; ii(1779), no. 8; iv(1782), no. 10. Steffan is generously represented in *DTÖ*, 54.
6. 1778, no. 14: p. 8 in *DTÖ*, 54.
7. 1778, no. 9: *DTÖ*, 54, p. 5. Steffan heads the song 'Die Cidly'; usual title: 'Das Rosenband'.
8. *Lieder aus Österreich*, Vienna, 1964, p. 37.

9. See too Friedlaender, vol. i, part 1, pp. 286ff.

10. E.A. Ballin's edition of the songs (see Bibliography) gives the original texts, with Jäger's 'improvements' in an Appendix. Until this critical edition appeared, most editions, whether of collected songs or single items, had followed Jäger.

11. Weiße's 'Die Zufriedenheit' (K473) is the one that got away; Jäger missed the 'subversive' third stanza, with its reference to bloodthirsty rulers.

4
Song-texts in the Latter Part of the Eighteenth Century

From about 1770 at the latest, hardly any poets of note continued to write in the Arcadian strain except very occasionally, in a spirit of play. This *Schäferpoesie* was now regarded as a mere literary exercise, something divorced from reality (fit only to be stored away in museums for the benefit of 'childish scholars', says Bürger scornfully). Goethe illustrates the transition to a new style of poetry very well; a handful of his youthful works still linger in the graceful but artificial world of Arcadian shepherds and shepherdesses, but from quite early in the 1770s his short lyrics show increasing affinity with folksongs and folk ballads. Bürger, whose 'outpourings of the heart' on the subject of folk poetry we have already encountered, was also inspired both by the folk ballad and by the style and form of shorter folksongs. His 'Schwanenlied', quoted above in Schulz's setting, provides an example. Here is the complete first stanza, clearly related to the innumerable German folksongs which treat of blighted or abandoned love:

> Mir tuts so weh im Herzen!
> Ich bin so matt und krank!
> Ich schlafe nicht vor Schmerzen;
> Mag Speise nicht und Trank;
> Seh alles sich entfärben,
> Was schönes mir geblüht.
> Ach, Liebchen, will nur sterben!
> Dies ist mein Schwanenlied.

Compare:

> Mein Herzlein tut mir gar so weh!
> Das macht, weil ich in Trauren steh . . .

or:

> Mei Mutter mag mi net,
> Und kei Schatz han i net,
> Ei, warum stirb i net,
> Was tu i do?

Quite apart from such general thematic resemblances, Bürger also picked up specific attributes of folksong style and exploited them in his verses: the matter-of-fact concreteness of lines 3–4, the laconic style depending in part on elipses (line 7), and so on. But these similarities do not mean that Bürger has simply imitated folk poetry; he is not afraid to go beyond its expressive range, as when he goes on to describe the beloved as a vessel full of healing balm (stanza 2), or when he uses the quasi-mystical *zerschmelzen* to suggest melting away in the ecstasy of love (stanza 3). A similar coexistence of indebtedness to folksong with a poetic imagination which transcends the expressive limitations of the model can be found in ballads by Goethe, such as 'Erlkönig', 'Der Fischer' and 'Der König in Thule'.

These examples all come from the Sturm und Drang and are ultimately traceable back to Herder's championship of folk poetry. A further important impact was made on the development of German song in the closing decades of the century by the group of poets who in 1772 joined together to found the *Göttinger Hainbund*. This was a brotherhood of like-minded young men bound by friendship and common literary aspirations. Chief among them were Voß, Hölty, Stolberg and J.M. Miller. They too rejected the rococo-Arcadian strain in favour of an altogether more earnest type of poetry. The chief impulses which fed their verse came from Klopstock on the one hand, folksong and hymns on the other. Their favourite themes were friendship, love, God-in-nature, mortality and love of fatherland.[1] Many poems were elegaic in tone, bewailing the loss of dead friends or meditating on the transience of earthly things by the sympathetic yet melancholy light of the moon. Germany now has its own Parnassus, says Bürger, greeting the foundation of the *Bund*. But it was shortlived: by

1776, Hölty was dead and the other members dispersed. Yet the poetic styles which it had encouraged lived on, to become of great importance in the history of German song.

The musical vogue for 'Lieder im Volkston' naturally led composers to simple texts, whose form resembled that of folk poems. As Schäferpoesie was rejected by the poets, it fell from favour among the composers too; the days in which Hagedorn, the 'German Horace', was the most set of all German poets, were past and new kinds of texts were preferred. Of the older generation, Klopstock came into his own, with his intense poems of friendship and love, of death and transience, of near ecstatic religious faith. But, given his daring style, his sometimes arcane metres and excursions into free verse, only a small minority of his shorter poems were found suitable for song. Much more popular were the simpler lyrics of the Hainbund: Hölty's fresh and graceful springsongs, Miller's famous expression of idyllic contentment ('Was frag' ich viel nach Gut und Geld'), Stolberg's quietistic hymn to death ('Des Lebens Tag ist schwer und schwül'), and so on.

In so far as one can generalise, the secular texts chosen by composers in the 1770s, 80s and 90s became markedly more serious, sentimental and, in many cases, moralising in tone. Titles like 'The Kiss' or 'To Chloe' give way to 'The Praying Girl', 'To the Evening Star', 'To the Moon', and so on. The transition from one poetic style to another had, in fact, helped the song-composers out of a dilemma. Song, theoretically speaking, had been supposed to appeal to the heart, to mirror, encourage or soothe the listener's feelings. But poetic fashions in the early decades of the Lied had more or less pushed the composers in the direction of the scherzhaftes Lied and impelled them to reserve their more serious efforts for settings of sacred texts.[2] The sentimental, pious or morally 'improving' poems in simple, songlike form which were produced in increasing numbers from the early 1770s onwards made it much easier for composers to put the Affektenlehre into practice, paying due heed to the deeper and more earnest emotions, while still setting their share of lighter texts.

It seems no coincidence that Goethe's novel *The Sorrows of young Werther* (1774), which most people would take as the epitome of German sensibility (*Empfindsamkeit*), should have inspired J.H. von Reitzenstein to write a poem entitled 'Lotte bei Werthers Grab' and that this text should have been taken up by half a dozen composers between 1775 and 1790. In it, Lotte stands at Werther's grave, reflecting on his suffering and, at the same time, regretting that he had fastened his attentions on a girl already betrothed to another: 'Ausgelitten hast du — ausgerungen/Armer Jüngling, deinen Todesstreit ... Hätte nimmer von den Mädchen allen/Das verlobte Mädchen dich entzückt!' (stanza 1, lines 1–2; stanza 2, lines 3–4). Compassion and stricture are so exactly balanced that the reader or singer can partake of the grief without any feeling of conniving at Werther's illicit passion or uncritically sympathising with his emotional self-indulgence. I cannot readily think of another poem in which the emotionalism of German Empfindsamkeit is combined with the eighteenth-century tendency towards moral didacticism in quite that way. It may be added that many of Reitzenstein's composers try to match the 'sensibility' of the text in their music. This is particularly marked in the anonymous 1775 version, with its chromatic rise on 'armer', immediately followed by a slurred fall through a fifth on '*Jüng*ling':

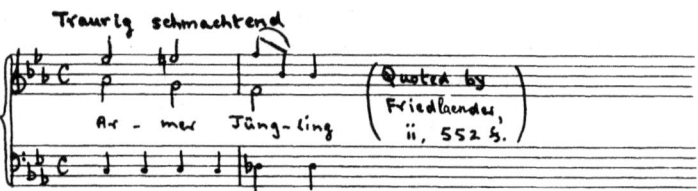

A similar attempt to match feeling with feeling can be seen in many of the settings from the 1780s of the then popular odes to the fortepiano ('An mein Klavier', etc.), in which the instrument was praised as sympathetic companion, able to match the singer's moods and help him or her to overcome sorrow or suffering.[3] One of these poems, 'Sey mir gegrüßt' by J.T. Hermes, may be singled out as typical. Here the piano is greeted as confidant and companion, responding to and echoing feelings which no language can adequately express:

Sey mir gegrüßt, mein schmeichelndes Klavier!
Was keine Sprache richtig nennt,
Die Krankheit tief in mir,
Die nie mein Mund bekennt,
Die klag ich dir!

The term 'Empfindsamkeit' is often applied to German music from the 1750s on, to designate a turning against pedantry and the quest for an emotive musical language by which the composer would reach out and touch the listener's heart. C.P.E. Bach's keyboard fantasias and slow movements are among the most expressive manifestations of this trend. In secular song, musical Empfindsamkeit only really began to make itself felt when Empfindsamkeit as a poetic fashion had come to influence the composers' choice of texts. The link can clearly be seen in Joseph Kraus's setting of 'Der Abschied' (Parting), no. 7 in his *Airs et Chansons* of *c.* 1785. Here we find an extreme of chromatic poignancy very rare in the songs of the day. Since this collection also contains a setting of Hermes's 'Sey mir gegrüßt', it is possible that Kraus has taken a hint from that poem and is attempting to imply that there is a musical language that goes beyond words. This is how the piano 'speaks' to us before the first entry of the voice:

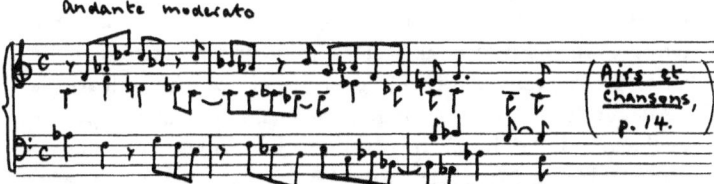

The links with Empfindsamkeit in purely instrumental music are clear, as the following short extract from a keyboard work by C.P.E. Bach will show:

It thus seems clear that the swing from 'scherzhaft' to 'empfindsam' affects both poetry and music. The new approach is mirrored in the titles of song-books published in the 1780s and 90s. Although song was still obviously intended to afford pleasure, words like 'scherzhaft' or 'Belustigung' are now rare on the title-pages. Some composers make a moralising intention quite explicit, as in G.F. Hillmer's *Oden und Lieder Moralischen Inhalts* of 1781. Such titles do not mean any open teaching of moral lessons (except in the many collections of children's songs), rather an innocent or lofty tone, as in songs which praise God through nature, idealise and sentimentalise human relationships or hymn the solemn notion of death's inevitability. It could even be argued, with no more than slight exaggeration, that 'moralisch' says as much about what the buyer is *not* to expect as about the things that he will find in the collection: here there will be no poems advocating a thoughtless *carpe diem* and nothing erotic.

More common is the sort of title which directly appeals to 'feeling':

M.J. Hitzelberg, *Für fü[h]llende Seelen* . . ., 1784
F.B. Benecken, *Lieder und Gesänge für fühlende Seelen*, 1787
J.F. Reichardt, *Gesänge der Klage und des Trostes*, 1797

Benecken's collection is particularly interesting in our present context. The composer's Dedication to Elisabeth Sophie Wilhelmine von Knigge and her sisters is full of appeals to the tenderest and most refined feelings and scorn for fashionable 'frivolity'. In a Preface, this clergyman and amateur composer talks of the supremacy of feeling in terms that show clearly how the Affektenlehre could be tinged by sensibility: his compositions have been guided by feeling rather than rules, the songs are intended for 'feeling souls', kindred spirits who will sense and share the emotions that prompted the composer. The general situation is very similar to that described by earlier, more sober theorists who had applied the Affektenlehre to song, but an almost tearful note has crept in and the impression given is that the poet, composer and performer(s) rather enjoy their melancholy. The instructions to player and singer at the head of the songs also belong to the realm of sensibility: 'Gently, with intimate feeling'; 'In a tender and melancholy manner'; 'Slowly, in deepest melancholy'; 'In an intensely motherly style' (this as the heading to a lullaby). In Benecken's collection of fourteen songs from which the above examples are taken, only two headings are simple indications of tempo; the rest hint at the nature of the emotional realm shared by poet, composer and performer(s). Unfortunately, it must be added that the songs in such collections do not always live up to the claims thus implicitly made for them. M.J. Hitzelberg, the daughter of a famous singer, often sets the melting poems in a decidedly florid manner, while Benecken is guilty of a fussy and mannered style which is anything but an expression of 'tender feelings'.

I have already hinted at some of the links between song and middle-class values in eighteenth-century Germany. This is not, of course, meant to imply that song was exclusively a middle-class affair. Subscription lists show that there were many aristocratic patrons, while the courts also supported song indirectly through the chance circumstance that many song-composers were directors of music at court or held other posts by virtue of aristocratic patronage. But in general the upper classes had their own forms of music, more elaborate, formal and public than the modest drawing-room song. There seems no doubt that the collections of songs were mainly aimed at, bought and performed by the middle classes and that one's mental picture of a young lady seated at the harpsichord or fortepiano in her bourgeois drawing-room, singing for herself or for the delectation of an intimate circle, is broadly accurate.

Walter Wiora makes the important point that song — while obviously a source of harmless pleasure — was also part of a process of social and moral education.[4] This is easily perceived in the *Moralische Lieder* and *Lieder für fühlende Seelen* of the age of sensibility, but what about the songs of earlier decades? No doubt, the Anacreontic songs in which shepherds and shepherdesses neglect their flocks in order to kiss and flirt were simply taken in a spirit of play, as 'Scherzlieder' in the most literal and obvious sense. But a poem like Stoppe's 'Das vergnügte Schäferleben' (The contented shepherd's life), set by Telemann in 1741 to an infectious tune in 6/8, could be, and probably was, implicitly related to middle-class life. Stoppe's poem sets off a happy rural life against the luxurious but discontented existence of towns-people. I believe that the manifest popularity of such pieces, as shown by the frequency with which they appear in books of poetry and collections of song, suggests that the middle-class reader, singer or listener was able to transpose the terms slightly, to cast himself or herself as the contented rural type. The implication that there is something wrong with town life *as such* will have been conveniently overlooked and the fact that the reader or singer did not live in a hut and drink water will not have prevented him from seeing his life as natural and casting those richer and grander than himself in the role of the epicureans, boasters and capitalists denounced in the poem. The eighteenth-century reaction to the 'humble shepherd' type of poem will probably not have been dissimilar to that displayed by a man of the twentieth century, as he ponders on the stressful and discontented life of oil-millionaires as shown in a television serial. Songs like 'Das vergnügte Schäferleben' or Gleim's famous 'Ich hab' ein kleines Hüttchen nur' were thus not as totally divorced from middle-class experience as might appear; they represented an encoded version of it.

This notion of an encoded social message may help to explain the otherwise slightly puzzling popularity of Bürger's revolutionary poem 'Der Bauer. An seinen durchlauchtigen Tyrannen' (The Peasant: to his most gracious Tyrant). The poem, which appears in many collections of songs in the 1770s and 80s, contrasts the peasant, who produces without the chance of consuming, with the prince, who consumes without producing. I cannot believe that middle-class performers and listeners can have unreservedly identified themselves with Bürger's radical sentiments — but they will have been confirmed in their virtuous feeling that they, unlike the aristocrats, earned what they consumed. Again, a sort of mental transposition will have taken place, by which 'peasant' will have come to mean merchant or professional man, 'sweating in the fields' will have stood for labouring in counting-house or law-court and 'crops trampled by noble huntsmen' will have seemed like a symbol of taxes exacted to pay for the ruler's extravagance. The villain of the piece will have been common to both schemes. This is impossible to prove, of course, but without some such theory it would seem highly incongruous that stanzas such as the following should have been sung in bourgeois drawing-rooms:

> Du Fürst hast nicht, bei Egg' und Pflug,
> Hast nicht den Erntetag durchschwitzt.
> Mein, mein ist Fleiß und Brot!

(You, prince, have never worked with harrow and plough and sweated through the harvest-time. Mine is the labour and mine the bread!)

Thus, in a variety of ways, song can be seen as bolstering up the social confidence of the middle classes, encouraging them in the view that hard work in a context of modest prosperity was admirable and that the honest merchant was at least as valuable and estimable as a prince. The Hamburg trader or Leipzig court-official, listening to his daughter singing of humble contentment, of the evils of ostentation and envy, of joy in nature, simple religious faith and unclouded human relationships, would feel the same mixture of well-being, moral rectitude and psychological stability as he gained from the pages of *Der Patriot*, *Der Biedermann*,

Das Reich der Natur und der Sitten or whichever of the scores of moral weeklies he happened to favour. A close relationship existed between the world of the moral weeklies and that of the Lied. It seems no coincidence that Johann Mattheson, who assures us that the 'moral ode' helps to conquer vanity and ward off melancholy and dissatisfaction,[5] was also the first German to publish extracts from *The Tatler* and *The Spectator* in translation, thus helping to establish the vogue for German periodicals based on such models.

Songbook-titles like *Lieder zur Beförderung der Tugend* have their parallel in the names given to many of the moral weeklies by their editors: *Der Tugendfreund, Der redliche Deutsche*, etc. The composer C.F. Weisinger incorporates into the title of his 1793 collection a statement of intent which would exactly apply to the moral weeklies too: *Gedichte mit Musik dem bürgerlichen und häuslichen Glück, der liebenswürdigen Sittlichkeit und schuldlosen Freude geheiligt* (Poems with Music, consecrated to middle-class domestic happiness, lovable morality and innocent joy).[6] Composers took poems from the weeklies, acknowledging this on the title-pages or elsewhere, thus underlining the almost symbiotic link between middle-class domestic music and middle-class secular reading-matter.[7]

The tone and implications of the morality furthered by the song-composers in their choice of texts vary from the exacting and disturbing to the anodyne. Let us return to J.T. Hermes, whose poems, mostly scattered about in his novels, were popular among eighteenth-century composers. 'Verdankt sei es dem Glanz der Grossen' seems at first sight one more conventional eulogy on humble sufficiency:

> Sie sind mir wert, die engen Grenzen,
> Wo ich so unbeträchtlich bin.
> Hier seh' ich Stern und Orden glänzen,
> Und Band und Stern reißt mich nicht hin.

(The narrow boundaries of my insignificant existence are precious to me. I see the glitter of orders and decorations but am not attracted to them.) But a later stanza shows how the preservation of integrity in a humble sphere involves a delicate psychological balancing act:

> Doch ließe sich zu meinem Kreise
> Ein Großer ohne Falsch herab:
> Erfahrung! dann mach' du mich weise
> Und zeichne meine Grenzen ab
> Und lehre mich, niemals zu klein,
> Doch auch nicht kühn und eitel sein.

(Yet, should one of the great descend to my level without false intentions, may experience make me wise and show me my proper bounds, teaching me never to be too lowly nor yet bold and vain.) That is an exacting psychological lesson in poetic form. By contrast, the 'happy shepherd' or 'simple hut' songs are invitations to complacency. Some poets, composers and publishers seem to have regarded song as an innocuous activity which should avoid anything challenging or even mildly disturbing.[8] But the explicit or implied morality of eighteenth-century song, whether conventional and unproblematic (as in the majority of cases), defiant (as with Bürger's rebellious peasant) or psychologically and spiritually demanding (as with Hermes) all seem to appeal to middle-class values.

This brief account of how song supported social values has necessarily been concerned with some of the minor poets, if only because major poets are much less likely merely to reinforce received opinions or provide support for commonly held prejudices. But the German song-composers did not limit themselves to what was comfortable and soothing and were certainly not content to set only the works of poetasters. As I have said, a respectable minority of good and very good poems were steadily chosen as song-texts. The point bears reiteration in view of what was said in Chapter 3 regarding the contrast between German and Austrian song; any contradiction is more apparent than real.

In Chapter 5 we shall say a brief word about the standing and professions of the composers and the probable performers whom they had in mind when they wrote their songs.

Notes

1. A growing sense of patriotism and a quest for some sort of national identity are common to the *Hainbund* and the writers of the Sturm und Drang.

2. Busch (p. 278) touches on this point. Johann Mattheson's *Odeon*

Morale of 1751, a collection of mainly secular songs in which the moral lesson conveyed by each is precisely defined in the list of contents, is an exception, an attempt to convey a practical philosophy for daily living in song.

    3. See my article on this in *Music and Letters*, lxvi (1985), 228–40.

    4. *Das deutsche Lied*, Wolfenbüttel and Zurich, 1971, pp. 113–16.

    5. *Odeon Morale*, 1751, Introduction.

    6. No copy of this work seems to have survived.

    7. See W.A.T. Roth, 1757. Marpurg, 1758, has many texts from the moral weeklies.

    8. For a bowdlerisation of poems by Hermes and others in a posthumous edition of Mozart's songs, see Chapter 3.

5

Composers and Performers

Of the hundreds of song-composers working in German-speaking countries in the second half of the eighteenth century, only a handful are still household names: C.P.E. Bach, Gluck, Haydn, Mozart, Quantz, Telemann. Among these it is only Bach whose keyboard songs form a really important part of his total output, both as regards intrinsic worth and historical impact. By contrast, Gluck's Klopstock-settings, although far from negligible, fade into insignificance beside his operas.[1] It is impossible to bring to mind a great composer who achieved a major and revolutionary development in the eighteenth-century Lied as did, say, Mozart with the piano concerto or Haydn with the string quartet. It is probably not unjust to say that the German songs of Haydn, Mozart, Quantz or Telemann are no more than an interesting and attractive sideline when related to the composer's *oeuvre* as a whole. Towards the turn of the century and slightly beyond, we find a number of gifted minor composers who, to a greater or lesser extent, concentrated on solo keyboard songs (Reichardt, Zelter, Zumsteeg), but in general the development of eighteenth-century German song is the joint achievement of a large number of composers, most of whom made their modest contributions unobtrusively. Few were full-time composers; they usually combined their activity with some salaried post, as orchestral player, court or municipal music-director, teacher, organist or choirmaster.

A substantial minority were musical amateurs, many of whom had studied music formally for a time side by side with their professional studies. The majority of these part-time composers seem to have been clergymen, but there were also lawyers, court and municipal officials, doctors of medicine, army officers and aristocratic dilettanti (often slavishly over-praised in their day). One interestingly quirkish composer, Christoph Rheineck, was an innkeeper. Many of these amateur composers claim in their prefaces that the songs were originally composed for the amusement of a circle of friends who then urged the reluctant composer to publish. That some of the professionals looked down on these amateur activities is documented by Zelter who, in his autobiography, recalls how one of his early teachers denounced the folly of trying to earn one's living in some non-musical professional while playing at being a composer in whatever spare time remained ('das geht nicht und gibt am Ende Unglück').[2]

Why *did* so many amateurs try their hand in this field? A clue lies in their prefaces, which reject 'virtuosity' and 'pedantry' and often aver that the composer owes more to nature than to art. The following two extracts, one from a clergyman who composed 'in his hours of leisure' and one from a self-styled dilettante, illustrate the point:

> . . . light and artless songs with which one may content oneself occasionally when no operatic arias by world-famous composers are at hand . . . (Flörke, 1779)

> . . . a young dilettante from Swabia . . . whose songs are offered to the public just as dear Mother Nature taught them to him in his little village . . .
> ('Dilettante aus Schwaben', 1778)

It seemed easy to write songs, given the modest scale, the apparently undemanding texture and the rejection of complexity and virtuosity even by the professionals among the song-composers. The Affektenlehre, coupled with countless appeals to 'nature' from the 1740s onwards, made possible the notion that you had only to immerse yourself in the text, wait for a melody to suggest itself and let nature do the rest. If there remained a sneaking suspicion that the correct rules of composition were sometimes broken, disarm critics by reference to the proverbial saying that apprentice work cannot be expected to produce a masterpiece ('Lehrwerk ist kein Meisterstück' — Flörke) or by claiming that an amateur should not be judged by the strictest professional criteria. Hence, it was that many composers (or would-be composers), who would certainly have hesitated to publish sonatas or symphonies, cheerfully sent their collections of songs out into the world.

More important in the long run than questions as to the proportion of amateur to professional composers is the fact that eighteenth-century song-composers, amateurs and professionals alike, aimed their works at amateur *performers*. Title-pages and prefaces constantly stress that the songs are intended for 'beginners' or 'those unpractised in singing and playing'. As we shall see, this mental picture of modestly gifted amateur performers influenced composition quite radically.

As well as collections of songs intended for singing in solitude or in a small circle of family or friends, there was much convivial song of a technically undemanding nature (often involving a solo verse plus a refrain), composed for students' gatherings, glee-clubs and similar groups. Books of song for Masonic lodges were common; this was a period in which Freemasonry played a very important part in German urban life. Since the movement was at the time in a pronouncedly idealistic, cosmopolitan and humanistic phase of its development, many of the songs in these volumes express the most elevated moral sentiments. Hölty's 'Der alte Landmann an seinen Sohn', with its emphasis on constancy, honesty and the need to follow Divine ordinances, is the most famous example; it was set many times as well as being sung in the lodges to Papageno's tune 'Ein Mädchen oder Weibchen' (!) from *The Magic Flute*. A more typical example of 'social song' used in the lodges would be the anonymous 'Die Entschließung', set by J.G. Naumann and included in his *Freymaurerlieder* of 1782. Here a solo voice sings the verse, lamenting the disappearance of good faith from the world, and the chorus joins in a refrain praising moral rectitude.[3]

In addition to songs which were quite specifically aimed at groups with a common interest or purpose and which in many cases, as in the last example cited, would simply not make sense as straightforward solos, there were collections which left open the question of how and indeed where the songs were to be performed. Thus Reichardt said that his *Lieder geselliger Freude* (1796–7) could be sung as solos, in chorus or as solos with refrain. They could be performed indoors or in the open air, with or without accompaniment. Other song-books carry titles which clearly signal two different types of song, intended for two different purposes. J.K.G. Assmuss's collection *Lieder für Gesellschaft und Einsamkeit* (*c* 1795) shows the distinction with great clarity: the one group of songs is cheerful and extrovert both in text and music, the other tends towards idyllic or elegaic expressions of solitary moods and experiences:

The great majority of eighteenth-century songs, however, are collections of solos to be performed in the home. Internal evidence suggests that singer and player were usually one; a glance at the titles confirms this. It cannot be a coincidence that by far the most common formula suggests singing *at* the piano (*Lieder am Klavier zu singen*), while the phrase 'songs with piano accompaniment' (*Lieder mit Klavierbegleitung*) comes into common usage only towards the end of the century, as the accompaniments gradually become more complex and demand more than half of a performer's attention. Paintings and engravings seem to bear this out. In the eighteenth century we are usually shown a young lady seated at her instrument; by the early nineteenth century the pictures tend to show a couple performing the song in collaboration. Further evidence is provided by the frequent episodes in sentimental novels from the 1770s to the 90s, where the hero or heroine sits at the keyboard and pours out ardent feelings in song. The many poems in praise of the piano nearly always imply a quiet communion, as the singer confides his or her sorrows and joys to the instrument. Thus, the sum of the evidence strongly suggests that most of these songs would have involved a singer who was also the accompanist.

There are indications that the composers did not have much confidence in the ability of the amateur performers for whom their works were intended, for the prefaces often contain information on the simplest matters. For instance, J.A. Hiller laboriously explains that in strophic song the singer will sometimes need to make slight adjustments to the note-values from stanza to stanza in order to accommodate the words. It is *not* superfluous to explain these things, he adds, as long as the Germans are so weak in song.[4] It is significant too that the instructions to the singer which head the songs are almost invariably in German. One motive behind this may be to distance the music from any foreign taint, but the main reason will probably have been a fear that German middle-class amateurs would not understand technical terms in Italian.

The prefaces are full of assurances that the music demands no more than modest ability:

> My tunes are intended to be of a kind that can be played and sung without much labour. (C.F. Endter, 1757)

> Each song will be gentle and easy and will not present difficulties even to beginners in playing and singing.
> (E.C. Dressler, 1774)

> The greater part of my public consists of amateurs who like something easy to play and a melody which easily and quickly impresses itself on the memory and is consequently easy to sing. (S.F. Brede, 1786)

Aristocratic dilettanti and middle-class amateurs alike will commonly have owed their musical knowledge and ability to private tutors. Since everything depends on the quality of the teaching and the gifts and determination of the pupil, it is impossible to generalise about likely standards. But the composers' views as stated in their prefaces and elsewhere, together with the obvious pains they took to keep their songs at a technically simple level, give us important indirect indications. It may seem odd to us today that the Lied, which was to become so complex in the hands of some nineteenth-century composers, should have gone through a long period of comparative technical simplicity. But this was certainly the case and it affected all aspects of song. In Chapter 6, I will take the main ones in turn, beginning with the limits placed on the types of text which were thought suitable for musical composition, going on to the more technical questions of form, relationship of vocal line to accompaniment and harmonic vocabulary, to conclude with a word on the general tendency to subordinate music to poetry.

Notes

1. Some critics perceive stylistic links between Gluck's songs and his

operas. But this does not affect the question of relative importance.

2. C.F. Zelter, *Darstellungen seines Lebens* (= *Schriften der Goethe-Gesellschaft*), xliv, Weimar, 1931, p. 46.

3. Given by Friedlaender, vol. i, part 2, ex. 183. Mozart, of course, set many Masonic texts. Masonic song in German-speaking countries would merit a detailed study of its own.

4. Hiller, 1772, Preface. C.P.E. Bach, 1774, finds it necessary to give somewhat similar guidelines. By contrast, Neefe has rather more confidence in the performers (1776, Preface).

6
Simplicity as an Ideal

Our starting point must be to consider what sort of poetry was regarded as suitable for song, a topic on which the theorists and composers of the eighteenth century held pronounced views. We have seen that at first the stress was on light and playful texts. By the 1760s disagreements are noticeable. Ramler's Preface to the *Lieder der Deutschen* still favours 'scherzhafte Lieder':

> We could have made our collection bigger, if, as well as these playful songs, we had included the solemn and elevated odes of our lyric poets, odes which for the most part are better suited for declamation than for song.

Zachariae would disagree: 'even music at home should not serve merely for pleasure; we can perform an act of worship and occupy ourselves with serious thoughts at the keyboard too' (*Sammlung*, Part ii, Preface). Serious and lighthearted songs are in fairly exact balance from about 1770 onwards; by the 80s the serious probably predominate. Apart from this point, debate centred on two issues.

Firstly, there was general agreement that song appealed to the heart rather than to the head. Gellert, whose poetry was repeatedly set to music in the middle decades of the century, speaks for many when he says that 'Lehroden' (not only didactic poetry, but any elaborate argument in verse) are less well suited to song than 'Oden für das Herz' (Preface to the *Geistliche Oden und Lieder*, 1757). Wieland ('Versuch', 1775) makes the point in an almost caricatured way when he argues that music, being 'the language of the passions', should not concern itself with political debates. C.G. Krause is the most exact and judicious writer on this topic, showing how music can appeal to our emotions in the obvious sense of setting up sympathetic vibrations in us, but can also reinforce a poetic argument by its emotional power; the reasons to which the poem appeals and the feeling which the music enlists on the poet's behalf thus complement one another (*Von der musikalischen Poesie*, 1753, iv. *Hauptstück*). So the composer who wishes to set 'Lehroden' to music should choose texts in which the argument is never so abstract, impersonal or detailed that it would fail to benefit from, and find expression through, the emotional language of music: that is what Krause implies. Were this not so, song would be limited indeed. For instance, Bürger's 'Der Bauer', being a personal and emotional response to class differences rather than an abstract sociological statement, is saved for song according to Krause's criteria, whereas Wieland would have disqualified it. The situation would be similar with some of Hermes's texts. In the religious realm, songs will be more likely to succeed if they contain a personal or lyrical note (the poet's personal faith, his wonder at the universe, his sense of sin). By contrast, versified theology makes for poor song.

Thus far, few people would disagree. It is when we go on to examine which emotions were considered unsuitable for song by the eighteenth-century theorists that we may find their views somewhat restrictive. As early as the 1720s Johann Mattheson had argued that violent passions do not lend themselves to musical setting (*Critica Musica*, 1722–3, i, 98). Half a century later Wieland repeats the point, basing his view quite explicitly on the aesthetic argument that music must not offend against the laws of beauty ('Versuch', 1775). Krause excludes not only violent moods, but irony (*Von der musikalischen Poesie*, iv). On this question of irony he may have had right on his side, at least for that stage in the development of the Lied. But for the rest, the exclusion of so much led to a huge concentration on poems which sang of wine and innocent conviviality, of the joys and sorrows of love (but not its frenzies), of the solemn or melancholy thought of death (but not man's occasional naked terror of it), and so on. Two poems on death will illustrate this last point. 'Das Grab', by J.G. von Salis, expresses the sinister mystery of the grave and the anguish of the bereaved, but manages to end with a wisp of comfort, for the grave at least offers peace after life's tempests:

Simplicity as an Ideal

Das arme Herz hienieden
Von manchem Sturm bewegt,
Find't nirgends wahren Frieden,
Als wo es nicht mehr schlägt.

That poem was first published in the *Göttinger Musenalmanch* in 1788 and was to be set to music at least twelve times before 1800. By contrast, Claudius's grim lines on death had to wait over a century[1] to find a composer:

Der Tod
Ach, es ist so dunkel in des Todes Kammer,
Tönt so traurig, wenn er sich bewegt
Und nun aufhebt seinen schweren Hammer
Und die Stunde schlägt.

(It is so dark in Death's chamber and sounds so mournful when he stirs and lifts his heavy hammer and strikes the hour.)

As a natural consequence of the choice of texts and the generally accepted Affektenlehre, the great majority of eighteenth-century songs are relatively straightforward and unified expressions of some basic human experience or emotion. As we have seen, the composer was supposed to capture this Hauptaffekt without worrying about the specific realisation of the various motifs in the poem or the stages in its story or argument (see the quotation from Görner, above, p. 16). Composers' instructions to the singer often define the Hauptaffekt, leaving him to judge the appropriate tempo. Thus, one encounters 'mood-words' such as *spöttisch, schmeichelnd* or *unschuldig* at least as often as *langsam* or *geschwind*.[2] Sometimes the way in which this is done will provoke a smile today. C.F.F. Paulsen heads his setting of Goethe's 'Mailied', 'Von der Schönheit der Natur berauscht'. How one is expected to sing his utterly vapid tune as if intoxicated by the beauty of nature is beyond conjecture. The unison accompaniment only enhances the cheerlessness and emptiness of the effect:

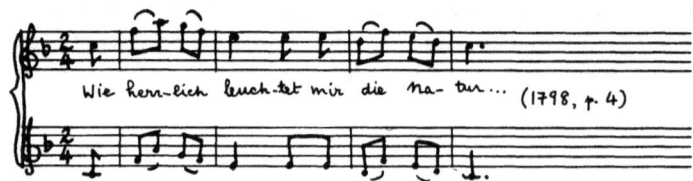

Simplicity as an Ideal

Reichardt goes even further in introducing his setting of 'Die Schiffende'[3] to the performer. In this poem, Hölty describes how the boat containing his beloved floats gently past in the moonlight. She seems half-goddess, half-mortal; the terms in which the poet describes her are exactly balanced between earthly love and the veneration due to a divine being. Reichardt's instructions read: 'In sweet ecstasy, gently floating as the girl floats on silvery waves, quiet as the rustle of evening breezes'. This is as much a paraphrase of Hölty as an indication of how to perform the song.

A conception of song as an uncomplicated and unified expression of the poem's basic mood was obviously well suited to an age in which the genre was aimed mainly at modestly gifted amateur performers. Such instructions as those just cited imply that even here the composer felt that the singer needed some hints. We may well think that a simple 'Sanft. Ziemlich langsam' might have been more helpful than Reichardt's ardent instructions, but it should not be forgotten that this was an age in which everything concerning the conception, composition and performance of a song was seen to flow necessarily from a proper understanding of the Hauptaffekt.

Insistence on the composer's duty to realise the dominant mood of a poem without concerning himself about the painting-in of details was bound up with the preponderance of simple strophic forms in the half-century under discussion. (I say 'bound up', because there was certainly a mutual influence at work: the Affektenlehre encouraged the composition of strophic songs which in turn seemed to validate the doctrine that had given rise to them.) From about 1780 onwards, the fashion for 'Lieder im Volkston' will have reinforced this tendency, since it is obviously very difficult to evoke the strains of folk melody in elaborately through-composed song.

A successful strophic composition must steer a middle course between two treacherous rocks. If you set the first stanza of the poem in a particularly eloquent and expressive way, there is a danger that some part of the melody will be wrong for the corresponding words or phrases in subsequent stanzas. If, on the other hand, you adopt a more cautious approach and produce a melody to which all stanzas may safely be sung, the result may well be tame. Eighteenth-century theorists and composers were well aware of the dilemma, and there is evidence that some of the composers chafed under the restrictions of strophic song; in 1759 J.G. Müthel notes that one could set the words in a much more exact and lively fashion if one did not have to think of the succeeding stanzas. C.P.E. Bach too felt that strophic composition imposed a constraint on the composer and blamed his amateur public, who would be incapable of performing more extended and elaborate songs (1774, Preface). J.P. Kirnberger solves the problem in an ingenious, if somewhat impertinent, way. In the Preface to his *Oden mit Melodien* (1773), he explains that he has printed only the first verse of the poems; this is not only to save space, but also because that is the verse for which he devised his music and therefore the basis on which his song is to be judged. Of the twenty solo songs in this collection, eighteen are given with just the first stanza!

But Kirnberger is the only composer to have cut the Gordian knot so ruthlessly.[4] Other composers at least printed the remaining stanzas underneath their music or on the facing page, leaving us to perform them as we may and judge them as we will. Where eighteenth-century composers tried more experimental types of song, there is evidence that this was done reluctantly at first and only with poems that positively demanded it.[5] J.A. Scheibe had already pointed the way in his *Critischer Musikus*, 1739, no. 64. In poems where a simple strophic setting is impossible, one may alternate between two melodies (Scheibe's term for this kind of song is *Wechselode*, a word that was taken over by C.P.E. Bach and achieved wide currency). Further, Scheibe mentions the possibility of devising fresh material for each stanza. He does not use the word *durchkomponieren*, however; this was to come into fashion only very much later. The various ways in which composers departed from simple strophic forms will be discussed presently; at this stage we may merely note that, for all their awareness of the problems involved, eighteenth-century song-composers cast the great majority of their Lieder in strophic form and that there is some evidence that this practice was, at least in part, due to a suspicion that more elaborate songs might be beyond amateur performers.

We have already heard Telemann assuring the purchasers of his *Oden* that these will be easy on the vocal cords. One needs only to contrast Telemann's songs with his solo cantatas and the surviving arias from his operas — highly exacting, often requiring the singer to imitate and rival the runs and arabesques of the obbligato flute, violin or oboe — to realise that the assurance is broadly true. The contrast becomes even more marked if we compare the cantatas of J.S. Bach with the Lieder written by

Simplicity as an Ideal

various of his sons. Solicitude for the amateur performer is expressed time and time again, as in Krause's ideal that a song should be within anyone's reach, and Schulz's declaration that his songs are intended even for unpractised amateurs.[6]

The one serious reservation that has to be made is that a good deal of early song contained unvocal, 'instrumental' features (see above, pp. 14f). But this became much less frequent as the vogue for 'Lieder im Volkston' spread; most eighteenth-century songs were truly accessible to any reasonably competent amateur singer. Zumsteeg's shorter songs illustrate the trend well; for all their subtleties, the great majority are quite easy to perform. There are only isolated cases where Zumsteeg clearly had a more practised singer in mind and permitted himself runs and embellishments of a mildly operatic nature.[7] In general, there is a freshness and directness about much late eighteenth-century song which does indeed vaguely remind the listener of the strains of German folksong without in any way being a pastiche; such simple and eminently singable songs continue to be written well into the next century and certainly influenced Schubert's simplest type of strophic composition.

In the early decades of the history of the Lied, as we have seen, the right hand of the accompaniment usually doubled the vocal line and the player seldom had to cope with more than two parts. There might be a middle part of the simplest nature (parallel thirds or sixths), there might be a somewhat fuller chordal accompaniment in settings of sacred or solemn texts, but that was all. The accompaniment emancipated itself only very gradually from its enslavement to the vocal line and, even where it took on an independent existence, it was rarely difficult to play. Fleischer apologises for the fullness and difficulty of some of his accompaniments (Preface to the *Oden und Lieder*, i. 1756), justifying any difficulties with the claim that his writing is pianistic (this is true) and is at any rate more interesting than a bare two-part style. But even here a pianist with a reasonable ability to play thirds and simple three-part textures plus a degree of agility in the left hand will not meet with any difficulty.

Early through-composed settings of long ballads will occasionally contain *agitato* passages in the accompaniment to match dramatic points in the narrative and Zumsteeg is capable of making demands on the player's agility, above all during his rare attempts at 'pictorial' keyboard writing.[8] But the fact that one has to *search* for examples of songs with technically exacting

Simplicity as an Ideal

accompaniments in the literature of the period is in itself significant.

As anyone experienced in the performance of nineteenth-century song knows, it is in the relationship between voice and accompaniment that difficulties abound, even when both performers have fully mastered their individual parts. The problems are most likely to be bound up with harmonic or rhythmic complexities or with the question of balance and 'togetherness' in passages where the composer exploits the extreme registers of the piano or otherwise experiments with its tonal and expressive potentialities. Such difficulties hardly exist in eighteenth-century song, even where the accompaniment is independent of the vocal line. Nor, since composers and theorists tended to the view that music was best suited to express general notions and would do better to avoid pictorial details,[9] were the song-composers given to the sort of 'representational' writing for the piano which often presents performers of, say, Schubert with considerable problems of tone-colour and balance. Since solo keyboard music was subtle, varied and often technically difficult in the latter part of the eighteenth century, we must again assume that the virtual absence of technical problems in the songs of the day resulted from a deliberate attempt to accommodate amateur performers. Even where the accompaniment liberated itself from the vocal line, it tended to support the singer with triplets or simple broken chords which mirrored the harmonies expressed in or implied by the voice part with the most reassuring directness.

Of the thousands of songs composed between the 1740s and 1800, comparatively few venture beyond the most immediate and obvious harmonies and modulations. Now it may well be that when we think of the chromatic experimentation of the late Renaissance and Baroque periods and the wholesale expansion of harmonic vocabulary in the Romantic era, we must concede that the second half of the eighteenth century was *in general* a comparatively unenterprising period, harmonically speaking. Nevertheless, the paucity of unexpected or unorthodox elements in the Lied is very marked. Modulations are nearly always from the tonic to the dominant and back again, or from the major to the tonic or relative minor. 'Die Verschweigung' from Ramler/Krause's *Lieder der Deutschen* (iii, 1768, 37), which moves from A major to F sharp minor, thence through E major and B minor before returning to its point of departure, although in no way surprising in the general context of eighteenth-century

Simplicity as an Ideal

modulation-practice, is unusual for a song of that day.

The question of modulation is linked, of course, to the prevalence of short strophic forms, since adventurous key-patterns are very difficult to achieve within a 16 or 24-bar form, even assuming that the composer had any such ambition. But this is only one aspect of a general tendency towards harmonic orthodoxy. Examination of the chords commonly used seldom reveals anything more venturesome than the diminished seventh or, more rarely, the various types of augmented sixths — and these are saved for especially dramatic or expressive moments.

C.P.E. Bach stands out among his contemporaries in respect of harmonic variety and unexpectedness as in other matters. The sacred songs are richest in experimental touches, often designed to seize the listener's attention in the very first notes of a song. 'Jesus in Gethsemane' (text by Sturm) opens dramatically with a rise of an augmented fourth and presently passes from G minor to D flat major(!), E flat minor and F minor back to the home key; the setting of Cramer's paraphrase of the 23rd Psalm even *begins* with the third inversion of a dominant seventh. Or a song may start innocuously enough, but go on to surprising things; this is the case with the setting of Stolberg's 'Lied' ('Ich ging unter Erlen') where, after a deceptively orthodox beginning, Bach combines a semitonal descent in the bass line with chromaticisms in the voice part. Most striking of all, however, is his treatment of Eschenburg's poem 'Die Trennung',[10] with its rocking diminished fifth in the bass, supporting a restless and shifting vocal line.

To turn from C.P.E. Bach to eighteenth-century song in general: here too the most interesting harmonies are usually to be encountered in sacred songs, where they are employed to underline a state of spiritual tension or anguish.[11] Such moods provoke Schulz to some of his rare harmonic adventures. My first example is taken from a song of penitence ('Bußlied'), at a point where the singer refers to sins which 'desecrate' ('entweihen') his heart, as if it were a holy place, previously consecrated to God's service:

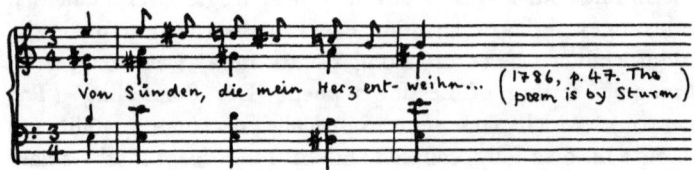

The second extract is from 'Beharrlichkeit im Guten' where the poet (Eschenburg) addresses God, who witnessed the fervour of the penitent's tears and bestowed grace upon him:

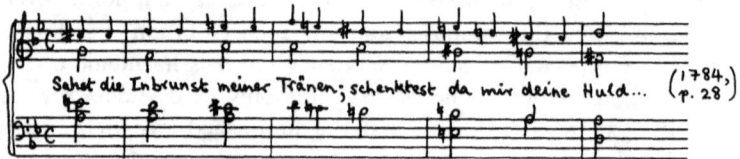

We have already seen how the general form and texture of the chorale could be taken over for certain types of secular text; similarly, the chromatic expressiveness which we have noted in sacred songs by Schulz could be employed in profane contexts, where the emotions to be expressed in music were gloomy or turbulent enough to warrant it. Thus we find closely similar passages in J.C.F. Bach's setting of 'Der Kranke' (The Invalid), where the text refers to the sufferer's fever:

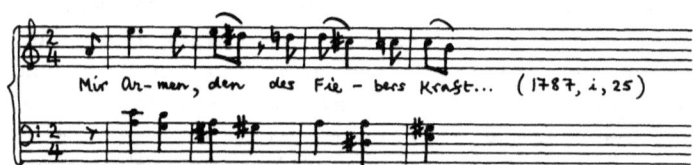

— and in Türck's song 'Denk, o Lieber!', at the moment where the singer looks back tearfully on past times of happy love (1780, p. 7). It may be noted that such chromatic progressions are rather backward looking than innovative, reminding one of the fugues and fantasias of J.S. Bach's predecessors, of the near-obligatory piece of chromatic 'daring' in seventeenth- and early eighteenth-century sets of keyboard variations, even of the fancies and *ricercari* of the sixteenth century. But they introduce a welcome note of harmonic diversity into eighteenth-century song and are very well suited to certain types of text.

However, such strains are not encountered solely in songs of spiritual anguish, fear of death or in near-tragic lover's laments. The strangest series of harmonic experiments known to me in the field of eighteenth-century song occurs in a *comic* song: J.G. Schmügel's setting of Lessing's poem 'Der Sonderling' (The Eccentric), which comments satirically on man's ability to recognise his own folly, coupled with his resentment if others dare

Simplicity as an Ideal

to point it out:

> So bald der Mensch sich kennt,
> Sieht er, er sey ein Narr;
> Und gleichwohl zürnt der Narr,
> Wenn man ihn also nennt.

The quirkishness of Schmügel's treatment matches the subject matter exactly. Marked *spöttisch und geschwind* (mockingly and quickly), the song[12] is characterised by interrupted cadences — rare in the *Lieder* of this period — and by rapid alternation of the major and minor modes.

The examples mentioned have all been concerned with extremes, whether of serious emotion or of whimsy. It is rare to encounter a song which possesses genuine harmonic interest without in any way partaking of this extreme quality. Such a song is J.M. Wiedebein's setting of Claudius's serene and popular little hymn 'Täglich zu singen' (1779, p. 8). Here the harmonic effect of a sequence of dominant sevenths is enhanced by the passages in canon in the two upper parts, and is combined with a limpid vocal melody. The harmonies shift rapidly, yet the effect is curiously peaceful:

Two other such examples are love poems, settings of Gleim and Klopstock. In 'Zwei verlorne Tage', Gleim speaks of the bittersweet experience of love in tones too light for any really forlorn musical treatment, but none the less touched with melancholy and regret. André's elegant little setting (*Lieder, Arien und Duette*, i, 1780 p. 30) achieves the right colouring through falling sequences, touches of minor harmony, generous use of the German sixth and, by contemporary standards, frequent modulations. Carl Preuß's Klopstock setting, 'An Lyda',[13] is on a more ambitious scale, with a harmonically adventurous passage of eight bars carefully placed between stretches of perfect orthodoxy. The poet carries the vision of his beloved in his mind's eye at all times. The climax of the poem comes when he challenges this vision to transform

Simplicity as an Ideal

itself into reality:

> Beschwör ich dich Erscheinung,
> Auf, und verwandle dich!
> Verwandle dich Erscheinung,
> Und werde Lyda selbst!

Rightly seeing that this passage must carry the heaviest emotional weighting, the composer sets it by means of what in his age must have seemed a vertiginous series of harmonic progressions: from F minor to D flat, to the dominant 7th of E flat, thence, via the second inversion of the chord of D minor, two diminished sevenths and an enharmonic change, to A flat. Here is the passage reduced to its harmonic skeleton; it may be noted that the camouflaged German sixth which leads to the chord of D minor is clearer to the ear than to the eye:

In fact, when associated with Klopstock's emotive lines, this progression works perfectly well. Preuß then sets the final words of the text as a brief passage of recitative, and wittily treats the conventional dominant and tonic chords which follow as a means of progressing to a postlude of eleven bars which puts us back most solidly into the home key of E flat:

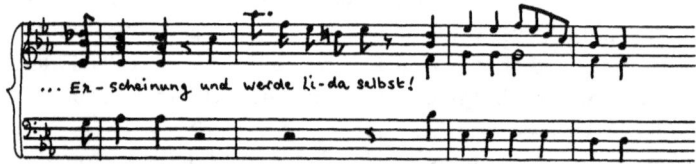

Unusually then, the postlude is employed to allow the ear to recover from all the harmonic surprises to which it has just been subjected and to re-establish the basic tonality of the song.

It is worth repeating that the songs just described form a tiny minority of the total. The paucity of harmonic experimentation will undoubtedly have been partly due to contemporary theories

Simplicity as an Ideal

of song, which encouraged the composer to seek out and express the general mood without attempting to paint in all the details. This was linked with a preference for strophic songs, in which unusual harmonic colouration, like all highly specific expressive devices, might fit the first stanza but be quite inappropriate for succeeding ones. Hence, composers played safe in this, as in other respects. An awareness that interesting effects could be achieved by adhering to the same tune and altering the underlying harmonies in the different stanzas of a song seems to have been lacking. Zumsteeg's setting of Kosegarten's 'Nachtgesang' (*Kleine Balladen und Lieder*, i, 22f), which does this at exactly the same place in each of the three stanzas with an effect which is both *piquant* and moving, seems to be an isolated example.

Of the composers working in the latter part of the century, it is in fact Zumsteeg who, harmonically speaking, is the most enterprising. It is not simply that we find in his songs chromatic progressions, diminished and augmented chords, dramatic interrupted cadences, even the occasional enharmonic change — in fact all the devices mentioned hitherto; the important point is that he uses harmony as the *major* expressive and interpretative device in a song much more often than his contemporaries. The following examples, all from the *Kleine Balladen und Lieder*, may serve to illustrate this. In Kosegarten's 'Erscheinung', where the beautiful apparition is shown to have nothing to do with earthly phenomena but to symbolise transcendental values, an effect both wistful and elusive is achieved through rapid progressions from G major to the tonic minor, thence to B flat and, surprisingly, back to G *minor* at the end (iii, 18). In a more playful poem, 'Macht der Sinne' (iv, 1), the singer's disorientation as he bewails his inability to resist the girl's attractions is conveyed by a series of modulations and constantly shifting harmonies.

In his setting of Overbeck's ecstatic song of praise, 'Hochgesang' (v, 14), Zumsteeg achieves an awe-inspiring effect through the abrupt use of the chord of the flattened submediant at the point where the poet speaks of the whole universe resounding to God's praise:

Simplicity as an Ideal

My last example shows what the composer can make of an interrupted cadence. Herder's ode to sleep 'An den Schlaf', v, 35) claims that sleep transposes us to a better world illuminated by a fairer light. Zumsteeg sets the poem in E flat and presently interrupts the expected and conventional close in B flat with the chord of G flat (flattened submediant again!). He proceeds for two bars in this remote key, to transpose us back into B flat on the words 'a more beautiful light'. The bright awakening into this 'other world' is exactly matched by the modulation into a brighter key after the muted effect of the passage in G flat.

These examples from Preuß and Zumsteeg[14] seem to anticipate Schubert, who was to make much of the surprise progression from the chord of the tonic major to that of the flattened submediant and would show himself unequalled in his exploitation of the 'ambiguities' of the German sixth. But Preuß and Zumsteeg are untypical. To return to the rather unadventurous norm: another factor limiting the frequency of harmonic experiments may have been the tendency to avoid poems which expressed violent emotions; it is certainly no coincidence that, of the examples I have been able to cite, several are settings of poems expressing some sort of spiritual anguish. Again, there may have been a measure of deference to amateur singers who, rightly or wrongly, were probably thought liable to become confused or disorientated by anything too unexpected. Such misgivings, if they existed, will not have been wholly unfounded. Even today, competent amateur singers can be left stranded by some of the harmonic surprises that Schubert springs on them.

We have seen, then, that the comparative simplicity of eighteenth-century song has much to do with the real or supposed limitations of the performers. It is also directly bound up with contemporary theories of song. Practically speaking, the Affektenlehre requires the composer to subordinate his invention to the demands of the poem and the interests of the poet in a quite radical, even restricting way. Here the images used by eighteenth-century theorists and composers to define the relationship of words to music give a significant pointer.

Music and poem, says J.N. Forkel (*Musikalisch-kritische Bibliothek*, i, 1778, p. 212), relate to each other like garment and soul. Translated into the more expected antithesis of garment and body, this metaphor is elaborated on by J.A.P. Schulz, when he lists among the criteria of a good song 'a striking similarity of musical and poetic tone, a melody which fits the declamation and the metre of the text as a garment fits the body' (Preface to the 2nd edition of the *Lieder im Volkston*, dated 1784). Maria Theresia Paradis makes the metaphor sound quaintly literal when she talks of clothing Bürger's 'Lenore' ('das gute Kind') according to her (the composer's) taste, and J.A. Hiller takes the notion to the point of voluntary enslavement when he argues that each poem has its latent, 'natural' melody and the music simply takes this up and adorns it ('bearbeitet diese natürliche Melodie und putzt sie aus').[15]

One very obvious consequence of this subservience shows itself in the reluctance of eighteenth-century composers to alter or otherwise tamper with the texts that they set to music. To be true, Ramler, when editing the poems which form the collection *Lieder der Deutschen*, altered some of them to suit the composers' convenience, claiming to have the poet's permission in most cases. Where not, he blithely assures us, the poet will no doubt turn a blind eye in the interests of the music-lover (Vorbericht). But this is very untypical and is in any case the action of an editor, not a composer. The great majority of composers set the words exactly as the poet had written them. It should perhaps be recalled that part of the reaction against the extravagances of opera and cantata had been a rejection of vocal writing that made it impossible to understand the words. This was not simply a recoiling from florid singing, but also from what was widely regarded as senseless textual repetition.[16] To treat a poem with respect did not only involve adopting a simple (often virtually syllabic) vocal style which did not get in the way of the words; it demanded a form of composition which allowed the verse to proceed at its natural pace and preserve its own proportions rather than having to conform to arbitrary patterns dictated by musical considerations.

Apart from conventional repetitions of the last line or couplet of a stanza, especially in 'gesellige Lieder', alterations to the text seem to have been made chiefly to solve the structural problems which are created when irregular poetic forms (e.g. sapphics) are

Simplicity as an Ideal

set to a musical language dominated by symmetrical phrase-lengths. This could involve the composer in (to us) wholly arbitrary textual repetitions.

The much discussed question of whether a song realises, transforms or even 'destroys' the poem was to be fuelled by nineteenth-century composers, many of whom were to rearrange or expand their chosen texts quite drastically. If such practices were rare before 1800, the main reason was undoubtedly that stated, namely that the melody was widely regarded as the 'garment' of the text, implying that the basic poetic contours should not be obscured. A further factor may be the close contacts that existed between poets and composers, between the members of the Göttinger Hainbund, for example, and the composers who set their works when they first appeared in the *Musenalmanach*, or between Goethe and his early composers. For Goethe, as is well known, threw all his authority behind the view that music should be the handmaiden of poetry and resented any attempt on the part of the composer to claim parity, let alone hog the limelight. But this is exactly what the composer does, if only implicitly, when he arrogates to himself the right to alter the structure of the poem in any but the most conventional way (repetition of closing line or refrain).

Although I may have devoted more space to the exceptions than to more orthodox productions (if only because exceptions are generally more interesting), it will have become abundantly clear that the simplicity which ruled in all departments of eighteenth-century song was the result of deliberate policy and, if one excepts the work of amateurs and very minor talents, of an artificial self-restraint.[17] Indeed, we sometimes find the paradoxical situation where minor composers overreached themselves in experimentation (harmony, form, the expressive use of the keyboard accompaniment), while greater men who showed great boldness and originality in other fields, were content with a fairly simple and undemanding style in their songs.

However, in the last two decades of the century, many more composers began to chafe at these restraints, as a consequence of which we see the Lied moving towards greater complexity in a number of ways. Chief among these are the increasing prominence given to the accompaniment and various types of formal experimentation. I will begin with the matter of the accompaniment — and here the popularity of the early piano as opposed to harpsichord and clavichord seems to have been a decisive factor.

Simplicity as an Ideal

Notes

1. Challier's *Großer Liederkatalog* records no settings at all up to 1888.
2. For expression marks that clearly reflect the values of Empfindsamkeit, see above, p. 54.
3. *Oden und Lieder*, i, 1779, p. 6.
4. Elsewhere, however, he says that one should have the whole poem in mind when devising the tune — *Anleitung*, p. 11.
5. See the Prefaces to Gräfe, *Fünfzig Psalmen* (1760) and Brede, *Lieder und Gesänge* (1786).
6. For Krause, see Marpurg's *Kritische Briefe*, i, 1759, no. 22; for Schulz, the *Vorbericht* to the *Lieder im Volkston*.
7. See *Kleine Balladen und Lieder*, ii, 6 and iv, 39.
8. Ibid., vii, 4f.
9. Cf. H.W. von Gerstenberg, *Briefe über Merkwürdigkeiten der Literatur*, 1766-7, no. 20.
10. Given by Friedlaender, ex. 79. 'Jesus in Gethsemane' is the last of the *30 Geistliche Lieder* (edn. Peters, 3748). For Cramer, see *Herrn Doctor Cramers übersetzte Psalmen*, 1774, p. 12. The setting of Stolberg is given by Friedlaender, ex. 166.
11. For an early example, see Marpurg's setting of Gellert's 'Bußlied' in *Geistliche Oden*, 1758, no. 21.
12. It can be found in Friedlaender, ex. 75.
13. 'Dein süßes Bild, o Lyda!', in *Vermischte Oden und Lieder*, 1783, pp. 10f. A variant is: 'Dein süßes Bild, Edone'. Schubert sets this latter version.
14. See too *Kleine Balladen und Lieder*, i, 8; ii, 13; iv, 26f.
15. For Paradis, see *Lenore*, Vienna, 1790, Dedication; for Hiller, see the 'Abhandlung von der Nachahmung der Natur in der Musik', in Marpurg's *Historisch-kritische Beiträge*, i, 1754, p. 526.
16. See Gottsched, *Critische Dichtkunst*, ii, 3, para. 6.
17. 'Selbstgewählte Schranken' (Abert, *Goethe und die Musik*, p. 62).

7
The New Adventurousness in the Late Eighteenth Century

The accompaniment

In the second half of the century the piano gradually asserted itself as the main accompanying instrument. The earliest pianos (*Hammerflügel*) had the general shape of small modern grand pianos and looked, in fact, very like harpsichords. From about the 1760s onwards the square piano (*Hammerklavier, Fortepiano*) grew in popularity as a domestic instrument. Although these early square pianos had nothing of the ornate decorative frippery of the grander type of harpsichord, they were neat and elegant pieces of drawing-room furniture, often beautifully inlaid. But it would be wrong to see a late eighteenth-century square piano as primarily a middle-class status symbol. If it was a status symbol at all, then an emotional one, belonging to the age of sensibility, like the copy of *Night Thoughts* or *Werther* on the bedside table. Hammerflügel and square piano alike were exceptionally well suited to the sort of intimate early song where the singer usually accompanied himself or herself, in communion with the instrument as it were.

The tone of the early pianos was light and pure, often bell-like and lingering on the ear. By contrast, the bass-line was sharply etched, still with a marked resemblance to that of the harpsichord. Modern listeners who are not used to the early instruments may be struck by their limitations, but in their age they seemed to offer exciting new possibilities, especially in the way that they made possible rapid crescendos and diminuendos. They were both able to express changing moods and nuances better than the harpsichord and possessed greater range and power than the clavichord.

We have already heard Hermes claiming that the new instrument could express feelings that ran too deep for words (above, p. 52). There is, in fact, abundant evidence that poets and composers alike prized the early piano for its 'gentle' and 'silvery' tone and its almost magical sympathy with the moods of the singer.[1] Indirect proof of the composers' confidence in the instrument's expressive powers is afforded by the increasing use of dynamic and other indications in song accompaniments. Although I know of one isolated example of this in J.H. Hesse's collection of 1757, the usage became widespread only in the late 1770s and the 80s, by which time the piano had firmly established itself as the chief accompanying instrument for domestic song. Neefe's *Serenaten* of 1777, bold and unorthodox in all sorts of ways, contains independent and highly idiomatic accompaniments, often with very rapidly changing dynamics. Forte and piano markings, together with 'hairpins', are used sparingly by Reichardt in his *Oden und Lieder* (1779–81), but rapidly become common in the eighties, in J.G. Moses (1781), Boßler's *Blumenlese* (1782–3), J.W. Häßler (1782–6) and elsewhere. Some composers, among them G.F. Benda in 1780 and Zumsteeg a decade later, employ dynamic signs and other expression marks only during passages for piano solo, as if feeling that the performer needs some indication or encouragement at those points where the accompanying instrument is holding the stage on its own.

Awareness of the piano's expressive potential undoubtedly accelerated the trend towards more elaborate accompaniments after several decades of rather unenterprising keyboard writing. Although even late eighteenth-century accompaniments are hardly ever of any great technical difficulty, they certainly become much more interesting in the last two decades of the century. One can perceive two independent but related strands: the accompaniment gradually liberates itself from its enslavement to the vocal line and it acquires solo passages (preludes, interludes, postludes) while the voice is silent. The two developments often coexist in the one song or at least in one and the same song-book, but can usefully be treated separately.

It will be remembered that early accompaniments had merely doubled the vocal line, with the occasional addition of a middle part. Composers were slow to experiment with freer and more adventurous textures, possibly out of a feeling that the amateur singers needed the support given by the doubling. The first modest experiments known to me occur in J.E. Bach (1749), where we occasionally meet with a slightly ornamented version of the vocal line in the right hand of the accompaniment, or even parallel movement a third above the voice. The effect is not unlike that of an obbligato violin part. More dramatically, Herbing uses rapid demisemiquavers in both hands to suggest the violence of a storm (1759, p. 53). Even decades later, when a degree of independence in the right hand had become much more common, few composers ventured beyond the obvious device of using broken chords and arpeggio figures in one or both hands. Rust (1796), Häußler and others have a liking for little phrases in the treble part of the accompaniment designed to fill in gaps between vocal phrases and a number of composers resort to the 'oom-pom' type of piano writing, usually as a means of imparting a mood of restlessness:

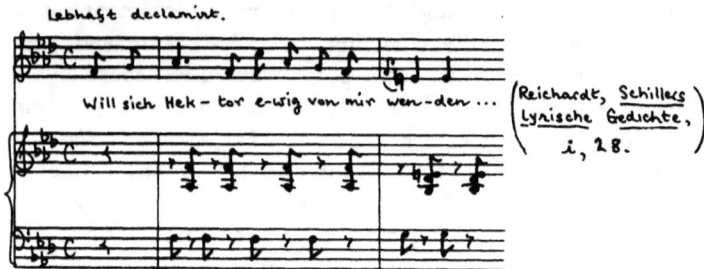

Swift broken triads may be used to achieve a similar effect, but we find little sign of the enormous and exciting variety which was so much to enrich and diversify accompaniments in the early part of the nineteenth century. Nor, in the two decades before the turn of the century, is there any great movement towards 'representational' piano writing. Early spinning-songs have accompaniments intended to evoke the movement of the spinning-wheel and some minstrel songs are accompanied by arpeggio figures suggestive of the harp. But the majority of cases are of the most naïve kind, usually attempts to summon up bird-song, an imitative device that has plagued European music since the 'birdcall' lute fantasias of the sixteenth century and the harpsichord pieces of the seventeenth.[2]

It will be recalled that most early Klavierlieder began with the first note of the vocal line and ended with the last; the accompanying instrument had no independent role. When short solos began to be written, they were clearly regarded as a novelty and were often labelled 'Cembalo allein' or 'Klavier allein'. Many of the early preludes are note-for-note anticipations of the singer's opening phrase (example: Türck, 1780, p. 12). It seems much more effective when the composer allows the piano to establish the mood of the song, using material which accords with what the voice will presently sing without pre-empting it. This is what happens with the clumping semiquavers that open E.J.B. Lang's setting of Bürger's defiant 'Der Bauer'; this is what Schubart achieves through the gentle pastoral opening to his 'Hirtenlied' (*Shepherds' Song*), anticipating Beethoven's *Pastoral Symphony* in the process:

Solo keyboard interludes are used sparingly, either to pass from one section to the next in a through-composed song, or to echo or otherwise round off the singer's phrase at an intermediate cadence. It is with the postlude that the accompaniment really comes into its own as an independent expressive element in eighteenth-century song. The earliest examples are no more than a conventional rounding-off, sometimes literally echoing the vocal line, sometimes in free imitation of it. J.H. Hesse (1757) marks his solo passages 'ritornello', thus clearly revealing their heritage. Here are extracts from his song 'An Doris' which show how the postlude elaborates on a phrase from the vocal line; in this early example, we could easily imagine that we had a continuo song before us, with a ritornello played on two flutes:

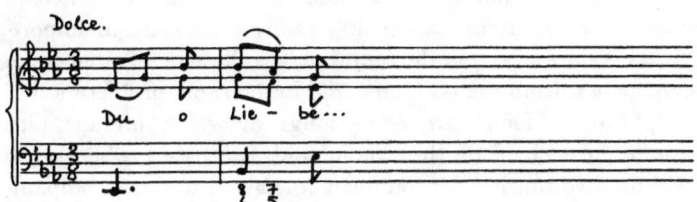

This use of the postlude as little more than an attractive way of saying 'that's that!' persists, of course,[3] but the postlude can also have a profoundly serious role to play, as in Schmügel's setting of Gleim's ode to sleep ('An den Schlaf'). The mood of the poem is dominated by the idea of slipping into weariness and gently dropping off to sleep ('Falle doch . . . sanft . . . drücke doch'). This mood, beautifully expressed throughout the song by means of falling quaver phrases, is enhanced by dreamily descending scale passages in the postlude (1762, no. 18: given by Friedlaender, ex. 73). The postlude can even have a harmonic and structural function, as in C.J.P.'s graceful setting of Stolberg's 'Daphne am Bach'. The composer, perceiving that the poem veers between memories of happiness and a sense of loss, devised a tune beginning in F major and ending in the tonic minor, a very unusual harmonic pattern in eighteenth-century song. The postlude then had the function of bringing us back, by way of the German sixth, to F major, both between verses and at the end of this (strophic) song.[4] These examples, although interesting and in some cases eloquent and beautiful, do not of course do more than herald a rather tentative awareness of what could be achieved in terms of expressive power by the piano after the voice had fallen silent. Although Hermes had declared that the piano could evoke feelings inexpressible in words, we will have to wait until the Romantic era before the full implications of that claim will be realised.

It will have become clear that the second half of the eighteenth century saw the accompaniment steadily increasing in importance, as is shown both in the (admittedly still modest) attempts to emancipate it from the vocal line and in the rapid proliferation of solo passages. There are even songs in which prelude plus postlude form half of the whole and two cases where they constitute two thirds![5] A prominent role given to the accompaniment does not, of course, of itself make a good song; E.A. Foerster (1791) was given to writing quite elaborate and sustained solo

The New Adventurousness

passages in his songs, but the songs as a whole are relentlessly trivial. An even crasser example is afforded by Gruber's setting of 'Der Bauer'.[6] For here the long prelude is exactly like a passage from one of the keyboard sonatas obsequiously turned out by court composers for the very princes who are pilloried in the poem:

Examples such as those should warn us against any simplistic 'evolutionary' view, according to which growing complexity might automatically come to be equated with an advance in intrinsic musical value. Nevertheless, the advantages of expanding the role of the accompaniment are manifest. A keyboard part that does not merely double the vocal line with the addition of a bass both has greater expressive possibilities and avoids that conflict of interests between two media that had led many earlier composers into hopelessly instrumental styles of writing for the voice. A well-conceived solo prelude can establish the mood of a song in advance of the singer's first entry, while a postlude allows the burden of the song to continue after the last words have been sung. In a song like Schmügel's 'An den Schlaf', the emotional reverberations are very considerable. By the turn of the century it was generally realised that voice and accompaniment were independent but interlocking and related parts of the song. Thus, the wheel had come full circle, for in the 1750s it had been a *divergence* from complete agreement that had been the exception. Goethe, conservative in this respect as in all things concerning song, distrusted this emancipation of the accompaniment,[7] but in general it was felt to be a liberating and expanding influence. Although, as we shall see, many nineteenth-century reviewers came to fear that the accompaniment was being taken too far in the direction of complexity and virtuosity, no one wished to return to the tame simplicities of earlier periods.

The development towards independent piano writing was paralleled by a growing tendency to write in three staves. Early attempts to introduce independent material into the accompaniment had used small notes which had to compete with the larger notes of the vocal line in one and the same stave. This crowded and rather confusing method was obviously irksome, and composers soon formed the habit of writing in three staves where the accompaniment made it necessary. Parallel to this development was the change from the old soprano clef to the modern treble clef. Since some composers, when writing their songs in three staves, reserve the new clef for the right hand of the accompaniment, it seems likely that in the first instance the change occurred chiefly for the convenience of the player; the singer, it was assumed, would manage with the traditional 'singer's clef'. This in turn is an important further indication of the fact that singer and player were increasingly expected to be two people; it is unlikely that a composer would expect a singer to read the vocal line from one clef and accompany himself or herself from another. Thus, notation followed developments in composition and performance.

The gradual emancipation of the accompaniment is one of two clear signs that, as the century drew to a close, song-composers were becoming increasingly dissatisfied with the largely self-imposed restrictions that had governed the Lied for nearly half a century. The second manifestation of this is the spread of formal experiments, evidence of a growing desire to escape from the tyranny of straightforward strophic song. Such experiments could go in two directions: an expansion of strophic form and an attempt to develop the through-composed song ('das durchkomponierte Lied'). Although in each case the process starts long before the end of the century, it is the 1780s and 90s that saw rapid advances in formal enterprise. I will take the two aspects in turn, beginning with the expansion of strophic song.

Expansion of the simple strophic form

J.G. Gräfe, in the Preface to his *Fünfzig Psalmen* of 1760, had talked of the stultifying effect of always adhering rigidly to strophic composition pure and simple. In fact, where the mood or the content of a poem changed from stanza to stanza or between groups of stanzas, composers were quick to see the advantages of devising two different tunes and using these in various combinations: a binary version (in which the first group of stanzas was set to tune A and the rest to tune B) or a ternary variant (in which tune A returned for the closing stanza or stanzas). A less common device was to maintain the basic melody in its essentials, but to modify it and/or its accompaniment at need. (It may be mentioned in passing that Scheibe's scheme of a strict ABABA alternation is rarely encountered.)[8] Taken together, these methods represent an opportunity to expand the range and flexibility of song-form quite radically.

The subtlest example known to me of strophic variation on a single tune is C.P.E. Bach's 'Nonnelied' (first published in 1789: in Friedlaender, ex. 78). The folksong text is the nun's lament over the love which she has had to renounce. (There are so many similar poems in the folk tradition that one asks oneself whether there was ever such a thing as a willing nun.) Bach varies both verse and refrain throughout the song, with subtle and at times poignant effect, showing how much can be achieved in expressive terms through very little. The type of setting in which the tune remains the same and the accompaniment varies is surprisingly rare in the eighteenth century. Yet the first of C.F. Teumer's *Sechs Oden von Klopstock* (1797) shows its potentialities clearly enough. The limpidly appealing but rather conventional tune is repeated note for note throughout the four stanzas, but the texture of the accompaniment, aided by changes of tempo, gives the necessary variety. Here are the opening bars of the first and second stanzas, evocations of peace and of a violent storm respectively:

The technique came to be widely practised in the nineteenth century, of course; perhaps full exploitation of this means of achieving diversity within a framework of strict thematic unity had to wait on further developments in piano writing.

Binary form, often involving a transition from major to minor or vice versa, was the most popular variation on the strophic in the eighteenth century and it is easy to see why. Many poems have a clear cut change of direction or mood which can be effectively rendered in music by this method. Salis's poem 'Das Grab' is an example, for the first three stanzas concentrate on the fear of death and the grief of the bereaved, while stanzas 4 and 5 treat of peace and man's entry into his true 'home', the hereafter. The contrast is matched in the setting by W.G.M. Jensen (1799) by a switch from minor to major, while the essential unity of the poem is preserved through very clear thematic links between the two tunes.[9] The same technique can be employed within the wider span of narrative ballad, as in C.G. Eidenbenz's setting of Hölty's 'Die Nonne' (*Musikalischer Potpourri*, 1791). The ballad tells of the seduction of a nun and of the terrible way in which she exacts vengeance. The song begins in the major (setting of scene, wooing, seduction), to move into the relative minor for the bloodthirsty events of the final stanzas.

The ternary form is obviously appropriate only for poems which begin and end more or less in the same mood and have a contrasting middle section. J.M. Miller's 'Was ist Lieb?' is eminently suitable and was, in fact, set in this way by D.G. Türck (1780). The sequence of ideas and events in the poem is as follows:

Stanzas 1-2: Love is equated with a spring day; an Arcadian scene of dalliance is conjured up.
   3-4: There is a violent storm and the lovers scatter in terror.
   5-6: The weather clears and we return to the opening idyll.

Türck gives a convincing realisation of the poem by setting stanzas 1-2 and 5-6 to a gentle pastoral tune, with a turbulent section in the relative minor for the middle stanzas.[10] Further possibilities include orthodox rondo-form (ABACADA), obviously of very limited use in song,[11] and a freer type in which successive stanzas or groups of stanzas are given successive tunes, usually in response to each fresh turn of events in a narrative poem. This device, which obviously points one way forward to through-composed song, was used by J.E. Bach in his settings of fables (1749), where we may encounter three or even four melodies in the course of a piece. (It may be noted that Scheibe had singled out the fable as appropriate for setting in the form of a 'Wechselode'.)

A rather more daring formal variant involved a combination of song, in the accepted sense of that word, with recitative. This device is usually associated with Zumsteeg, who influenced Schubert here as in other respects.[12] But experiments with this type of mixed setting go back to the 1750s. The first seems to be a setting by W.A.T. Roth of an untitled satirical poem 'Es floh Belisens erste Jugend' (1757, no. 5). In each stanza some sort of folly or pretence is described in the first half, with the concluding lines satirically prophesying the consequences. The refrain ('Das kann ich prophezeyn') epitomises the cynical worldly wisdom of the anonymous poet. It is this second half of the stanza that Roth sets in mock-sententious tones in the form of recitative, with the conventional pair of chords which follows seeming to confirm the truth of the prophecy:

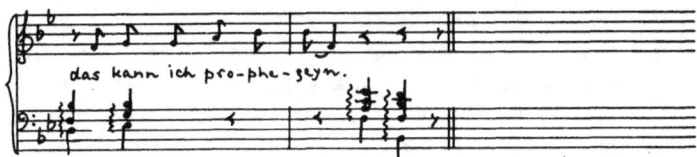

It would appear that this hybrid form continued to be seen as a comic possibility, for the next example known to me (J.G. Müthel, 1759, no. 5) again treats a satirical text (this time making fun of Stoicism and asceticism), as do Georg Benda's two experiments with this form (*Sammlung*, iii, 26 and iv, 10). Since the second of these involves a poem later made familiar through Beethoven's setting, it may be interesting to see what Benda does with it.

C.F. Weiße's poem 'Der Kuß' ('Ich war bei Chloen ganz allein') tells of a young man who, alone one day with Chloe, wants to kiss her. Despite her threat to cry out for help, he persists. 'And did she cry out?' — 'Yes, but a long time after'. Beethoven will extract the maximum comic potential from that last phrase ('doch lange hinterher') through almost interminable repetition, requiring 'lange' to be sung thirteen times. Benda's setting is more economical, rather ironic than broadly humourous. Note the slight suspense occasioned by the pause before 'doch lange hinterher':

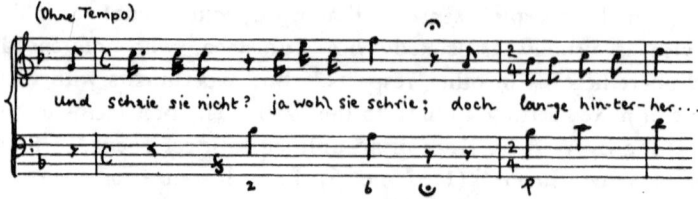

As far as I know, C.M. Wolff was the first to use this form for a serious poem, in his setting of an anonymous ode to sleep ('Komm, süßer Schlaf': 1777, p. 18). The poem, in three stanzas, takes the form of a dialogue. The first stanza praises sleep as source of rest and reinvigoration. In the second, an imaginary interlocutor asks, 'What if you fell asleep, never to reawaken?', to be given the answer: 'Ultimately I would awaken into a brighter, eternal day'. Wolff sets the first stanza calmly, in a faintly hymnlike style (in E major). The middle stanza is set as recitative, the question ending on the dominant chord of the relative minor. For the final stanza, Wolff returns to the opening key and the original material, so that the confident answer that sweeps away the doubt also resolves the slight harmonic uncertainty attaching to the G sharp chord. The impression given by this ternary form — that we are, melodically and tonally speaking, 'back home' — undoubtedly strengthens the point of the closing stanza, the sense of finding a home beyond the grave.

Later composers certainly had no hesitation about using this hybrid form for serious purposes. The importation of recitative not only into long ballads but also into quite short songs made available a more radical and dramatic contrast than was afforded even by orthodox ternary construction. The expressive possibilities opened up by this form could range from satire of folly to the contemplation of death, from dramatic narration[13] to earnest questioning.

These attempts to diversify and expand the basic strophic form are intrinsically interesting and of great importance for the future development of the Lied. It should not, however, be forgotten that they form a small minority of the huge number of songs composed between 1750 and 1800, most of which were written in an absolutely straightforward strophic manner. There is, as I have shown, some evidence to suggest that departures from the norm were at first undertaken only when the composer had satisfied himself that a strict strophic treatment would not work; there are even hints that such experiments were made with some misgivings as to the ability of amateur performers to cope with them. These factors apply with yet greater force to early experiments in through-composed song.

Through-composed song: 'das durchkomponierte Lied'

Early through-composed songs, although relatively uncommon and very uneven in quality, are again of great historical importance. Such songs were understandably slow to establish themselves in a context where the strophic variants just described already offered opportunities for the setting of texts that did not seem to lend themselves to simple strophic composition. The time needed for through-composed songs to establish themselves and become fully accepted is mirrored in the terminology. Although Türck uses the term 'durchkomponiren' in 1780,[14] Gruber in the same year uses 'ganz componirt' and Brandl (1793) prefers 'durchaus in Musik gesetzt'. Goethe, whose resistance to this newfangled device is well known, could hardly bring himself even to write the word without a preceding 'so called'.[15] As late as 1814, an anonymous reviewer in the *AMZ* speaks of this 'strange expression' ('Das Stück ist . . . wie nun einmal der wunderliche Ausdruck lautet, durchcomponirt' — xvi, 427).

Since a good through-composed song combines unity and variety in a unique way, treating musical material in an almost symphonic manner while always heeding the exigencies of the text, it is not surprising that many of the early experiments fail to solve the formal and interpretative problems satisfactorily. Many early attempts are still written in an operatic style or resemble little solo cantatas; except where parody was the aim, this would necessarily appear retrograde in an age in which the Klavierlied had been dominated by a desire to escape from the associations of these virtuoso and 'unnatural' forms. Through-composed songs in a recognisably operatic manner persist until the end of the century; Rheineck (1779) and Gabler (1795) offer examples which, formally and stylistically, recall *da capo* arias, the first of these examples involving a senseless repetition of the opening stanza of the poem.[16] Flörke (1779, no. 1) has a song which resembles nothing so much as the piano reduction of an operatic *scena*. Viennese song-composers were understandably given to operatic styles in their Klavierlieder (examples in Grünwald, 1785; Hackel, 1786; Holzer, 1787).

The most common failing of early through-composed songs is a lack of unity, a loose and episodic form. If a composer decides to depart from strophic form, a natural temptation is to do the job comprehensively, inventing new material for each stanza, each change of mood or, if the text is a narrative ballad, each turn of events. This method, unless very skilfully employed, can destroy both the listener's sense of musical logic and his perception of the text as a formal unity. One early hint as to how song might progress towards freer forms without sacrificing musical logic and unity is provided by C.P.E. Bach's setting of 'Die Küsse', an Arcadian poem by Gisecke (Ramler and Krause, i, 1753, no. 14). An old man criticises Thyrsis for over-indulgence in kissing (stanza 1). Hereupon, Thyrsis takes his doubts to Neära (st. 2), who comforts him, saying that she is the only competent judge in this matter (st. 3). A simple strophic setting was ruled out by the irregular stanza-lengths (eight lines — six lines — seven lines). So Bach sets freely, casting his song as a sort of extended slow minuet — although that is not intended to suggest that there is anything 'instrumental' about the vocal line; the whole is eminently singable. The three sections which correspond to Gisecke's three stanzas are linked by freely varied melodic motifs and follow a careful tonal pattern. The poem is trifling, but the way in which Bach has devised musical structures to fit its irregularity, its natural transitions and subdivisions and its inner logic is masterly.

However, song-composers much preferred more symmetrical texts, and the subsequent history of through-composed song is bound up with longer poems of regular structure but changing content. In these, the sort of motivic and formal unity which characterise Bach's 'Die Küsse' are much more difficult to achieve, so that a disjointed and episodic form became depressingly common. G. Bachmann's 1790 setting of Bürger's ballad 'Lenardo und Blandine' contains twenty-four distinct sections; a through-composed song by Fleischer (1788, pp. 2–9) has seventeen indications of tempo in eight pages.[17]

Many of Zumsteeg's longer songs (mostly settings of ballads) suffer from this episodic character. Since some of these works influenced Schubert, the fact is obviously of historical significance. Zumsteeg's method involves a free alternation of recitative and arioso passages, the different sections sometimes being linked by rhythmic or melodic similarities.[18] The longer the text, the more likely is the setting to lack unity as the composer searches for suitable expressive equivalents to each stage in the poet's

The New Adventurousness

argument or narrative. 'Colma', one of the *Ossian* settings (Leipzig, 1794) has thirty-three sections, including fourteen passages of recitative. Here there is little organic link between one section and the next and the result is hopelessly episodic. A much more successful experiment in this field is Zumsteeg's setting of Schiller's 'Ritter Toggenburg' (*Kleine Balladen und Lieder*, vol. i). This ballad is a simple and direct retelling, in the dramatic present and using eight-line stanzas, of a legend which existed in various forms in different parts of German-speaking Europe. A knight, disappointed in love (stanza 1) goes to the Crusades (st. 2–3). Returning years later to find that the lady has become a nun (st. 4–5), he lives a hermit's existence in a spot from which he can at least observe her daily (st 6–10). Let us turn to Zumsteeg's musical realisation of this popular ballad.

He sets the first stanza at moderate tempo in 4/4 in the style of a simple but affecting eighteenth-century *Stimmungslied*. After a very brief passage of recitative (the knight's grief at realising that his love cannot be returned), the composer continues in quicker tempo, maintaining melodic, tonal and rhythmic links with his opening material:

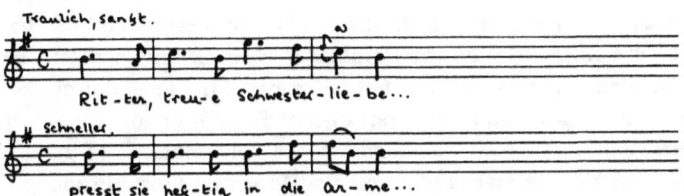

There follows a march-like piano interlude before the third stanza which tells of Toggenburg's heroic deeds in the Holy Land. Vague reminiscences of the earlier sections are skilfully integrated into this more martial section. Stanza 4, which deals with Toggenburg's homesickness and return, is set to new material in a new key, but here too there are sufficient reminders of previous motifs to hold the song together. Now follows a second interlude for piano solo, suggesting his hopes of a joyful reunion. The grievous revelation — that the beloved had taken the veil only the day before — is set as recitative, and the remaining stanzas, devoted to the hero's last years as a hermit, are composed strophically in a style and key which contrast strongly with what has gone before. This setting makes perfect sense. While the arioso sections (st. 1–4) necessarily have motivic similarities, the break before the

The New Adventurousness

passage of recitative is justified, since it heralds a dramatic new twist to the story. And since the closing stanzas deal with a quite different way of life for this hitherto tempestuous knight, the new, calmer material is exactly right. The rhythmic unity of the piece is, no doubt, largely due to the fact that Zumsteeg decided to reproduce Schiller's trochees conventionally by ♩♪ or ♩.♪ , but the effect is never undifferentiated or tedious. It has seemed both more charitable and more rewarding to concentrate on one of Zumsteeg's successes than on his comparative failures. It must, however, be said that — apart from an obvious indebtedness to Zumsteeg in his own setting of 'Ritter Toggenburg' — the young Schubert seems to have taken the least unified compositions as his models; indeed, comparison of his setting of 'Hagars Klage' with Zumsteeg's reveals him as *plus royaliste que le roi* in his determination to devise new material for each episode in the poem.

The problems posed by the through-composed song were not to be fully solved until Loewe appeared on the scene. But there are isolated examples in the eighteenth century which show that a few composers were as capable of achieving diversity within unity as was Zumsteeg on his best days.[19] Although most composers of the age resorted to such forms only when the poem demanded it, Neubauer (1788) and Brandl (1793) are exceptions in that through-composed songs predominate. While Brandl's efforts are inept, Neubauer shows considerable grasp of the formal problems involved — although it must be conceded that his chosen texts are mostly fairly short. If one turns to the contributions of greater men, it remains a matter of regret that Mozart's short life and vast range of interests prevented him from developing techniques of through-composed song further, since his 'Abendempfindung an Laura' (K523) is so obviously a masterpiece. If we further bear in mind his extraordinary skill in carrying operatic action onwards in a succession of symphonically conceived ensembles, there seems no doubt that he could have effortlessly solved all the problems posed by the long, through-composed ballad.

The question of Beethoven's position in the development of through-composed song is slightly more complex. He can write in a decidedly operatic style ('Mit einem gemalten Band') or produce what is virtually a miniature cantata with piano accompaniment ('Adelaide'). His finest achievement in *Durchkomponieren* is, in my opinion, his setting of Goethe's 'Neue Liebe, neues Leben' — at least, if one disregards the rather cavalier treatment of the text. The song is a highly unified construction, all in the same rushing tempo, with the exception of the retarding moment afforded by a *quasi-recitativo* passage as the poet asks himself how things ever came to this pass ('Ach, wie kamst du nur dazu!'). What Beethoven does is to repeat the first two stanzas with some melodic variation and modulation before setting Goethe's third and final stanza to a new tune, but one which quickly shows itself as related to that which opened the song. Thus, we have a pattern loosely related to the rondo-form. Although not a virtuoso piece, the song is vaguely operatic in tone — and the textual 'tampering' is certainly nearer to operatic practice than to anything yet current in song-writing. It would be accurate to describe this work as on the borderline between through-composed song and aria.[20]

It is very debatable whether Beethoven's contribution to the through-composed song had much impact on future developments. His influence, as has often been pointed out, is rather to be seen in the expansion of the role of the accompaniment and of harmonic vocabulary and to a lesser degree with the popularisation of the song-cycle (see below). But with Beethoven we are already bridging the eighteenth and nineteenth centuries; let us return to the closing decades of the eighteenth. It will have become evident that these decades saw a quite decisive movement towards more complex and enterprising songs, above all in the development of piano-writing and in various kinds of formal expansion, although not yet to any great extent in harmony.

Notes

1. See *Music and Letters*, lxvi, 231–4.
2. For a comic instance of representation in the accompaniment, see Haydn's use of drumming chords to suggest knocking at the door in his setting of C.F. Weiße's lighthearted 'Eine sehr gewöhnliche Geschichte'. Pohl suggests a rustic dance in his accompaniment to 'Amor im Tanz', 1785, no. 12.
3. See Preu, 1785; Baumbach, 1792, p. 20; Neubauer, 1788, p. 53.
4. C.J.P., 1782, p. 16. Other composers with a liking for postludes include Neefe, Pohl and F.X. Weiß. See too the account of Preuß, 'An Lyda', above.
5. Half in songs by Hurka, Nauert and C.M. Wolff; two thirds in Benda's 'Betrachtung einer Schönen' (given by Friedlaender, ex. 115) and in Benecken's 'Abschieds-Lied' (1787, pp. 26f).
6. Gruber, 1780, i, p. 41.
7. See F. Biedermann, *Goethes Gespräche*, 2nd edn Leipzig, 1909, ii, pp. 460f.

8. For Scheibe and the 'Wechselode', see above, p. 70. F.W. Rust has an ABAAABA pattern: see 'Bey Annäherung des Frühlings' in *Die Muse*, 1776, ii, 23. Reichardt, in his setting of 'Der Pilgrim', has AABBAABBA: *Schillers lyrische Gedichte*, ii, pp. 8f.

9. See too F.L.A. Kunzen, 1788, pp. 32f, where the switch is from major to tonic minor. Other examples of 'binary strophic' in Tag, 1783, pp. 19–21; F.W. Rust, 1784–96, i, no. 4; J.B. Hummel; Reichardt.

10. *Was ist Lieb?* is given by Friedlaender, ex. 197.

11. Examples: Gräser, 1785, pp. 3–5 and 26f; Schubart, 1782; Thonus, 1792, no. 1. The last-named example involves a nonsensical sacrifice of poetic logic to the exigencies of the rondo-form.

12. For Zumsteeg, see *Kleine Balladen und Lieder*, ii, pp. 26f; vii, pp. 1f and 20–2. There are several instances in early Schubert: see, for instance, 'Der Geistertanz', D116.

13. For Mozart's 'Veilchen', see above, pp. 44f. It seems immaterial whether one labels this as a miniature operatic *scena* or a song expanded by the insertion of a passage of recitative.

14. In the Preface to his *Lieder und Gedichte aus dem Siegwart*.

15. See Goethe to W. von Humboldt, 14 March 1803 and to Zelter, 23 May 1807.

16. *Lieder mit Clavier Melodien*, i, pp. 26f; *Zwoelf Lieder*, no. 12.

17. For further examples of episodic through-composed songs, see Wiedebein, 1779, pp. 2–7; J. André, 1783–4, ii, pp. 9–18; Queck, 1792. Most settings of Bürger's ballads share this characteristic.

18. Some critics over-charitably see this as a general feature of Zumsteeg's through-composed songs; would it were so!

19. See Romberg, 1793, no. 1 for an example. But Romberg is not always so successful.

20. Beethoven's long through-composed setting of Bürger's 'Seufzer eines Ungeliebten und Gegenliebe' (rather operatic in style and unappealing from a melodic point of view) was published posthumously in 1837 and remained without influence on the development of song-form.

8
The Eighteenth Century — A Summing-up

There was then, an extraordinary proliferation of songs in the second half of the century: thousands of works by composers ranging from the greatest of the age to shallow dilettanti. They virtually all aimed at a simple and technically undemanding style, reacting against the complexities of opera and cantata and apparently distrusting the capabilities of amateur performers. Only gradually, in the latter decades of the century, did any significant movement towards a richer and more demanding style of song occur — and even here a fairly simple type of strophic song continued to dominate.

In the nature of things, much that was written was mediocre. The earliest composers, although usually technically correct, were often stiff and pedantic, at times showing scant awareness of the difference between instrumental and vocal styles. As song became more and more popular, an increasing number of amateur composers had tried their hand at it, often betraying their lack of professionalism through inept bass-lines or clumsy word-setting. Two fallacies seem to have been at work here: the belief that what goes for a circle of indulgent friends is suitable for publication and the pious hope that a 'natural' (i.e. spontaneous and melodious) effect can be achieved without technical correctness and unobtrusive hard work.

Perhaps a more substantial criticism is that much eighteenth-century song was technically unexceptionable but colourless. We should remember here that many of the avowed aims were negative ones: song should not be florid or showy, it should not attempt to match each motif in the poem with any too exact musical equivalent, it should contain nothing difficult to sing or play, etc. Moreover, the reliance on strophic form encouraged a

A Summing-up

sort of neutral, general-purpose melody, if it was to fit all stanzas of the poem. Could anyone guess that this is the tune to which Bürger's grisly ballad 'Lenore' was to be sung? —

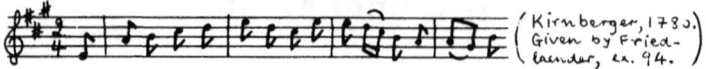

'Cold and arid', says a reviewer in the *AMZ* (xv, 675).

For all that, the music-lover will find much to delight him in eighteenth-century song. Many of the simple strophic works, above all the settings of serious and meditative texts, have great charm. A good example would be F.W. Weis's setting of Philippine Gatterer's tribute to the piano, 'Mit stillem Kummer in der Brust', first published in the *Göttinger Musenalmanach* for 1779.[1] But not all the outstanding songs are slow and elegaic. Although it was all too easy to fall into a sort of cheerful and empty patter in the 'scherzhafte Lieder', there are many good examples in playful vein too. Here is part of Marpurg's setting[2] of a paraphrase of Anacreon, in which Elisa and Corydon barter sheep for kisses:

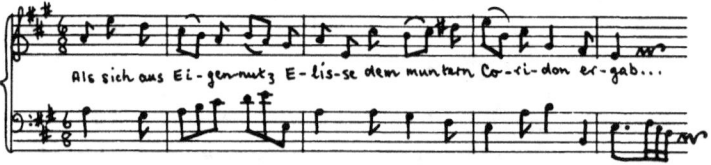

Thus, one finds occasional very good songs by quite minor talents. A small number of composers are consistently outstanding: C.P.E. Bach (whose experimental daring has been commented on often enough in preceding chapters), Schulz (whose notion of the 'Volkston' continued to influence song far into the next century), F.L.A. Kunzen, Neefe and others. Three important figures straddle the two centuries, growing up in the atmosphere of eighteenth-century song but influencing composers in the nineteenth. Zumsteeg, whose importance for Schubert has already been touched on, survived the turn of the century by only two years, but his influential collection *Kleine Balladen und Lieder* continued to be published posthumously, the final volume appearing in 1805. Reichardt and Zelter both lived well into the new century, Reichardt until 1814, Zelter until 1832, the year in which his close friend Goethe also died. Each of these two composers can range from totally straightforward strophic settings to much more elaborate and dramatic works (although Zelter, like Goethe, preferred the strophic form). Reichardt's and Zelter's ability to find the common touch is shown by the fact that works of theirs appear in virtually all the popular anthologies of song throughout the nineteenth century and well into the twentieth — they are almost invariably represented by Klärchens song from *Egmont* ('Freudvoll und leidvoll') and 'Der König in Thule' respectively. But we should not overlook the almost Brahmsian tones of Reichardt's 'Rhapsodie' (with text from Goethe's poem 'Harzreise im Winter') and the tempestuous through-composed setting of the same author's 'Rastlose Liebe' by Zelter.

Reichardt's and Zelter's dates are sufficient to show that any division into centuries is artificial. But a convenient break must be made somewhere — and it is not unreasonable to treat the century of Marpurg, the Bachs, Kirnberger, Gluck and even Zumsteeg as different from that of Schubert and those who followed him. As we shall see, certain things will persist and provide continuity: the phenomenal popularity of the Lied will not flag; new songs will, as previously, be accompanied by renewed efforts to define what song is and what it ought to do; the veneration for folksong and the quest for a 'Volkston' will colour a good deal of German song for at least a century to come; a significant minority of songs will continue to draw on good texts by Germany's leading poets. But some aspects of eighteenth-century song will disappear or become relatively unimportant: no longer will dilettanti make any notable contribution; no longer will we see that close and active collaboration between poet and composer which can be witnessed in the eighteenth century in the links between Voß and Schulz, Zumsteeg and Matthison or between Goethe and first Reichardt, then Zelter. With a few exceptions, such as the friendship between Schubert and Mayrhofer, the connection between the great nineteenth-century song-composers and their favourite poets is more likely to be an intangible, spiritual one.

Notes

1. Part of this song is given in *Music and Letters*, lxvi, 236. For other examples of strophic songs in similar vein, see André, 'An die Natur' (1800, p. 8); Kayser's setting of Goethe's 'Der du von dem Himmel bist' (first published in 1780 and included in innumerable anthologies); the

slow songs in Kriegel's anthology of 1790; Marpurg's 'Sinkt nur hin, ihr matten Glieder' (1758, no. 14); Weis's setting of Klopstock's 'Im Frühlingsschatten' (*Lieder mit Melodien*, i, 1775, p. 20). Many songs by Reichardt, Schulz, Zelter and Zumsteeg fall into this category too.

2. *Historisch-kritische Beyträge*, ii, 1756, no. 3. See too Weis's setting of Bürger's 'Mädel, schau mir ins Gesicht', in *Lieder mit Melodien*, iii, 1779, p. 9.

9
From the Turn of the Century to Schumann, Mendelssohn and Franz

Immediately before Schubert

Songs were produced in almost unimaginable profusion throughout the nineteenth century: one could cover the whole of Germany with song, says Schumann in 1837. The term 'Liederflut' (flood of songs) becomes a common trope among the reviewers in the *AMZ* and elsewhere.[1] Many hundreds of composers, the great majority of whom are unknown today, wrote Lieder: most histories of the genre are thus like maps with only the high mountains drawn in. Occasionally, half a dozen of the less familiar composers will be disposed of in a paragraph. Even the big music encyclopedias have little or nothing to say about most of these minor figures as song-composers, even where their eminence in other fields merits a few column-inches. But a view of nineteenth-century song based solely on the small minority of obviously great composers is in danger of overlooking some quite important considerations and trends. So, in the account that follows I will try to pay due attention to some of the forgotten composers, in order to reveal a picture of nineteenth-century song rather different from, perhaps even rather more interesting than, that possessed by someone who knows only Schubert, Schumann, Brahms, etc.

The distinction according to countries which was useful and necessary in our discussion of eighteenth-century song is no longer of great consequence. Apart from settings of folksong — obviously governed to some extent by local considerations — German, Austrian and Swiss song can now be seen as parts of one cultural phenomenon, governed by broadly similar factors and, on the whole, involving settings of the same poets and types of poem.

The situation is also different from that obtaining in the eighteenth century in that there are now composers of the first rank whose songs are absolutely central to their musical output (Schubert, Schumann), and other composers of considerable stature who composed little *but* songs (Franz, Wolf). This in itself is a pointer to the prestige enjoyed by the Lied as a genre. But who were the great mass of forgotten composers?

Such data as one can garner from encyclopedias, journals, etc. (and it must be admitted that many composers are now no more than names) suggest that we are dealing with professionally trained musicians whose main activities were often concentrated in fields other than composition but who were quite prolific and, in their day, well respected part-time composers. Many combined public careers as virtuosi with teaching and composing. Others were conductor/composers, the two activities often complementing each other, as when the conductor of a theatre or opera house would concentrate on writing stage-music, or the director of a *Gesangverein* or *Liedertafel* would keep his choir supplied with part-songs. But such men also invariably contributed their few strands to that carpet of song which, according to Schumann, was spreading over Germany. Many professional singers whose working lives were largely centred on the opera houses wrote songs — and it is interesting to note that these works seldom presuppose any great virtuosity on the part of the singer; we shall see the significance of this when we come to examine the Lied as an aspect of amateur domestic music-making. A few of the song-composers were (and are) chiefly renowned as scholars, editors and theorists, but the great majority were performers and/or teachers. The switch from court music to municipal music can be traced very clearly when one examines the careers of these men: the grand-sounding title *Musikdirektor* persists, but now more often applies to the directorship of a town orchestra, theatre or choir than to court appointments.

The picture one gains is of an age in which music was highly prized and practised with prodigious energy: the sheer volume of teaching, playing, conducting, founding and organising choral societies, composing, reviewing and editing is staggering. It seems that these men quite happily combined composing with the more mundane and practical activities by which they earned their bread. I have not come across much evidence of tension between the 'creative' and the 'practical' sides of their lives.[2] In this they resemble the writers of Poetic Realism (Stifter, Keller, Storm, etc.) rather than the German Romantic authors.

There was a small minority of amateur composers drawn from the middle classes and a few noble dilettanti, of whom by far the most important is Johann Vesque von Püttlingen, a high-ranking court official in Vienna who, under the pseudonym of J. Hoven, published many Heine-settings of great interest and, sometimes, marked eccentricity. But we no longer find, as we did in the eighteenth century, a host of clergymen,[3] schoolmasters and noble amateurs who tried their hand at song-writing and were then 'reluctantly' persuaded to publish the results. A consequence of this switch to greater professionalism is that, apart from lapses in word-setting (usually misplaced stresses) and a few misguided harmonic experiments, the *average* level of competence in the nineteenth century was much higher than it had been in the eighteenth. Most shortcomings are now errors of poetic judgement.

Among these hundreds of minor composers there were a few who concentrated on song and whose repute mainly rested on their achievements in this field: Norbert Burgmüller, Curschmann, Conradin Kreutzer. Others were chiefly famed (as far as composition went) for their work in other genres: H.A. Marschner for his operas, Scharwenka for piano music. But this does not mean that their songs are of negligible interest. Other composers seem to have written a few songs in their youth (in an adolescent spell of Romanticism, if one may so express it without sounding patronising) and to have abandoned the Lied thereafter. Apart from these, however, it was nothing for an energetic man to produce a hundred or more songs in the course of a long career devoted to various forms of musical activity, so that Schumann's vision of a Germany carpeted with song is not outrageously hyperbolic.

The conditions governing music publishing have changed somewhat by the early decades of the century. The cumbersome and rather informally organised system of publication by subscription has yielded to a more modern type of commercial, speculative publishing in which full-time music dealers and publishers come to play a much more prominent role than in the preceding century.[4] At the same time, the eighteenth-century custom of producing songs in bound volumes gave way quite quickly to the publication of single opus numbers in flimsy paper editions. (This has not aided survival!) In addition, there were numerous anthologies, sometimes of new or newish songs by living composers, sometimes combining anonymous folk-tunes with popular Lieder by named eighteenth or early nineteenth-century composers. Titles were often high-sounding and romantic: *Arion, Orpheon, Lieder Tempel, Musikalische Gartenlaube* and so on.[5] Such collections were specifically intended to provide technically undemanding domestic music with immediate appeal. Their appearance is often sentimental; thus, for example, the *Musikalische Gartenlaube* shows a young lady in her best frock performing at a cottage piano for the benefit of her admiring parents. But the presentation should not blind us to the musical and cultural importance of such anthologies. Side by side with trivialities one finds examples of the finest eighteenth-century Lieder im Volkston, together with contributions by Heinrich Marschner, Mendelssohn, Schubert, Schumann, Wilhelm Taubert and many other esteemed composers of the day. The first printing of Heinrich Werner's setting of Goethe's 'Heidenröslein' (which appeared thereafter in virtually all nineteenth-century anthologies and temporarily eclipsed Schubert's version) is to be found in the seventeenth volume of *Arion*, by the way, in 1830.

The chief composers whose work extends across the turn of the century and who influenced the course of nineteenth-century song in various ways (Beethoven, Reichardt, Zelter, Zumsteeg) are, of course, familiar to students of song. In addition, hundreds of songs were produced by more obscure composers between the turn of the century and Schubert's appearance on the scene. Their songs were mostly strophic or in some extension of strophic form; through-composed songs were still in a small minority. Although offering the listener few surprises, the songs of Ludwig Abeille, Franz Danzi, I.F. Eunike, G.C. Grosheim, F.W. Grund, Albert Methfessel[6] and others are charming and elegant works, still capable of giving pleasure to amateur singers and players. Rather than attempting further generalisations, I will take one of Abeille's songs and examine it in a little detail.

Abeille, who was for many years concert-master and organist in Stuttgart, provides us with an example of the best kind of short through-composed song to be encountered just after the turn of the century. It shows the full extent of the composer's artistry better than one of his simpler strophic efforts could do (although the best of these are very good). The poem, Schiller's 'Der Jüngling am Bach', has four eight-line stanzas. A young man sits by the stream, lamenting the passing of his days (stanza 1) and contrasting his melancholy with the joyful mood of nature (st. 2).

The third stanza explains this melancholy as being due to fruitless longing for his beloved who, as the final stanza tells us, is of higher birth than he. Let us see how Abeille, whose song appeared in Leipzig in 1812, approaches this poem.

Seeing that the stanzas are independent entities, he gives fresh material to each, returning to the tune of the first stanza at the end in order to round off the song. Piano interludes further separate stanza from stanza, except at the transition from stanzas 2 to 3, where the change of direction is signalled by a pause and a dramatic change of key. Unity is provided by the characteristic shape of the vocal phrases, the close links between these and the solo passages for piano and, of course, by the recapitulation at the end. Diversity is ensured by two means: by variations in the texture of the accompaniment and by an interesting but never laboured pattern of modulations (A — F sharp minor — E — A minor — A major — D — thence, by turning the dominant note of that key into the mediant of F major, into F and, by way of A minor, back to the home key). Although, as I have said, Abeille knits the song together by means of characteristic rhythmic patterns in the vocal line (♪♪ | ♪♪♪ ♪ | ♫ ♪ and similar), he shrewdly picks those phrases in the poem which call for more expressive or melismatic phrasing, for instance, the evocation of spring (3,2) and the reference to the 'infinitely distant' beloved (3,4: it is a measure of his poetic judgement that this 'ewig' is the only word in the poem which he requires the singer to repeat):

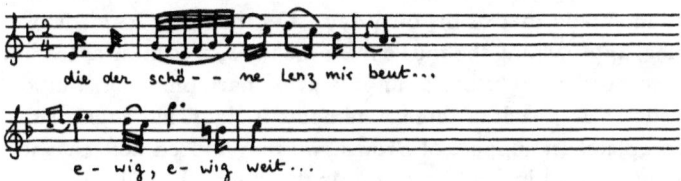

This song is not a work of genius, but it is highly competent, melodically attractive and sensitive to the nuances of the text.

Schubert

Such experiments in short through-composed song, together with Zumsteeg's more ambitious attempts to set long ballads and the simple but melodious and accomplished strophic songs referred to above, obviously prepare the ground for Schubert. Hence, accounts of Schubert that represent him as the 'father' of German song and suggest that he virtually invented the Lied are greatly over-simplified. It is probably more correct to see him as assimilating within himself everything that had gone before, while showing, at least in potential, much of what was to happen in nineteenth-century song after him. It is fitting to borrow the label that Germans were wont to apply to Shakespeare and call Schubert a 'universal genius', for his songs do indeed seem to offer a complete universe, both in terms of emotional experience and of technical possibilities. (Furthermore, as we shall see, Schubert did not escape the strictures of the more 'correct' type of critic any more than Shakespeare had done in the previous century).

If, then, we survey the history of the Lied from the mid-eighteenth century onwards, it is clear that Schubert is the first composer to have *radically* affected its development singlehanded. To put the matter in evolutionary terms: it is no longer (as arguably in the eighteenth century) a gradual and fairly smooth process, but a sudden big jump — rather akin to the evolutionary process as scientists now tend to see it, in fact. Although Schubert seems to break through all conventions and inhibitions that had hitherto obtained in German song,[7] the areas where his influence was most revolutionary and far-reaching are, I believe, in harmony, the role of the accompaniment and the development of the song-cycle. I will take these in turn.

It may be instructive to start with two apparently contradictory statements. M.J.E. Brown declares that 'Schubert's harmony is fundamentally that of his own day'. On the other hand, Moritz Bauer, approaching the music from the texts, sees these as leading the composer to hitherto undreamt-of harmonic possibilities.[8] Paradoxically, each of these statements is right, although neither is complete. In support of Brown, we may indeed note that it is difficult to find in Schubert any single chord which did not exist elsewhere in his day. But the combination of all available harmonic means, as prompted by the dramatic and expressive demands of the chosen poems, created what seems like a new harmonic language, unprecedented within the field of Lieder.

Yet the ingredients seem unsensational enough. To say that Schubert is fond of sevenths and ninths, of augmented fifths and of German and Neapolitan sixths is not apparently to say very much. But when we note how he uses these, both to achieve colour and atmosphere and as pivotal or passing chords, we realise that we are in the presence of something new. 'An den Tod' (D518) offers marvellous examples. When in the third bar the voice rises from the tonic to the flattened submediant, this is placed above a dominant seventh chord, leading us quickly from B major into the remote key of C major. Later, a series of augmented fifths is used to urge the music to modulate dramatically upwards:[9]

E.G. Porter[10] gives many examples of Schubert's harmonic richness, adding that to explain these technically would often need a very complicated nomenclature which might well give a false impression. For there is no reason to suppose that such effects did not suggest themselves naturally to Schubert — and their impact on the hearer is certainly immediate and spontaneous, with no hint of calculated artifice. It is in this sense that Fischer-Dieskau talks of Schubert's 'natural style'.[11]

Some of Schubert's most dramatic effects rely less on unusual chords or on a complex web of passing notes than on the unexpected juxtaposition of chords which, in themselves, are totally conventional. A wholesale expansion of harmonic vocabulary is made possible when the 'natural' and expected relationships between common chords in a given tonal context are so extended that any one can be followed by virtually any other one:[12]

In each of the examples just quoted, the ear would expect a major chord at the point marked by the asterisk.

In 'Das Heimweh' (D851b), the process is taken yet further. Here the progression is from a major tonic chord to the minor chord of the flattened submediant. A chromatic drop in the bass — ambiguous to the ear — helps to produce a truly vertiginous effect:

From 1800 to Schumann, Mendelssohn & Franz

It seems that doors leading to 'unacceptably' remote regions, doors previously held to be closed, had been open all the time; Schubert gives a gentle push and walks through. Less dramatic but no less effective is the way in which he moves in and out of the major and minor modes,[13] often with important implications for his (and our) reading of the poem (see *Die schöne Müllerin*, nos. 6, 10, 15 and 17 and *Winterreise*, no. 1, especially the postlude).

Music is ambiguity made into a system, says Thomas Mann in *Dr Faustus*. No composer has exploited this ambiguity more frequently and more subtly than Schubert. Even the individual note can be made to sound ambiguous and shifting if the supporting harmonies are changed abruptly. (The device is such a favourite one with Schubert that examples are superfluous.) The ambiguity of certain chords is constantly exploited. We have seen how Schubert precipitates us into C major at the beginning of 'An den Tod'. But that same chord (were the F natural written as an E sharp) should equally well take us back to B major, either as the home key or as the dominant of E major/minor. The chord of the diminished seventh is, as is well known, highly ambiguous; it can go (and in Schubert does go) almost anywhere.

Many of Schubert's most abrupt and mysterious progressions involve enharmonic changes, often via the German sixth. It should not be forgotten that this device is a notational convenience, but one which, since it provides a means of linking two remote chords or keys, nearly always produces some sort of uncertainty or shock effect, changing the meaning and function of a note in mid-stream, as it were. In 'Das Heimweh', the G flat in the bass could be heard as an F sharp, especially coming after a C sharp in the same bar. Were that so, we would expect a shift into B minor; instead, the new 'meaning' placed on the bass note (G flat) determines events and drives us into the remote region of E flat minor.

The discussion of these processes is necessarily technical. But it must be stressed that the listener does not need to understand such matters in order to appreciate the harmonic subtleties and ambiguities of the song. It is the ear, not the analytical intellect, that takes these in; it is above all the ear that relates them to the particular stage in the unfolding of the text and thus gives them their true and complete meaning. The above examples have given only the merest hint of this complex subject; hundreds of pages have been written on the subtleties of Schubert's harmonic language as displayed in his songs. But every lover of Schubert will recognise the devices to which I have referred, will have his or her own favourite examples and will have come to savour their function as one more factor contributing to the composer's interpretation of the poem.

Schubert's contemporaries, for all that they recognised in him an exciting talent, were often alienated by the harmonic progressions and modulations that they found in his songs. 'Original but horrifying', 'desperate', 'offending the ear': these are some of the phrases used. The harmonic restlessness and constant desire to modulate are seen as a disease of the age, a 'mania'.[14] From our more distant perspective, the musical and poetic logic seems clearer — but the disquiet felt by conservatively minded reviewers used to the uncomplicated harmonies and conventional key-patterns of Schubert's immediate predecessors in song-writing is understandable. It is, in fact, part of a widespread opposition to formal and harmonic experimentation in song, an opposition to which we shall have to return presently.

We have seen that as musical interests came to demand parity of esteem with poetic ones, the accompaniment gradually became more varied and adventurous. But it was Schubert who revolutionised the role of the piano *vis-à-vis* the voice. His accompaniments show an infinitely greater variety of textures and tonal effects than had ever existed before. Towards the end of his life, in the thirty-eight songs which make up *Winterreise* and *Schwanengesang*, a universe of phenomena and emotions seems to be epitomised in the piano parts.

Perhaps Schubert's most important contribution was to show how a song can be given unity by means of a ruling motif (or, occasionally, a cluster of related motifs) suggested by something in the poem. He mastered the principle, says Tovey, that, 'wherever some permanent feature can be found in the background of the poem, that feature shall dominate the background of the music'.[15] Against this background we may find the straightforward repetition of a strophic melody, or the voice part may modulate and vary freely, following the emotional rise and fall of the poem. The persistent figure in the accompaniment *can* become obsessive, but this is rare in Schubert, given his almost inexhaustible inventiveness.

This leads us to the question of the 'representational' function of the piano part in Schubert. In a way, the word 'representation', together with 'Schilderung' and 'Malerei' as commonly used by German critics,[16] is misleading, for rippling semiquavers do not actually sound like a running brook, nor does even the interval of a minor third, when played on the piano, sound like the call of a cuckoo. It is more accurate to say that the hearer gradually comes to accept various musical devices as setting up associations with things and events in nature. The fact that the pianistic motif usually coincides with mention of the relevant phenomenon in the voice part aids identification. (To take the obvious example, 'Bach' and 'Bächlein' are almost invariably accompanied by broken-chord figures throughout *Die schöne Müllerin*). In Schubert, the device is usually employed to reflect within the vocal part and the accompaniment the relationship existing in the poem between human emotions (the 'I' of the poem) and a non-human, usually natural, world. At its simplest and most direct, this is shown in the various note-patterns used to evoke wind, water, etc. But it can be employed to much more elaborate and subtle effect, as in 'Die junge Nonne' (D828) and 'Die Wetterfahne' (*Winterreise*, no. 2). When described — or even, perhaps, when seen in the musical score — the device seems simple, but everyone who has listened to or performed Schubert knows that it can sound magical. It must be stressed that this is a *major* contribution to song, for the huge majority of accompaniments hitherto had offered little more than the necessary harmonic support for the voice.

Just as Schubert was censured for his excessive fondness for modulation, so too did reviewers pick on his 'immoderate' style of piano-writing, his too independent and over-rich accompaniments ('obligate, wohl auch bis zum Uebermaaß volle Begleitung' — *AMZ*, xxviii, 480). Again, this is a manifestation of a widespread conservatism among the critics, a trend which will presently be discussed in more detail. *Die schöne Müllerin* and *Winterreise* have figured a number of times in this discussion. We must now turn our attention to Schubert's role in popularising the song-cycle and helping to determine its future development.

Although Beethoven's *An die ferne Geliebte* helped to set the fashion for song-cycles, it is untypical of what was to follow in two respects. The more obvious one is that Beethoven uses bridge-passages in order to create an unbroken flow of music. Add to this the thematic recapitulation at the end, and we have a large organic structure. This is certainly one possibility — and an exciting one — of creating unity out of diversity. But most later composers preferred to set the successive poems as independent entities, trusting that the story would provide the unity, while contrasts of mood in both text and music would ensure diversity. The second way in which *An die ferne Geliebte* turns out to have been untypical in the history of the song-cycle concerns the nature of the narrative content. Indeed, 'narrative' is hardly the word to describe such a static situation: we hear of the lover's grief at being separated from the beloved and at being able to bridge the distance only by pouring his feelings into song. But it seems that later composers, where attracted to the idea of the song-cycle, would regard it as a means of *telling a story* through song. It is here that Schubert's influence combines with that of Conradin Kreutzer to become decisive.

The pairing may seem strange to the modern reader, but Kreutzer's settings of Uhland's *Wanderlieder* enjoyed great popularity in his day and encouraged many imitations. It may be noted that Kreutzer and Schubert have an important thing in common: their chosen texts do not only tell a story, but tell a story of *wandering*. In Kreutzer/Uhland, we begin with a parting kiss (*Lebewohl*), after which various moods and experiences on the journey are recorded: loneliness, renewed hope, defiant optimism against the odds, the cheerlessness of tramping through an icy winter landscape, gratitude for the tranquillising and restorative effect of nature, etc. This is not such a clearcut story as we have in *Die schöne Müllerin* and *Winterreise*. For instance, there is not a clear relationship between wanderer and distant beloved. Indeed, songs nos. 5 and 9 are incompatible unless one postulates two girls! But the inner resemblance to the Schubert/Wilhelm Müller cycles is manifest; as in the more famous works, Uhland's poems record the moods and experiences of the lonely wanderer parted from his beloved and examine his relationship to nature and his fellow men.

After Kreutzer and Schubert, the history of the song-cycle in Germany is very largely bound up with the notion of 'Wanderlieder'. In cycle after cycle we encounter a young man who, either disappointed in love or forced into parting for some reason, sets off on a journey through lonely landscapes. Other cycles take a particular social or human type (the student, the apprentice) and follow him on his peregrinations; yet others use the motif of wandering as a pretext for the glorification of a particular region

— for a display of local patriotism, in fact. The attractions of such a framework are obvious: it gives the composer opportunities to treat a variety of human emotions and an equally great variety of natural phenomena and nature's moods. The work is held together, almost like a novel, by its narrative thread; indeed, a reviewer in the *AMZ* talks of the 'song-novel' ('Lieder-Roman').[17] The journey as a framework in which to accommodate a cycle of songs did not fall into disuse after the end of the nineteenth century; Ernst Krenek, in his *Reisebuch aus den österreichischen Alpen* of 1929, continues the genre in what is arguably one of the major contributions to the literature of the Lied in our century.

The importance of Wanderlieder in the history of the song-cycle can easily be underestimated, simply because of the accidental fact that most of the famous post-Schubertian cycles do not fit into this mould. But statistically the Wanderlieder-cycles form the great majority. Why this popularity? The song-cycles came into favour at a time when the German Romantics were obsessed with the figure of the Wanderer, who seemed to embody all their restless longings for something distant from, and superior to, their familiar environment and range of experience. To escape from daily routine as traveller, itinerant musician, wandering student, etc. or to be rejected and forced into a restless, wandering existence — these were two of the commonest themes in German Romantic literature. And they were no mere conventional tropes; many of the poets and composers set out on their travels as young men in just such a way. To what extent the roving prompted the poetry or the poetry the roving is an unanswerable question. But there seems little doubt that the popularity of the Wanderer-type in literature (and especially in poetry) helps to account for the large number of song-cycles which revolve around such a type. For there is no compelling intrinsic reason why a cycle of poems dealing with a wanderer should be any more suitable for this purpose than a set of poems on any other theme, provided that it had a clear shape and offered opportunities for musical diversity.

If Schubert has limitations — and it almost seems like *lèse-majesté* to suggest such a thing — it would be in the field of through-composed song and in his choice of texts. Spitta pointed out long ago that many of the ballad-settings destroy the stanzaic form of the poem, have no discernible formal principle, and demonstrate how the composer — especially in his early years — was inclined to squander his ideas rather than husbanding them in the interests of musical unity.[18] Although there are many subtly constructed short and medium-length ballads, the criticism certainly applies to many of the large-scale works. The episodic structure reveals the influence of Zumsteeg with the result, noted by one contemporary reviewer after another, that the provision of new material for each new twist in the story sacrifices unity in the quest for dramatic effects which are, frankly, often trumpery.[19]

The above strictures concern only a very small part of Schubert's enormous output. The question of his choice of poetry is more far-reaching. It has often enough been said that he could set anything to music and make the result melodious. Given the number of his songs and the speed at which he turned them out, it is hardly to be expected that he would subject each text to rigorous aesthetic scrutiny before deciding to set it, even if he had been so disposed. The poems which he set as solo songs certainly include many good and very good texts: by Goethe and Schiller, the poets of the Göttinger Hainbund, Klopstock, Shakespeare (in translation), the Romantics, Heine and others. But Schubert also set many sentimental, or even occasionally vapid, lyrics by Kosegarten, Leitner, Schlechta, Seidel and others who would be deservedly forgotten today but for the chance fact that they provided a great composer with material for song.

Perhaps it is unreasonable to expect a song-composer to be guided wholly by questions of aesthetic merit in this matter. Schubert set 'Erlkönig', but also Matthäus Casimir von Collin's 'Der Zwerg' (D771), which suggests that a good dramatic story appealed to him, whether or not it was told with any great *poetic* power. Similarly, if the general mood or message of a poem attracted him and something in it set his imagination working, a song resulted, regardless of whether the text contained a sonorous and eloquent philosophical message (Goethe's 'Grenzen der Menschheit', D716) or the homespun assurance that sometimes a good cry relieves your feelings (Leitner, 'Das Weinen', D926). Often it seems to have been a motif from the natural world, with its invitation to write 'pictorially' for the piano, that drew him. Or, more subtly, the possibility of relating voice to accompaniment in ways that would bring out the pathetic fallacy expressed in the poem, as in 'Die junge Nonne'.

Discussions of Schubert's poetic taste often revolve around the Wilhelm Müller cycles, for obvious reasons. It must be conceded that the poems making up *Die schöne Müllerin* are poor; the story is routine for the day, the poet makes constant use of the most conventional figures and motifs (miller, hunter, brook, colour-symbolism, etc.) and the cycle is full of mechanical applications of the pathetic fallacy, here far less interesting than in 'Die junge Nonne'. It is, of course, easy to see the appeal of these texts to the composer, but the kindest thing to be said of them is just that: they are serviceable song-texts. (Having said that, I would add that they never reach the almost unbelievable bathos of the poems making up *An die ferne Geliebte*.) *Winterreise* is a more complex matter. Here, I believe, the poetry is sometimes underrated. The reason is clear; since the cycle contains some of the greatest songs ever written, the texts are by definition the weaker half — and it is easy to exaggerate by how much, especially if one has *Die schöne Müllerin* in mind and recalls that the same poet wrote both cycles.[20]

It must be confessed that some of the *Winterreise* texts are built on mere poetic conceits ('Wasserflut', 'Frühlingstraum'). Others are straightforward examples of the pathetic fallacy, adequate as song-texts but indifferent as poetry ('Letzte Hoffnung', 'Der stürmische Morgen'). But there is much genuine poetry in *Winterreise*. The beginning is deceptively simple, as the young man recalls that he arrived a stranger and is departing a stranger: 'Fremd bin ich eingezogen,/Fremd zieh' ich wieder aus'. The repeated word has subtly shifted in meaning; our curiosity is aroused and only the sequel will tell us exactly what the second 'fremd' means. The next song ('Die Wetterfahne') expresses genuine bitterness, 'Der Lindenbaum' genuine nostalgia, 'Mut' genuine cosmic defiance. Towards the end of the cycle there is an overwhelming impression of world-weariness, resignation and longing for death. Here too Müller is capable of a simplicity that is far more telling than rhetorical pathos, as when the wanderer asks himself why he avoids his fellows and seeks the remotest paths; he is not a guilty man ('Habe ja doch nichts begangen,/Daß ich Menschen sollte scheun': 'Der Wegweiser'). The story is half told, half hinted at, with the stages in the journey caught up in little episodes or tableaux, often linked to bleak or dramatic natural phenomena. We almost share the sense of physical weariness in 'Rast' and 'Das Wirtshaus'; we almost *feel* the cold in 'Der Leiermann'. It is worth stressing that these are all things which are in the poetry, not put there by Schubert's music. The music certainly enhances the effect, but that is another matter; Müller would have been the first to admit that his poems were potential song-texts, waiting on a composer who would show himself to be a kindred spirit.

The problems surrounding the relationship of a great composer to indifferent or even poor texts are too complex to examine in detail here. It is obvious that a great song can come of an indifferent poem, even that the music can carry us along to a point at which we are literally no longer able to approach the poem objectively, *as a poem*. But it is equally obvious that, for anyone who loves both poetry and music, the most satisfying experiences come from a wedding of great music to great poetry. It is impossible to listen to, say, the Harper's songs and then to Leitner's 'Die Sterne' (D939) or Schlechta's 'Fischerweise' (D881b) without wishing that Schubert had set rather more of the first kind and rather fewer of the second.

There is a related question. A composer who does not always exhibit fastidious taste in what he sets may also strike a false note in his treatment of the finest poetry. While it is easy to think of Schubert songs where magnificent poetry is magnificently set ('Erlkönig', 'An Schwager Kronos', 'Der Doppelgänger'), some people would question whether Schubert's settings of 'Ganymed' or 'Prometheus' measure up to the grandeur of Goethe's texts.[21] Similarly, it is arguable that Schubert's setting trivialises Schiller's 'Elysium' (D584) and that the tone of the music is at odds with the poetry in some of the Novalis settings.

Loewe, Schumann, Mendelssohn and Franz

Now we must turn to Loewe and Schumann, two composers who — quite apart from the intrinsic beauty of their songs — had an important influence on future developments. Loewe's impact was mainly in the realm of long through-composed settings of narrative ballads. Here, as has been noted, Schubert's touch was sometimes less than sure and his over-readiness to follow Zumsteeg's example could lead to disunity. Loewe seems to have avoided the pitfalls almost intuitively, and shows himself equal to the formal demands of the large-scale ballad quite early in his career.[22]

Two factors aided him: a clear awareness of how the ballad derived from, and depended on, the stanza as a structural unit and an intimate knowledge of the German folksong tradition. The first led him to devise musical forms which, while seeking variety, never lost sight of basic poetic structures; the second encouraged him to write unaffected and 'catchy' tunes, even when operating on a level of musical sophistication very far from the simple melodies and plain strophic form of folk balladry. In short and medium-length ballads, he often found it possible to employ one melody throughout, but tended with longer texts to divide the poem into groups of stanzas — roughly analogous to the acts of a drama — and to give each group its characteristic melody. These melodies are not repeated mechanically as in orthodox strophic song, but are varied and modified in all manner of subtle ways. The resulting pattern may be like the song-equivalent to a set of variations; it may resemble a rondo or share some of the basic features of sonata-form. The unity of the text may be underlined by a literal repetition of the opening melody at the end of the song. But whether or not this occurs, the musical processes of variation and modification are never taken to a point where we lose sight of the basic melody and the basic poetic unit (usually the stanza) which it represents in musical form.

Loewe's accompaniments, while seldom taking on an absolutely central 'representative' function as do Schubert's, are independent, idiomatic, occasionally brilliant and often witty. Formally they strengthen the impression of diversity-within-unity by providing a changing undercurrent to a persistent melody or small group of melodies in the vocal line. Voice and piano fuse into an artistically satisfying whole which never slips into tedium (as the less imaginative sort of strophic composition had so often done in the case of long ballads), and never allows us to lose our sense of the fundamental one-ness of the poem (as we are in danger of doing with Zumsteeg and his imitators).

Schumann is quite different from Loewe. He prefers short lyric poems to longer narrative pieces (although some of his settings of Heine ballads are unsurpassed) and goes much further in his musical realisations of extreme states of mind than any previous song-composer.[23] By use of syncopations and tiny rhythmical dislocations between vocal line and accompaniment, he is able to create elusive and ambiguous effects. Unexpected modulations, interrupted cadences, chromaticism and bold discords (always carefully placed and used economically) combine to communicate uncertain or restless states of mind. Some of the most remarkable and moving moments in his songs derive from the piano-writing and the subtlety with which he combines vocal line and accompaniment.

Most critics, listeners and performers would agree that in Schumann piano and voice are in perfect balance. (In fact,

Schumann saw the domination of the accompaniment as a potential evil and rebuked more than one of his contemporaries for offending in this respect.) Although a minority of his accompaniments are 'representational', this is not an aspect of songwriting in which he was particularly interested; he saw the essential role of the piano as helping to bring out the mood or moods of the poem, as pointing to inner states rather than externals. It is noteworthy how he will resist what other composers would regard as a positive invitation. 'Auf einer Burg' (opus 39, 7) contrasts the stillness of the ruined castle, broken only by the 'lonely' song of birds, with the cheerful music of a wedding party sailing past on the Rhine far below. But the bride is weeping. One would expect a composer to make much of the contrasts in the poem, between the stillness above and the noise and movement below. Above all, one would expect him to respond to the totally unexpected final twist: 'Musikanten spielen munter,/Und die schöne Braut, die weinet' (Musicians play gaily and the lovely bride weeps). But Schumann's setting is all of a piece, austere and chill: exactly the same musical phrase is used for the music-making of the wedding party as had figured in the description of the old knight, turned to stone in his lookout and holding his silent watch through the centuries:

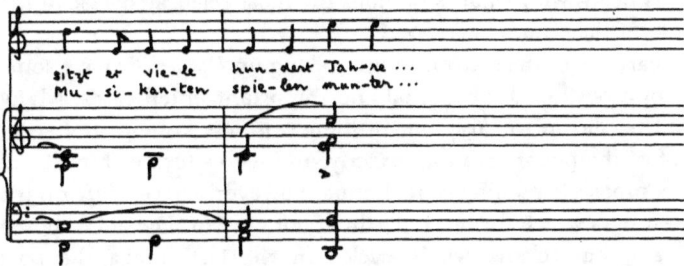

That must be the strangest setting of 'munter' in the whole of German song!

Perhaps the most distinctive feature of Schumann's accompaniment is the prominence which he gives to the postlude. To explain this fully we must, I believe, glance at contemporary conceptions of music as an art. The German Romantics made much of the notion that music, in its expressive power, went beyond words. E.T.A. Hoffmann, a man who was both writer and composer, speaks for many when he says:

> Music opens up to man an unknown kingdom, a world that has nothing in common with the external world of the senses that surrounds him and in which he leaves behind him all *definite* feelings, in order to surrender himself to an inexpressible longing.
>
> ('Beethovens Instrumentalmusik')

It is worth examining the implications of that passage. If music has nothing in common with the world of empirical reality and leaves far behind it everything definite and definable, it must indeed begin where language leaves off.

Examples of such views could be multiplied at will and Schumann, very much a product of the Romantic era as far as his aesthetic views are concerned, will unquestionably have been impressed by the Romantics' exalted conception of music. It may be added that the works of his favourite novelist, Jean Paul Richter, are full of ecstatic testimonies to the power of music. It is not coincidental that the postlude comes to play such a vital part in Schumann's songs and that so much is hinted at in the music after the voice has fallen silent. Postludes had figured in songs since the eighteenth century, of course, and are important in Schubert, but never before had they been given such prominence. Let us begin with what is perhaps the most celebrated case in the whole of Schumann's *oeuvre*.

Nearly all of the sixteen songs making up *Dichterliebe* have some sort of a postlude, substantial and important in ten cases. Many could be shown to carry on, in their wordless fashion, the argument of the poem or, more exactly, to give us further hints as to the composer's reading of it. Let us, however, concentrate on the fifteen bars which form the postlude not only to 'Die alten, bösen Lieder', but to the whole cycle. In the last stanza the poet proclaims his intention of burying his songs in a huge coffin:

> Wißt ihr, warum der Sarg wohl
> So groß und schwer mag sein?
> Ich senkt auch meine Liebe
> Und meinen Schmerz hinein.

(Do you know why the coffin should be so great and heavy? I placed my love and my anguish in it too.)

Until now the poem has been characterised by a self-mockery which takes the form of hyperbole: the coffin must be bigger than

From 1800 to Schumann, Mendelssohn & Franz

the great barrel at Heidelberg, the bier stronger than the bridge at Mainz, the only grave wide and deep enough is the ocean itself. Schumann, as is well known, sets all this to an extrovert and four-square march, with an uninterrupted movement of rapping quavers in the accompaniment. The effect is enhanced by emphatic rising phrases where Heine's hyperbole is strongest. But moods change more abruptly in Heine than in any other poet, and the final couplet (quoted above) is manifestly more serious and is treated seriously by the composer. He ends with a passage of 'quasi recitativo' over a minor subdominant chord with added sixth, a chord which resolves on to the dominant and takes us into the tonic major and the marvellously expressive postlude.

This begins with an echo of the postlude to an earlier song in the cycle (no. 12) and culminates in a 'quasi cadenza' of great tenderness. The song evoked is 'Am leuchtenden Sommermorgen', in which the poet, blind to the joys of a brilliantly sunny morning, broods on his grief over woman's treachery. The final bars of the cycle thus renew our memory of the sad, pallid lover ('trauriger blasser Mann') and it is with this sadness, rather than with self-dramatising exaggeration, that the work closes. Schumann, prompted by the final couplet of 'Die alten, bösen Lieder', evokes the 'Liebe' and 'Schmerz' for a last time before they are sunk in the oblivion of the ocean. Whether the mood of self-pity and resignation is indeed the ground bass of this sequence of poems or whether the note of irony and bitterness ought to predominate is a question tirelessly discussed by readers of the *Buch der Lieder* (from which Schumann took his texts) and listeners to *Dichterliebe*. But the point I wish to make here is that the final word in Schumann's reading of his chosen texts is no word at all, but the word*less* commentary of the piano. The 'definite' has been left behind, to return to Hoffmann's phraseology; the expression of the 'inexpressible' has become the responsibility of music. The postlude certainly means something, but the meaning cannot be verbalised; it defines itself as it is played.

But Schumann can make the postlude serve a lighter purpose too. In Rückert's little poem, 'O ihr Herren', the voice, the 'self' that speaks in the poem, is a nightingale: 'You fine gentlemen! Do you not need a nightingale for your beautiful gardens? Grant me a quiet refuge, and I will repay you in song'. A delectable little postlude of five bars follows. Since this is lyrical and songlike without in the least suggesting bird-song, we may assume that Schumann took the poem to have metaphorical overtones and assumed that the nightingale is also the poet in search of a patron. This is certainly a tenable reading; it is not easy to see why Schumann should otherwise have composed this particular postlude. Nor can I imagine how the metaphorical point could be implied within the song *without* some such postlude.[24]

It is safe to assume that most music-lovers, if they are interested in the Lied at all, will know some songs by Mendelssohn, Liszt, Brahms, Wolf and — spanning the turn of the century — Mahler, Reger and Richard Strauss. Songs by Robert Franz, Peter Cornelius, Hans Pfitzner and a few others are also heard from time to time. Most of these composers affected future developments. Liszt and Brahms in their different ways made exacting demands on the accompanist; Cornelius, especially in the late songs, is full of interesting harmonic experiments; Brahms and Mahler — again in very different ways — showed new possibilities for the setting of folksong; Wolf is as revolutionary in almost all aspects of song as Schubert had been in his day; Reger and Strauss push the Lied to extremes of textural complexity and technical difficulty that place much of their output beyond the reach of amateur musicians. Mendelssohn and Franz seem comparatively free of any desire to 'innovate', but this is not to say that their songs are dull or conventional.

Mendelssohn's songs — elegant, mellifluous, skilfully written for both partners in a way that makes them ideal for domestic performance — are well known and easily accessible. Robert Franz (1815–92) has suffered an undeserved eclipse, so that a word on him may not come amiss. During his lifetime his admirers included Schumann and Liszt.[25] Schumann's appreciation, dating from 1843, sees Franz as a fastidious composer who rejects all readymade formulae in the interests of expressing the essential nature and mood of each poem he chooses to set. He is perhaps best, adds Schumann, in his muted, dreamy songs which are admirably suited to a quiet evening's music-making. Liszt repeats the point about scrupulous realisation of the text and stresses the avoidance of ostentation in these songs, while pointing to the many subtleties of harmony and modulation that occur in them. One might add that virtually all contemporary reviews treat Franz with great respect, and augment this impression of an unassuming but exacting miniaturist of great poetic sensibility. Franz himself, in a letter of 11 February 1884, maintained that any *good* text (his emphasis) has a seed from which everything grows, so that an adequate setting of it will need to have a basic motif which similarly unifies the song. Everything superfluous must be rigidly excluded; there must be no unnecessary changes of rhythm or 'forced and foreign' modulations.

As might be expected, given this rather austere ideal, the songs are mostly to carefully chosen short lyrics of some literary merit, they are faithful to the spirit of the poems, are carefully constructed and devoid of superficial bravura. The accompaniments, although seldom demanding virtuosity, require to be played with great subtlety. They often have a marked contrapuntal nature, unusual in nineteenth-century song; this often provoked comment from Franz's admirers and led Schumann to single out J.S. Bach as one of the formative influences on him. In fact, a good grounding in Bach's keyboard music will certainly be of assistance to anyone who wishes to play these accompaniments properly. Although not averse to hunting motifs, rustling and rippling effects and so on, Franz is much less interested in 'pictorial' writing for the piano than were many of his contemporaries; his concern with the musical realisation of the poem's essence places him nearer to Schumann than to Schubert in his piano-writing.

As an example of Franz in his gentlest and dreamiest vein, one might single out the setting of Lenau's 'Bitte' (opus 9, 3), a prayer addressed to night: 'Rest your eye upon me, exercise your mysterious power to take the weight of the world from me':

Whenever Franz chooses a poem which shows obvious affinity with folk poetry, a general resemblance to the strains of German folk melody is likely to be discernible in his setting. In Mörike's 'Ein Stündlein wohl vor Tag' (opus 28,2), this Volkston coexists with the most extreme motivic economy and haunting contrapuntal textures in the accompaniment:

But it would be wrong to see Franz as a composer wholly given over to the gentle and the elegaic. Where dramatic effects are appropriate, he can supply them, as in his realisations of some of Heine's sea-poems ('Mit schwarzen Segeln segelt mein Schiff, An die bretterne Schiffswand') and, most notably, in 'Ja, du bist elend' (opus 7,6), also by Heine: 'we are both wretched, my love, and will remain so until death'. The song, marked 'largo appassionata', has a striding melody which matches the poet's relentless and doom-laden argument. The voice part is full of dramatic leaps against drumming triplets in the accompaniment. But the most remarkable feature is a series of bold modulations not equalled, as far as I know, in any other song by Franz. Here is the close, surely one of the most electrifying endings to a song to be encountered anywhere in the field of the mid-nineteenth-century Lied:

This song demonstrates that, for all his dislike of those who strove for an impression of originality by arbitrarily introducing unexpected harmonies or modulations into their songs, Franz was perfectly willing and able to startle us if the text required it; as he said in the letter already referred to, the music must grow out of the poem.

It is noteworthy how many short lyrics by Heine were set by both Franz and Schumann. Although some critics[26] seem to imply that a comparison always works to Franz's disadvantage, I would prefer to see the two composers as simply different in their approach, so that a comparison of the familiar Schumann song with Franz's lesser known version leads us to re-examine the famous song and, perhaps, Heine's text too. For the benefit of anyone who cares to put this to the test, here are some examples:

	Franz	Schumann (*Dichterliebe*)
'Hör' ich das Liedchen klingen'	opus 5,11	no. 10
'Allnächtlich im Traume'	9,4	14
'Am leuchtenden Sommermorgen'	11,2	12
'Im Rhein, im heiligen Strome'	18,2	6
'Im wunderschönen Monat Mai'	25,5	1
'Die Rose, die Lilie . . .'	34,5	3

Franz's fall from popularity after a long period of esteem among discriminating music-lovers and fellow-composers is to be regretted. Any amateur singer or player who values subtlety and truth to the text within a small compass will find much to delight and test him in these songs.

Notes

1. Schumann, *Gesammelte Schriften*, 4 vols, Leipzig, 1854, ii, 136. See too above, p. xi.

2. There were, of course, exceptions: see Walter Salmen, 'Social obligations of the emancipated musician . . .', in *The Social Status of the Professional Musician*, ed. Salmen, translated Kaufman and Reisner, New York, 1983, especially pp. 270-2.

3. One clergyman, J.L.F. Glück (1793-1840), made a name as a song-composer, notably for his setting of Eichendorff's 'Das zerbrochene Ringlein'.

4. See K. Hortschansky, 'The Musician as music dealer . . .', in

The Social Status of the Professional Musician, pp. 189ff.

5. For a representative selection, see Bibliography, section 2. Nineteenth-century periodicals, such as the *Zeitung für die elegante Welt*, continue to publish songs and some of the most important musical journals regularly include *Musikbeilagen*.

6. Heine wrote an appreciation of Methfessel, describing his songs as genuinely and deservedly popular by virtue of their simplicity and naturalness: see Heine, *Säkularausgabe*, iv, 1981, p. 221.

7. See Dietrich Fischer-Dieskau, *Töne sprechen, Worte klingen*, Stuttgart and Munich, 1985, p. 73.

8. M.J.E. Brown, *Schubert. A critical biography*, London, 1958, p. 220; Moritz Bauer, *Die Lieder Franz Schuberts*, Leipzig, 1915, p. 41.

9. In these and subsequent illustrations, I have simplified the texture, since it is the harmonies and modulations that concern us.

10. E.G. Porter, 'Schubert's harmonies', in *The Music Review*, xix, 1958, 20–6. I am indebted to this article.

11. Fischer-Dieskau, *Auf den Spuren der Schubert-Lieder*, Wiesbaden, 1971, p. 9.

12. For a technical discussion of how that expansion comes about, see Donald Tovey, 'Tonality in Schubert', in *Essays and Lectures on Music*, OUP, 1949; E.C. Bairstow, *Counterpoint and Harmony*, Macmillan, 1937, pp. 351ff; Arnold Schönberg, *Structural Functions of Harmony*, first published 1954, many editions, chapter 9.

13. See Eric Blom, 'His favourite device', in *Music and Letters*, ix, 1928, 372–80.

14. See *AMZ*, xxvi, 426f; xxix, 292; xxxi, 654, 658, 660f. It will surprise modern Schubert-lovers to learn that 'Schlummerlied' (D527) contains 'einige desperate Modulationen'.

15. Tovey, 'Franz Schubert', in *Essays and Lectures on Music*, p. 109.

16. See, for instance, Ernst Bücken, 'Franz Schubert und Robert Schumann als Naturmaler im Lied', in *Musikalische Charakterköpfe*, Leipzig, 1942, pp. 17–56.

17. *AMZ*, xxviii, 483 and xxxvii, 778. For a representative selection of Wanderlieder, see Bibliography, section 4. For an account of Kreutzer's *Wanderlieder*, see Luise E. Peake in *The Musical Quarterly*, lxv, 1979, 83–102. It was not only the reviewers who saw the cycle as a 'novel': F.H. Truhn describes his opus 64 as 'ein Liebes-Roman in 12 Liedern'. (I have not been able to locate a copy.) A good deal of work has been done in the last twenty years to show the derivation of the early song-cycle from the *Liederspiel*: a play with songs intended for amateur performers. But this point does not affect the importance of Schubert's cycles as a formative influence on later works for single voice and piano.

18. P. Spitta, *Musikgeschichtliche Aufsätze*, Berlin, 1894, p. 426. This is part of the article 'Ballade', to which I am much indebted. Many critics have echoed Spitta with varying degrees of emphasis.

19. See, for instance, 'Der Sänger' (D149a) and 'Der Taucher' (D77).

20. Some writers bracket the two Müller cycles together as far as poetic value is concerned. For A. Craig Bell (*The Lieder of Brahms*, Darley, 1979, p. 2) they are both 'slop'(!). By contrast, Klaus G. Just (*Übergänge*

..., Berne, 1966, pp. 133–52) treats the *Winterreise* texts with considerable respect.

21. For a discussion of 'Kennst du das Land' from this point of view, see below, p. 195.

22. Loewe lived from 1796 to 1869. He first published ballads in 1824, although some of these had been composed several years earlier. For his 'precociousness', see Spitta, p. 433. Some modern writers on song seem to me to underrate Loewe.

23. For more on this, see below, p. 128.

24. The song is no. 3 of Schumann's opus 37. For a discussion of a Schumann postlude which implies an interpretation of the text through dynamic contrast, see my article, 'The Composer as Interpreter', in *German Life and Letters*, n.s. xxxiii, 1982, pp. 224f.

25. Schumann, *Gesammelte Schriften*, iv, 262–5; Liszt, *Gesammelte Schriften*, Leipzig, 1880–3, iv, pp. 211–42.

26. For instance, D.W. Ivey, *Song: anatomy, imagery and style*, New York, 1970, pp. 217f.

10
The Development Towards Greater Complexity

German song rapidly became more adventurous throughout the nineteenth century after a long period in which, as we have seen, it had been subject to deliberate and almost dogmatic restrictions. This development influences all aspects of song: the choice of texts, harmony and modulation, vocal and piano-writing and their interrelationship. I will take these aspects in turn.

Texts

We saw that eighteenth-century composers and theorists held strong views as to what should and should not be set to music. Their objection to 'Denkoden', if suitably qualified, obviously retains some validity; no one would enjoy versified philosophy of a formal and abstract kind in song-form. But the banishment of emotional extremes from song in the interests of a rather blinkered notion of what was aesthetically tolerable did not long survive the turn of the century.[1] The irony, wild humour and occasional morbid fancies of Heinrich Heine, Lenau's black melancholy, the neurotic fears of madness and the agonies of mind expressed in some of Hans Andersen's poems (set by Schumann in German translation) — all were to seem fair game to the nineteenth-century song-composer. Perhaps the most startling illustration of my point is Andersen's 'Muttertraum'. The mother watches over her slumbering infant and indulges in fond dreams, while a raven gloatingly foresees that this 'angel' will grow up to be executed as a criminal: 'Dein Engel wird unser sein,/Der Räuber dient uns zur Speise'. Schumann's uncanny setting, with its wandering semiquavers and syncopated bass-line, exactly catches the gruesome atmosphere. It goes without saying that Andersen's 'Der Spielmann' and 'Muttertraum', Heine's 'Doppelgänger' and 'Am Kreuzweg wird begraben', etc. form only a tiny minority of the multitude of texts chosen by nineteenth-century composers — but the fact that they figure in song at all is a measure of a drastic change of attitude.[2]

Harmony and modulation

As the century progresses, the expansion of harmonic possibilities demonstrated by, above all, Schubert is further enhanced by ever increasing chromaticism. Wolf and, later, Reger develop a constantly shifting, nervous harmonic language well fitted to the expression of neurotic anxiety, restlessness, impatience and caprice. This enables Wolf to bring out, for instance, the edginess and tension that form the undercurrent to even so apparently lighthearted a poem as Goethe's 'Gutmann und Gutweib' (see below, p. 199), to find musical expression for the eerie atmosphere of Mörike's 'Die Geister am Mummelsee' or to match Goethe's extravagant daydreams in 'Der neue Amadis'. The danger is, of course, that such resources can be misapplied, squandered on relatively uncomplicated texts, so that the resultant songs strike the hearer as 'over-composed': this certainly applies to most of Reger's and Richard Strauss's folksong settings.

This brings us to a vital general point concerning the role of harmony and modulation in song. In a piece of 'pure' music, harmonic piquancy and unanticipated modulations must justify themselves and achieve their effect on exclusively musical grounds. But the song-composer has to satisfy two sets of criteria. His unexpected chord or shock change of key must make sense not only in terms of technical (musical) requirements, but also with reference to the mood of the poem or to the particular word or phrase being sung at that moment. We cannot, if we listen attentively to a song, simply surrender ourselves to appreciation of the harmonies as harmonies; a chord which might produce a delightful *frisson* in a piano solo could be quite wrong in the context of a song. Conversely, fairly conventional harmonic devices,[3] which would not raise an eyebrow in an instrumental piece, can have an altogether more striking effect if shrewdly used at a critical moment in a song.

Where technical competence and poetic sensibility are combined, an unlooked-for modulation or piece of harmonic colouring can contribute vitally to the process of interpretation through song. One of Goethe's most famous short poems, the first of the *Wandrers Nachtlieder* ('Über allen Gipfeln') will provide an example. The text describes the stillness of the natural world at night and goes on to promise that soon a like peace will come to the Wanderer: 'Warte nur, balde/Ruhest du auch'. But how soon is 'soon'? There have been almost as many implied answers to that question as there are settings of the poem. F. Siebmann, in a version dating from 1880 (opus 60,5), implies his understanding of Goethe's text at this point by purely harmonic means. He sets the closing words thus:

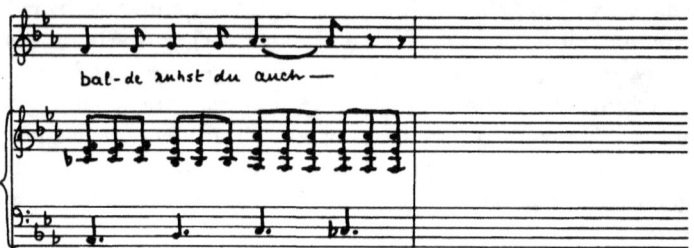

From here — were the peace as imminent as Schubert and some other composers evidently thought — it would be an easy step to the second inversion of the tonic chord of the home key (E flat) and thence to a 'resting place'. Instead, Siebmann requires the singer to repeat the phrase, proceeding by means of an enharmonic change in the bass to the distant region of E major, as if to underline the injunction to wait. This little harmonic peregrination tells us more clearly than ever words could that the wanderer still has a way to go before he finds peace:

A somewhat similar use of an unexpected modulation which cheats the listener's impression that he is headed for the home key comes in Schumann's 'Waldesgespräch' (opus 39,3). A wanderer in the forest at night encounters a woman and offers to escort her home as his bride: 'du schöne Braut! ich führ' dich heim!' Too late he realises that she is the Lorelei and that he, far from guiding her out of the forest, is destined to remain there as her victim. The words just quoted are set in a way that leads us confidently to expect a cadence in the home key of E major. Instead, on the very word 'heim', Schumann precipitates us into the remote key of the flattened submediant (bars 14-15). This is Schumann's way of implying, by harmonic means, that there is to be no homecoming, of giving a disquieting anticipation of the end of the poem: 'kommst nimmermehr aus diesem Wald' (you will never leave this forest).

Such examples (and they could be multiplied at will) bear out the point made concerning the dual function and dual justification of unexpected harmonies and modulations in song. Siebmann's abrupt shift from E flat to E major must not only satisfy harmonic logic, but must tell us something about his reading of the poem; Schumann's surprise modulation would not make much sense, were the encounter in 'Waldesgespräch' not a sinister and fateful one.

Schubert's influence in the matter of harmony was radical and long lasting. His demonstration of how the harmonic language of song might be extended through the use of chromatic triads, both for their intrinsic capacity to produce mysterious, exotic or romantic colouring and to facilitate surprise modulations, was seized on by later composers. Ludwig Hartmann's setting of Heine's 'Ich will meine Seele tauchen'[4] may serve as an example. On the words 'the song shall quiver and tremble like the kiss of her mouth', the composer relies *solely* on a succession of common chords — but the effect is anything but commonplace. This is the harmonic progression, reduced to its bare bones:

In Alfred Julius Becher's setting of 'Über allen Gipfeln' (opus 1,5), the insouciance with which the composer walks out of F sharp into F major is pure Schubert:

Since this is not a treatise on the influence of Schubert as harmonist, the above examples must suffice. But they are two of many.

Formal advances

As we have seen, eighteenth-century composers discovered quite quickly the advantages of expanding and diversifying simple strophic forms, thus creating variety within unity and providing a musical equivalent to the changing emotional or dramatic content of the different stanzas or sections of the poem. All the variants on the strophic form current in the eighteenth century were further developed in the nineteenth. (Most of them can be found, used with great subtlety, in Schubert's songs.) In addition, the greatly enlarged role now given to the piano meant that an unvarying tune could take on differing emotional or dramatic colouring through changes in the accompaniment from stanza to stanza. Brahm's folksong arrangements provide the most famous and possibly the most beautiful examples; further instances can be found in Beethoven, Schubert, Schumann and a host of less famous composers.

But the most dramatic formal advances came in the field of the through-composed song. We have noted that early attempts had, by creating new material for every twist in the poem, all too often sacrificed musical unity and destroyed the listener's sense of poetic unity in the process. Once the example of Schubert's short to medium-length through-composed songs ('Erlkönig', 'Der Zwerg', 'An Schwager Kronos', etc.) and of Loewe's ballads had been assimilated, the formal possibilities must have seemed virtually unlimited. Many nineteenth-century songs have shortcomings, no doubt — melodic tedium and ill-advised harmonic experiments among them — but formal miscalculations are rare, and the absurdly episodic through-composed form, depressingly common in the late eighteenth and early nineteenth centuries, rapidly became a thing of the past.

The vocal line

Eighteenth-century theorists of song had encouraged a vocal style which, if not wholly syllabic, imposed strict limits on decoration. We have seen in Schulz and the ablest of his followers how effective this modest style might be, but it could not long remain unchallenged as song-composers became increasingly eager to assert themselves *as composers*, no longer subservient to the poet. In the decade immediately before Schubert, it is already clear that many composers are aiming at a richer style which, while not putting the clock back by fragmenting the text into isolated expressive phrases, could do justice to its dramatic or emotionally charged moments.[5] Schubert shows prodigious inventiveness in this, as in all other aspects of vocal writing, but virtually always remains true to the general character of the poem and within the bounds of what is songlike. Florid and 'operatic' vocal writing, as in 'Der Hirt auf dem Felsen', is so rare as to be surprising (and that work is in any case not so much a Lied as a *Konzertlied*).

Throughout the century, the feeling persists that elaborate runs, trills and arpeggios have no place in song-writing, the exceptions usually being texts like Goethe's 'Die Bekehrte', with its 'la-la' refrain.[6] In general, however, melismatic writing is carefully controlled and used sparingly. As illustration of this, I will take two contrasting, but equally effective, examples. In 'Lieb' Liebchen, leg's Händchen', Heine equates the beating of his heart with the hammering of a carpenter mysteriously housed inside his breast. Typically, the revelation that it is his own coffin that is being fashioned is held up until the end of the stanza: 'der zimmert mir einen Totensarg'. In Schumann's setting (opus 24,4), the virtually syllabic writing is embellished at this point:

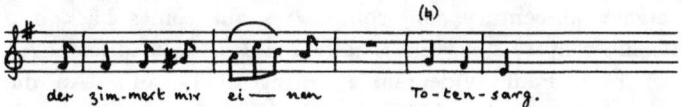

The music displays the same sort of disquieting wit as Heine's text. Just as Heine starts in a deceptively harmless tone (for the beating of the heart might be expected to lead to a declaration of love), introduces the first note of foreboding by saying that the carpenter is *malevolent* ('schlimm und arg') and saves up the worst for the end, so Schumann begins with a neutral rising phrase on 'Lieb' Liebchen . . .', introduces a note of misgiving through remote and mysterious harmonies at 'da hauset ein Zimmermann . . .' and creates a moment of suspense at the end of the stanza through the melismatic touch and the bar's rest in the vocal line. The effect is doubly remarkable in that the word stressed through the melisma is not, as would be normal, a key word, but an indefinite article: the carpenter is hammering away at a . . . a what?

For a more conventional type of melodic decoration, one could turn to Wilhelm Taubert's setting (opus 67,2) of an affectionate parody of folk-poetry by Hoffmann von Fallersleben, 'In der Fremde' ('Es steht ein Baum in jenem Tal'), in which the singer looks back on the past joys of love. Each stanza ends with a tribute to the beloved ('nach meinem Schätzelein', 'mein holdes Schätzelein', etc.) and it is these phrases that the composer draws out in the most delectable fashion in his strophic setting. The effect is decorative yet plaintive, motivically linked to the rest of the melody in such a way that the work remains a song and not a Lied with an operatic tail:

Melismatic writing, then, is restrained and accords with the general mood of the poem, while helping to stress a particularly important or emotive word, phrase or — as in Schumann's case — revelation. It is the same with that type of word-painting according to which, in earlier periods of Western music, it was almost mandatory to set the words 'rise' and 'fall' to rising and falling figures, 'sigh' and 'laugh' in a manner suggesting sighs and laughter, etc. The device had been comprehensively rejected by the eighteenth-century song-composers, but comes back into nineteenth-century song in a modified and disciplined form. An extract from Paul Widemann's setting of Lenau's 'An die Melancholie' (opus 1,1, 1875), at the point where the text reads 'whether my star rises or falls', may be regarded as typical. The vocal line certainly rises and falls, but in a way that does not cut across the general melodic and rhythmic character of the song or 'destroy' the poem:

A closely similarly passage comes in Wolf's setting of one of Goethe's mock-oracular utterances, 'Geh! gehorche meinen Winken'. In sententious tones that are deliberately made to sound like a parody of the professional sage and giver-of-advice, the poet proclaims that human fortunes never remain static; one must rise or fall, suffer or triumph, be hammer or anvil. It is again at the words 'rise or fall' that Wolf permits himself a modest degree of word-painting. But even such limited vocal 'pictorialism' as we find in these two examples is quite rare. Indeed, at one point Schumann seems to go out of his way to avoid it, as if ironically signalling that such direct parallelism of words and music is no longer *de rigueur*. The song is his witty realisation of Chamisso's 'Verratene Liebe',[7] at the moment when a star falls into the sea. There is something almost defiant about Schumann's use of a rising ninth on 'gefallen':

The use of expressive devices such as melisma, provided that they did not come to constitute a tyranny of music over poetry, was expressly countenanced by some nineteenth-century critics.[8] Similarly, the relationship of musical rhythm to poetic metre was no longer a question of slavishly matching ♩ ♩ against trochees or ♩ ♩ ♩ against dactyls, but of finding much more flexible associations between the two elements.[9] These could range from subtle variants on a dominant pattern, as in Schumann (see opus 24,4 bars 9–10), or the use of hemiola to create a passing tension between vocal phrasing and the basic rhythm of the piece (common in Brahms), to a technique whereby the vocal line floats freely above recurring rhythmic patterns (as in Wolf). The methods open to the composer were various, but the motive remained constant: to stay true both to the metre of the poem and to the rhythm and cadences of the German language without being tied down to one unvarying rhythmic figure.

The accompaniment and its relationship to the vocal line

As the piano developed greater power and hence greater possibilities of dynamic contrast, song-composers came to make greater demands on the instrument and consequently on the accompanist, although, as we shall see, they seldom demand extremes of virtuosity. The 'pictorial' function of the accompaniment in so many songs from Schubert onwards is another obvious way in which the piano's role was expanded and the accompanist's capabilities were stretched.

The extension of the piano's compass also added considerably to the composer's options. From Schubert ('Totengräbers Heimweh', D842) to Wolf ('Frühling übers Jahr', 'Nixe Binsefuß'), composers were quick to exploit the light and rarefied tones achievable in the top registers, while Brahms and Wolf are equally skilful at creating sombre effects by using the bottom of the range. Loewe's 'Ständchen' (opus 9, ii,4) is a striking example of a song whose accompaniment moves from the upper registers to the middle range and back again in direct response to the events of the poem. Uhland's rather lachrymose text, popular among nineteenth-century composers, tells of a sick child who imagines that she is hearing music. Her mother's rejoinder — that no one is likely to serenade her in her condition — leads the dying girl to assume that what she hears is no earthly music, but an angelic song of greeting. While the daughter sings, the ethereal music which she hears (or believes to hear) is hinted at by Loewe by equally ethereal effects in the piano (a); the mother's prosaic response is accompanied by deliberately prosaic chords (b):

One could obviously cite innumerable further examples showing how the accompaniment was used by nineteenth-century composers: to evoke objects or phenomena which figure in the poem, to create mood, to prepare us through a solo prelude for the opening words or, by means of a postlude, wordlessly to comment on the whole poem. Since anyone who is at all interested in the Lied will have his or her favourite examples, it seems superfluous to pursue the matter at greater length here. The central fact, that the accompaniment steadily becomes more complex and varied,[10] is incontestable, and is yet another manifestation of the general feeling among nineteenth-century song-composers that music and poetry should now be regarded as equal partners. Composers were no longer content to provide accompaniments that did no more than support the vocal line harmonically, but, here as elsewhere, wished to become co-creators with the poets rather than somewhat subservient collaborators.

The increasingly complex interplay of voice and piano is obviously of yet greater moment than developments in either individual area. Where a subtle vocal line and an intricate accompaniment are combined in unexpected ways, the expressive possibilities of song — and the demands made on performers and listeners — become far greater than ever before in the history of the Lied. For the performers, mastery of individual parts is only the beginning of a patient and challenging process of putting the song together. As for the listener, he must pick up the implications of the melodic ebb and flow of the vocal line, while also interpreting such information concerning the composer's reaction to the poem as is conveyed by the accompaniment in its relation to the vocal line. The piano may reinforce the sung melody in the most unproblematic way; it may, through disturbing harmonies or by means of syncopation, create an uncertain and elusive effect. The piano may evoke a background of natural phenomena at points where these are not mentioned in the text, thus inviting us to make connections between different parts of the poem (settings of Goethe's 'Der Fischer' provide examples of this: see below, pp. 184f). Or the accompaniment may take over a theme that originally belonged to the voice, while the voice is relegated to an inner part; this too will make us ponder on the relationship between different sections of the text (example: Schubert's 'Der Kreuzzug', D932). Going yet further, the accompaniment may virtually become an independent and self-contained piece with the voice floating freely above and within it, almost accompanying the accompaniment. Wolf is adept at this, as in 'Auf einer Wanderung' (*Mörike-Lieder*, no. 15), where the 'wandering' theme is given to the piano throughout, forming a background against which the singer 'talks' to us (see especially bars 55ff). This is an almost paradoxical reversal of the expected situation in a song; the words are delivered almost casually, and it is the accompaniment that communicates the interpretation put on the poem by the composer. Indeed, Wolf often surprises us by giving the 'juiciest' tune to the piano.[11]

Even if few composers are as unconventional and unexpected as Wolf, it is generally true to say that the interplay of voice and piano becomes more complex and challenging from Schubert on. The performer's task in satisfactorily combining and balancing voice and accompaniment was compounded in the latter decades of the century by the difficulty for the singer of pitching the notes with correct intonation against constantly shifting chromatic harmonies.

Too complex for the drawing room?

It seems at first sight, then, that the demands made on performers increase quite dramatically as the nineteenth century wears on. Even if one allows for the fact that many amateur players and singers were quite well trained and accomplished, there seems to be a possibility that the Lied might, for the first time in its century-old history, be about to pass out of reach of these amateur performers. Certainly one has to record signs of a bifurcation into domestic and concert song, one manifestation of which was the growing popularity of the *Konzertlied*, a work which was specifically intended for public performance and which often resembled a voice and piano arrangement of a virtuoso operatic aria. Title-pages began to distinguish between 'Lieder' and 'Konzertlieder'; the *AMZ* took to reviewing the two categories in separate groups.[12] We have moved a long way from eighteenth-century notions, which conceived of song as a reaction against florid and difficult vocal music.

Mention of Konzertlieder naturally leads us to the wider question of public performance. The exact process by which the modern phenomenon of the song recital developed is complex and, as far as I know, has yet to be charted in detail. Until about Schubert's day, vocal items — if they figured in public or semi-public concerts at all — tended to be showy operatic pieces; pre-Schubertian song was on the whole too intimate to benefit from public performance and too unpretentious to show off the singer's prowess. Soon, however, things began to change. The 'Schubertiaden', at which many of Schubert's songs had their first performance, were somewhere between informal music-making and concerts in the modern sense. In various German towns and cities, notably Berlin, quasi-public performances took place in the *salons*. Heine mentions such events in his *Briefe aus Berlin*, specifically noting that Lieder figured in the programmes. Carl Loewe was, of course, famous for public performances of his own ballads and (although this fact receives less emphasis in accounts of his achievements) of works by other composers whom he admired. Famous singers gradually found that there was a public willing to listen to songs and ballads, not only to *bravura* extracts from operas.[13] Of course, this fact is not in itself a precise measure of the movement towards complexity and technical difficulty. (We have all been to song-recitals which included items which could and should be performed quietly in the home; most of us too have suffered domestic performances of songs which ideally require more spacious conditions.) Our prime concern here must be not with the comparatively incidental question of conditions of performance, but with the intrinsic nature of the songs themselves, their accessibility to amateur performers and the extent to which this lessened as the century wore on.

One cannot reduce the question to statistics, if only because no two people will agree exactly as to what a typical amateur performer can or cannot do. But no one would deny that the great majority of songs by Schubert, Loewe, Mendelssohn, Schumann and Franz can, with a degree of determination, be performed by a reasonably competent pair of amateurs and that such songs are eminently suitable for a domestic ambience. Brahms is obviously a degree more difficult, Liszt yet more so. With Wolf, I would estimate that nearly half of his songs are virtually ruled out for purposes of amateur domestic performance and, as we reach the turn of the century with Strauss and Reger, a good deal more than half.

However, this trend is only a tiny part of the whole story; the more familiar part, no doubt, because many of the names associated with it are still famous today. But the great majority of the now forgotten *petits maîtres*[14] operate on a much less demanding technical level. It is lack of knowledge of these composers that enables writer after writer in our day to exaggerate the extent to which the Lied became a virtuoso and public genre:

> The great song-composers of the nineteenth-century, with Franz Schubert foremost among them, remove song from the realm of private, domestic music-making and raise (!) it to the level of concert-song.
>
> . . . once the solo song [attained] the rich and elaborate maturity enshrined in the nineteenth-century Lied repertoire, it was no longer accessible to those amateur singers and players who had seen its birth . . . Art-song . . . had again entered the closed province of the professional performer.[15]

But the contemporary observer will not have seen song according to this 'evolutionary' view. For him, song intended for amateur performance will still have seemed the norm, while difficult songs, beyond the reach of anyone not of professional or near-professional standard, will have been the exceptions, often disapproved of as foreign to the spirit of the Lied.

Although twentieth-century commentators often tend to chart the development of the Lied, formally speaking, as a movement away from the strophic towards the through-composed song, the majority of songs in the nineteenth century were strophic, often still visibly related to the eighteenth-century Affektlied or to the catchy tunes common in the *Singspiel*. A further important factor, as we shall see, is the persistent popularity of the Lied im Volkston. Moreover, even the piano virtuosi among the song-composers usually seem to have taken pains to make their accompaniments — varied and interesting as these may have been — accessible to amateur players.[16] Leopold Lenz even took his solicitude to the point of adding a note to one of his songs (opus 21,5), saying that weaker pianists could confine themselves to repeating the accompaniment to the first stanza (this in a strophic song in which the piano part grows progressively more strenuous and demanding from verse to verse). A similar concern can be seen in the songs of the famous bass singer J. Staudigl which are, as a contemporary reviewer points out with satisfaction, not difficult show-pieces, but well within the range of any reasonably competent singer (*AMZ*, xlvi, 71).

Notes

1. Stoljar (p. 137) seems to date the process from Beethoven's setting of a pair of poems by Bürger, 'Seufzer eines Ungeliebten und Gegenliebe' (op. posth., *c*. 1795). But I find her remarks both on the text ('almost savage erotic force') and the music ('emotional frankness') exaggerated.

2. 'Muttertraum' is no. 2 of Schumann's opus 40. It was to be set three more times before the end of the century, 'Der Spielmann' only once more. Six composers apart from Schubert set Heine's 'Doppelgänger'.

3. On the whole, it is true to say that most German song-composers between Schubert and Wolf reflect and exploit the harmonic trends of the day without showing any great desire to set up as innovators.

4. *Lieder und Gesänge*, Heft iii, 3.

5. See the account of Abeille's 'Der Jüngling am Bach', above, p. 107.

6. As well as the setting by Wolf, one could cite those by Robert Volkmann (opus 54, 1879) and Max Stange (opus 13,2, 1888), both with florid refrains. For the unusual spectacle of a miniature operatic cadence to close an elegaic song, see F.H. Himmel, opus 36,2 (1810).

7. Opus 40,5. Ludwig Hartmann (*Lieder und Gesänge*, ii,1) has a rise of a fifth on 'her*un*ter'.

8. See below, p. 145; also *AMZ*, xix, 764 and 1, 779.

9. *NZfM*, ix, 1838, p. 2; *AMZ*, n.F. ii, 1864, 472.

10. Nägeli, in his article 'Die Liederkunst' of 1817 (*AMZ*, xix, 765), already notes this phenomenon and greets it, albeit with caution.

11. See *Mörike-Lieder*, no. 13 and *Spanisches Liederbuch*, i,6 and ii,2.

12. Adolf Jensen calls his setting of 'Alt Heidelberg, du feine', opus 34, a 'Concertlied'. Carl Banck distinguishes between *Lieder* and *Salon de Concert. Dichtungen . . . mit Begleitung des Pianoforte* (opus 33). 'Konzertlied' in the *AMZ* can mean any of the following: songs demanding great agility, those requiring a strong, dramatic voice, show-pieces with obligato instrument in addition to the piano accompaniment.

13. See Grove, 'Concert' ii, para. 5 and Schwab, pp. 176-81. Jenny Lind, J. Staudigl, Julius Stockhausen and Gustav Walter were all famous in their day for public performances of Lieder. Wilhelm Kienzl, the Austrian composer, organised song-recitals in Graz in the 1880s. From the middle of the century onwards, title-pages occasionally mention singers who have performed the songs in public.

14. A few of the minor composers were, on occasions, quite demanding. For difficult piano-writing, see S. Herzog, *Vier Lieder* (no opus); Konrad Heubner, opus 4; Ferdinand Hummel, opus 6; Anton Urspruch, opus 23,5; A. Winterberger, opus 10. Urspruch was a pupil of Liszt — and the fact shows in his piano-writing. For a very florid vocal style, see Ernst Häußler's 'Kennst du das Land'. Ludwig Berger's opus 27,9 and some of Carl Engel's songs and Loewe's ballads presuppose considerable agility on the part of the pianist. But one has to search for really difficult songs.

15. *Das große Lexikon der Musik*, edited by M. Honegger and G. Massenkeil, Freiburg, Basle and Vienna, 1976, v, 117; Stoljar, pp. 12 and 17. See too Schwab, p. 176.

16. Apart from the famous and obvious examples, one might mention Theodor Kirchner, Lührss and Tomasek. Liszt stands out in this respect, in that many of his song-accompaniments demand considerable virtuosity. See too note 14 above.

11
Theories of Song and the Ideal of 'Hausmusik'

If the great majority of songs composed throughout the nineteenth century were neither unduly exacting as far as the performers were concerned nor particularly experimental in idiom, this would be in the main due to the temperament of the composers, few of whom were revolutionary in their approach. In part also, I would guess, it was due to the fact that they had an eye on the amateur market in an age when song enjoyed vast popularity in German-speaking Europe. But in addition, there was strong theoretical underpinning of conservative values in song and constant insistence on an ideal of unaffected emotional directness and ease of performance. For the reviewers in the most widely read and influential musical periodicals do not eagerly welcome new developments. On the contrary, they fear them and try to check experimentation and the movement towards technical difficulty. This approach is so consistently adopted in the main journals up to and somewhat beyond the middle of the century that the value-judgements so revealed almost coalesce into an editorial *policy* on song. (This is particularly marked in the *AMZ* and the *NrMZ*). Since the reviews, essays and treatises from which the following summary has been made were mostly written by men who were themselves song-composers, they are an invaluable pointer to the views current in this important period of expansion and experiment.

Much so-called 'progress' is only apparent, says A.E. Grell, while Selmar Bagge sees around him a ferment of experimentation in which composers reject traditional values and follow their personal whims.[1] The areas where reviewers concentrated their attacks were, understandably enough, harmony and the role of the accompaniment. One of Grell's examples of progress that is more apparent than real is that of the extravagant and over-complicated type of piano-writing that, he felt, threatened to drive the vocal melody into a subordinate position; the accompaniment had come to sound like fragments of a piano sonata or concerto. Such strictures were common.

Schumann and others explicitly relate this real or supposed danger — that the piano might come to swamp the voice — to recent advances in piano construction.[2] Indeed, some critics believed that the new potentialities for rich and complex accompaniments could camouflage an essential poverty of musical thought,[3] a point to which we shall have to return. A writer in the *NrMZ* for 1855, L. Kindscher, wittily takes up the image residing in the word 'accompaniment': the accompanist, whose task it is to escort the 'lady melody', has been ungallant enough to ignore her and pursue his own interests (ii, 324). Kindscher further reveals his somewhat backward-looking stance when he adds that melody too has lost her innocence and become a 'coquette'. The ideal still seems to be a simple tune supported by an accompaniment which is content to *accompany*; the underlying feeling in many of these mid-nineteenth-century reviews and articles — that 'progress' towards greater complexity is to be resisted and slowed down if possible — is quite apparent in Kindscher. But even Schumann, the least backward-looking of music critics and the man who believed the Lied to be the one department of composition which had made genuine strides since Beethoven, was aware of the dangers of overweighting the accompaniment, although his criteria are more exact than those of his contemporaries. Theodor Kirchner's opus 1 *Lieder* are criticised for being like Songs without Words, piano realisations of the texts in which the vocal line has become almost incidental (iv, 218). But when reviewing Koßmaly's third collection of songs, Schumann warns against hasty judgements: Koßmaly's piano-writing, seemingly too weighty for perfect balance at first glance, turns out to be exactly appropriate and organically linked to the vocal melody.[4] Hence, it is the accompanist's job to achieve balance and integration with the vocal line. But other critics and reviewers simply inveigh against the 'dominance' of the accompaniment or declare that it is too difficult (*AMZ*, xliv, 414; *NrMZ*, iv, 56). Perhaps they show too little confidence in the abilities and judgement of amateur pianists.

Since it is the vocal line that carries the text, the question of voice part versus accompaniment (the gladiatorial expression seems justified, given the tone of some of the reviews) leads us naturally to a more general question: the relationship of music to poem. Writing in 1811, H.G. Nägeli sees a new stage in the development of the Lied; where previously composers had been willing to subordinate themselves to the text, they now give freer play to their musical instincts in the matter of keyboard solos, more expressive vocal lines and melismatic word-setting (*AMZ*, xiii, 645–50). An article in the same review, 'Über einige Fehlgriffe in der Gesangscomposition' (signed 'CFM'), expresses a similar ideal, according to which parity of text and music results in a perfect fusion and mutual enhancement.[5] This is a clear abandonment of the rather inequitable eighteenth-century notion that the composer should content himself with tailoring a well-fitting and suitably unobstrusive garment for the poem in favour of a more confident and assertive musical-poetic ideal. Even before the turn of the century, Friedrich Rochlitz had maintained that music should no longer be the servant of poetry, but on an equal footing (*AMZ*, i, 433–5). But no more than equal: warnings against allowing the music to gain the upper hand at the expense of poetic values are common (cf. *AMZ*, xv, 674).

Developments in harmony were thought to be at least as great a threat to perfect balance as was the growing complexity of the accompaniment. Everywhere one finds denunciations of 'arbitrary' harmonies, of the 'craze' for surprise modulations and of what was seen as a dangerous fondness for enharmonic changes. Constantly to employ chromatic harmonies and enharmonic progressions is like substituting the spices for the dish itself, says Bagge (p. 132), singling out Liszt as culprit and comparing him unfavourably with Schumann, who always saves up special effects for special occasions. Other composers — technically less gifted than these two — are criticised for lack of skill or judgement in matters of harmony and modulation. A reviewer in the *AMZ* (ns, ii, 1864, 760) takes Louis Ehlet to task for his misguided efforts. Johanna Kinkel too is criticised for losing herself in 'harmonic labyrinths' (*NZfM*, viii, 77). The tone can be patronising: wild modulations are a fault of youth, something the composer grows out of (*AMZ*, xlviii, 690).

Whether the harmonic aberrations are seen as proceeding from artistic whim, technical incompetence or youthful high spirits, the underlying point is the same: harmony should be subordinate to melody ('die untergeordnete Begleiterin' — *NZfM*, i, 219). If it becomes dominant, the resultant song may amaze us or engage our intellectual interest, but will lose its hold over our emotions (ibid. see too *NrMZ*, iv, 203). Although the most common complaint concerns over-indulgence in modulation, there is also criticism of unexpected and 'alien' passing-notes which obscure the basic relationships between chords (*AMZ*, xli, 756). The reviewer would, on that basis, have to reject some of Schubert's most succulent cadential effects!

What general criteria emerge from a study of these nineteenth-century critical writings? How is the 'parity' of music and poetry envisaged?[6] The necessary starting-point is always seen to be the correct perception of the general mood of the poem; lacking this, the whole song will be a failure. (Considering that, even by the 1820s and 30s, famous texts had already been set by many different composers, one might expect some more searching investigation as to what is to be understood by 'the' mood of a poem, but I have not been able to find any such discussion. Indeed, some reviewers seem to imply that the existence of a successful and widely popular setting of a poem should preclude further attempts.)

As we have seen, melody is regarded as paramount, so that the mood will be primarily conveyed by the vocal line which should be genuinely songlike, simple and 'natural'. Scrupulous attention to correct declamation is invariably insisted on. Imaginative harmonies and elaborate accompaniments are tolerated only if they underpin the melody and enhance its power to communicate the mood of the poem. The ideal is therefore a modest and conservative one, although a few concessions have been made to recent developments in composition. The harmonic colouring which is accepted as not threatening the autonomy and unity of the vocal line is a good deal richer than would have passed critical scrutiny at the turn of the century, and the same goes for the accompaniment. In addition, much more painting-in of detail through characteristic melodic twists or 'pictorial' writing for the piano, together with somewhat more ambitious melismatic passages, are allowed — again provided that these do not threaten the ruling mood of the poem.

This insistence that the composer's main task is to capture mood in melody shows that nineteenth-century theories of song, in their basic assumptions at least, are a direct extension of eighteenth-century notions. To be true, the old term 'Hauptaffekt' yields to 'Hauptgefühl', 'Grundempfindung', 'Grundstimmung', 'Ton des Ganzen' or 'der innere Geist' — but the difference is only terminological.[7] In his article on Lied (*Encyclopädie*, 1840–2), Gustav Schilling makes the emotional effect of song depend on the musical representation of this mood ('darstellung nur *eines* Gefühls . . . welches die Seele sanft bewegt'). This is the old Affektenlehre in slightly different clothing. In other statements of the ideal, the traditional notion is combined with the Romantic conviction that music touches our emotions with a greater immediacy than any other medium ('die Musik, diese unmittelbare Gefühlssprache' — NZfM, viii, 86). So the theorists constantly and strenuously champion conservative values in song. They virtually equate simple with good; characteristic words of approval are 'schlicht', 'einfach, 'natürlich', 'gesund', 'anmutig', 'ungesucht' and 'faßlich' (easily comprehensible). Conversely, anything regarded as over-ingenious is condemned. Praise is often bestowed by listing what the composer *avoids*; thus, Silcher is described as a composer who can dispense with showy trimmings and gaudy ornamentation ('geschniegelte Verbrämungen oder bunte Verschnörkelungen').[8] Anything experimental or mildly daring tends to be written off as pretentious, a modish striving for effect.

In view of the respect enjoyed by at least the major periodicals and the prestige of their editors and reviewers, the theories and opinions put forward year after year in a ceaseless flood of articles and reviews cannot have been without influence, especially on young composers eager to establish themselves in this important niche of musical activity. Only gradually, and especially in the NZfM, do we find more progressive attitudes gaining ground.

Franz Brendel, who was to become an enthusiastic champion of the 'New Music', had taken over the editorship of this paper in 1845. Nine years later, in *Die Musik der Gegenwart und die Gesamtkunst der Zukunft* (Leipzig, 1854), he thundered against the triviality of much contemporary music which, he maintained, had become a fashionable commodity, hollow and frivolous. Nowhere was this more clearly to be seen than in song (p. 16). Such strictures were to become common in the song-reviews of the NZfM (cf. 'die Seichtigkeit . . . gewöhnlicher Unterhaltungslieder', liv, 222). By the early 1870s, reviewers show distinct signs of favouring the 'music of the future'. W. Otto praises Metzdorff for his 'original inventiveness', and in the same year of 1872 an anonymous writer, carrying on Brendel's tradition, notes with approval how the seeds of the New Music are taking root in the minds of young composers ('wie die ausgeworfenen Samenkörner eines *Wagner* und *Liszt* immer wieder Wurzel fassen, wie junge Talente in die Bahnen dieser Meister einlenken und Blüthen treiben').[9] The most radical statement I have come across was made by Emanuel Klitsch: the highest praise that one can bestow on a collection of songs is to say that they are in the vanguard of modern musical development (*NZfM*, lv, 41). This general attitude colours the assessment of various elements in the song: precision in matching musical accent against poetic stress is now to be measured against Wagner,[10] while a richness of modulation made possible by enharmonic changes is praised as being in accord with the modern spirit (1v, 232, lviii, 215). It may be recalled that composers had regularly been *rebuked* in the *AMZ* for surprise modulations and a fondness for enharmonic changes. Even in the *Musikalisches Wochenblatt* (Leipzig, 1870ff), which was anything but a revolutionary journal,[11] we find a reviewer praising the song-composer for his painting-in of detail (v, 534) — again in marked contrast to the more cautious attitudes of twenty or thirty years previously. But such reactions — undoubtedly an encouragement to the more experimental composers — were comparatively few. Even as late as 1882 we find it argued in a musical encyclopaedia that the Lied should be simple and natural in expression and form; the writer uses exactly the same words as were encountered in the *AMZ* half a century before: 'natürlich', 'einfach', 'ungekünstelt', etc.[12]

Yet it would be facile to regard this conservatism as mere blinkered opposition to everything that was most enterprising in mid-nineteenth-century song. In two respects the denial that greater intricacy automatically meant progress had some justice on its side. It was undoubtedly true that some composers resorted to 'fancy' accompaniments to bolster up feeble melodic lines. Siebmann's setting of Eichendorff's 'Intermezzo' (opus 60, 1) opens thus:

The composer evidently hoped to give some semblance of life to this moribund piece of vocal writing through the accompaniment:

The Ideal of 'Hausmusik'

That — and it is not an isolated example — shows what happens when a recurrent piano motif, such as had been employed since Schubert's day to impart unity to a song and liveliness to its accompaniment, is divorced from genuine melodic invention.

Nor were the frequent complaints of over-daring harmonies and modulations entirely without foundation. After the dramatic expansion of possibilities demonstrated by Schubert, it must have seemed as if anything was permissible, despite the fulminations of conservatively minded reviewers. Johanna Kinkel, whose harmonic peregrinations were criticised in her day, sometimes reminds one of a cat which, having got to the outer branch of a tree, cannot get down again. Her setting of Heine's 'Lorelei' (opus 7, 4) illustrates this.[13] The song is in E minor, from which key the composer passes by means of a camouflaged enharmonic change (A) smoothly enough into F major. But how to get back again? Another enharmonic change (B) is pressed into service, this time with a forced and displeasing effect. Here I simplify the piano figuration, in order to show the harmonic progressions quite clearly:

An ill-conceived attempt to revitalise a lifeless song can be seen in Friedrich Kempe's setting of 'Über allen Gipfeln', opus 12, 3. This proceeds in a dull, chorale-like style for fourteen bars until the following progression occurs: E flat, C minor, dominant seventh of G, G major and thence via another dominant seventh to the dominant of the home key, A flat. The words that provoked all this activity (in the course of five bars) are some of the quietest in the whole of German poetry: 'Die Vöglein schweigen im Walde'.[14] As the fondness for ever more expressive chromatic effects grew, we occasionally find the vocal melody quite subordinated to the harmonies, as in Eugen d'Albert's setting of Lenau's gloomy poem, 'Nebel', opus 3, 4 (*c.* 1886):

Even if we cannot, since Wagner, Wolf and Strauss, go as far as the theorists in the mid-nineteenth century in giving absolute sovereignty to the melodic realisation of the poem's mood, the above examples are salutory reminders of what can happen to a song (and its text!) when the harmonies are allowed to dictate events. The reviewers in the *AMZ* and elsewhere had some reason on their side. It may be noted that a cautious and conservative attitude towards song persisted in some of the music periodicals until the turn of the century: the musical works (*Musikbeilagen*) appended to the *Neue Musik-Zeitung* in the 1890s and singled out for praise by its editors are homely and traditional in style for the most part.

In addition to the critical pressures just outlined, there was energetic propaganda in the cause of amateur domestic music-making, *Hausmusik*. One of the most eloquent and persistent champions of this ideal was W.H. Riehl (1823–97), in whom a love for music in the home combined with an interest in musical education and a passion for folksong and Lieder im Volkston. In addition to two important polemical works, *Die Familie* and *Musik im Leben des Volkes*, he composed songs specifically designed for the home: *Hausmusik: Fünfzig Lieder deutscher Dichter.*[15] This has its 'accompanying letter' (*Des Tonsetzers Geleitsbrief*), a statement of faith and intent in the form of a short preface. The collection, says Riehl, offers simple German domestic music, originally written for performance in his own home. There has been no attempt at 'external glitter'; his songs would be quite unsuitable for the fashionable *salon*. The link between these sentiments and the theories of song propounded in the journals is manifest. Riehl has taken his texts from the seventeenth century and folk poetry, from

The Ideal of 'Hausmusik'

Claudius, Bürger, Goethe and Schiller, from the Romantics and other, later poets. A minor curiosity is one of the very few nineteenth-century settings of Hölderlin: 'Ehemals und Jetzt'. Most of the settings are very pleasing: not too exacting to sing and play, but certainly not 'easy' in any patronising way. This is the simplicity which hides art, so that the songs reveal hidden values as one gets to know them. Although players and singers of modest gifts can make a reasonable shot at them, more practised performers will find themselves tested if they are to achieve a subtle and truly adequate reading. (This applies to virtually all songs of great *surface* simplicity by masters of the genre, from Schulz, Reichardt and Zelter, through Schubert and Schumann to many of Brahms's folksong settings).

Riehl's disparaging reference to 'external glitter' hints at an important aspect of Hausmusik, which again goes back via nineteenth-century theories of song to eighteenth-century notions. There is, firstly, the familiar point that modest technical ability is quite compatible with profound musicality. Indeed, Riehl goes further: many amateurs with only moderate technique but genuine musical understanding are musicians in a much more profound sense than the most brilliant virtuosi (*Musik im Leben des Volkes*, p. 51). But the distinction between 'house' (= middle-class drawing room) and salon hides a nationalistic point too. To expound this, we have to turn to Riehl's other work, *Die Familie*, where he attacks the salon not only for its glitter and cleverness, but also for its preference for French fashions (p. 322). Here is yet another similarity to the eighteenth century, where the Lied, as a German form involving German texts, was set off against French and Italian models. That deep-seated German prejudice against the witty but facile French as opposed to the solid if less flashy Germans is also revealed in the constant references to German 'inwardness'.[16] August Härtel, in his *Deutsches Liederlexikon* of 1865, combines praise of simple and natural domestic song with admiring references to 'unser deutsches Volk'. This tone of national pride — harmless enough in Riehl, who is after all offering some of the finest short German lyrics for use in German homes where they would naturally be preferred to French *chansons* or showy *Salonmusik* — can take on rather more disquieting, chauvinistic overtones, as when Cyrill Kistler maintains that everything 'un-German' must be rejected, in music as in all other things, or when Paul Möbius, in a speech made in the flush of victory following the Franco-Prussian War, associates German

The Ideal of 'Hausmusik'

song with the Germans' sense of identity and national pride.[17]

To return to Hausmusik: innumerable anthologies of simple *Kunstlieder*, running series of domestic song and piano solos, popular voice and piano settings of folksongs and, more important, volumes of the *Deutscher Liederschatz* type, in which folksong arrangements coexisted with technically undemanding strophic songs by Schulz, Reichardt, Zelter, Schubert, Mendelssohn and others abounded throughout the century.

The collection *Neue Hausmusik* by Johannes Heuchemer and Bernhard Scholz illustrates the trend well: the texts are a mixture of folk poems and short lyrics by known poets in a popular, 'folkish' style.[18] Seven of the twenty-four texts are by Ludwig Uhland, a fact which testifies to that poet's skill in finding the popular touch. But the most interesting song in the collection from our point of view is Scholz's setting of Goethe's 'Mailied'. A comparison with Beethoven's version shows that Scholz's is similar in many respects, but notably simpler for both partners: the accompanist has no solo passages (contrast his extremely responsible role in Beethoven) and the vocal writing is virtually syllabic. Scholz is 'Beethoven für das Volk':

The above account of Hausmusik is not intended to suggest any absolute and rigid distinction between domestic music and that intended for the salon or concert platform. Some songs work in both settings, some composers write both types of music. But Hausmusik has its champions, just as 'public' music has its virtuosi — and in practical terms it is usually easy to see which setting is more appropriate for any given song. Certainly, the age perceived a rivalry and conflict of interests between domestic and public song; many people either took sides in active polemic or implicitly supported one trend or the other through their practice as composers. The active cultivation of Hausmusik continues into this century:

The Ideal of 'Hausmusik'

Otto R. Hübner, *Neue Lieder für die Hausmusik*, Breslau, 1907 or earlier.

―――― *Schlichte Lieder nach Gedichten erster Meister als neue Volksweisen*, 6 vols, Breslau, n.d. (*c*. 1905?).

R. Göttsching, *Fürs Haus*, Leipzig, 1913.

Ernst Pepping, *Haus- und Trostbuch*, Bärenreiter, 1949 (not so simple!).

By this time, of course, the gulf between the interests and technical capabilities of amateurs and the demands, both in terms of technique and of musical understanding, made by advanced *Kunstlieder* had become wider than in any previous period of Western music.

Rudolf Hemmleb, in the Preface (Geleitwort) to his *Feldblumen*, Langensalza, 1913, comes very close to the terms in which nineteenth-century champions of Hausmusik had expressed themselves: the songs are not intended for the concert hall, but as pleasing and easily performable domestic music for the great army of amateur music-lovers. In the same year Göttsching shows that this aim is compatible with the most fastidious choice of texts. *Fürs Haus* is certainly accessible to the 'great army of amateur music-lovers' and contains texts by Eichendorff, Rückert, Mörike, Nietzsche, Shakespeare and from the Bible. There is no trace of sentimentality such as one sometimes encounters in the 'Liederschätze' and 'Liederkränze' of the previous century; indeed, both poems and music are on the austere side. Heinrich Lemacher's *Aus Friedenszeit* (Mönchengladbach, mid-1920s) — part of a series entitled *Musik im Haus* — is not dissimilar. The texts include poems by Mörike, Keller and Walter von der Vogelweide (in the original Middle High German!) and the settings, although not technically difficult, are certainly not condescendingly simple. The phrase 'Musik im Haus' here seems to imply that the texts will contain fairly reassuring messages, also that the music will not be in any 'advanced' or experimental idiom.

As in the eighteenth century, the quest for a simple, national and popular style became inextricably linked with the enthusiasm for folk music. Suitably tailored for use in the drawing room, folksong became, together with Lieder im Volkston, a weapon in the battle against the growing professionalism of the *Kunstlied*. Brahms's superb settings of folk poems, both to traditional tunes and those of his own devising, are well known, as are Mahler's *Wunderhorn* settings. But scores of composers worked this vein, often with very beautiful results. A famous letter from Brahms to Clara Schumann of 27 January 1860, in which he describes the folksong as an ideal from which song-composers have much to learn, should put us on our guard against treating the question from too narrow a viewpoint and simply confining ourselves to a discussion of how composers arranged or reset actual folk poems. This is an important subject but equally important is the fact that Germany's most famous and best-loved poets adopted the style of folk poetry, thus tacitly inviting composers to set the resultant poems 'im Volkston'. In Chapter 12, I will take the main strands in this complicated pattern in turn, beginning with arrangements of folk poems to traditional melodies, passing on to similar poems reset to new tunes and concluding with a brief description of settings 'im Volkston' of lyrics by Goethe, Heine and others.

Notes

1. Grell, *Aufsätze und Gutachten über Musik*, Berlin, 1887, p. 174; Bagge, *Musik und Musikzustände*, Vienna, 1860, p. 131. See too Ludwig Rellstab, *Ludwig Berger . . .*, Berlin, 1846, p. 109.
2. Schumann, *Gesammelte Schriften*, 1854, iv, 218.
3. Oswald Lorenz in *NZfM*, ix, 2.
4. Vol. iv, 259. I have not seen this collection of Koßmaly's.
5. *AMZ*, xii, 257f. Similar in *NrMZ*, iv, 106.
6. What follows is put together mainly from these sources: *AMZ*, xii, 17f; xvi, 427f; xix, 761-7; xxii, 387; xxiv, 152. *NZfM*, ix, 2f. Schumann, ii, 133 & 140; iii, 148 & 261. But examples could be multiplied almost indefinitely.
7. See *AMZ*, xiii, 514 and xxxvii, 473; *NrMZ*, ix, 37; *AMZ*, iv, 205 and xiii, 171.
8. *AMZ*, xlii, 336. Similar: xxxii, 473, on Moritz Hauptmann.
9. *NZfM*, lxviii, 29 and 351. It must be added, however, that simple and traditional songs were also praised in the *NZfM*, provided that they were good examples of their kind.
10. See too Karl Metz, *Das deutsche Kunstlied . . .*, Leipzig, 1900, p. 56.
11. Witness Richard Pohl's thunderings against excessive experimentation, xi, 158.
12. Friedrich Bremer, *Handlexikon der Musik*, Leipzig, n.d. (Preface dated 1882), p. 400. Ernst Bücken (*München als Musikstadt*, Leipzig, 1923, p. 67) notes that the supporters of the New Music had only limited influence as composers. This would apply particularly to song. My account of this debate has of necessity been very brief. The history of Schumann's running battle against the ultra-conservative 'Philistines', together with a full account of the controversy surrounding the New

Music, are dispensed with, since interested readers can easily find this information elsewhere. Some commentators judge the *NZfM* to have become *less* progressive under Brendel's editorship, but I find this debatable; it would certainly not apply to the paper's attitude towards song and song-composers.

13. This is not to be taken as a general stricture, however. Her settings of 'An Luna' (opus 6,4) and 'An den Mond' (7,5) are harmonically enterprising in a much more technically accomplished way.

14. For a senseless helter-skelter of chromatic harmonies, see Hedwig Hertz, *12 Lieder von Heinrich Heine*, no. 5. Even as good a composer as Loewe can miscalculate: see the slither from the dominant of C sharp major to G major in 'Das Ständchen', opus 9, ii, 4, bars 28f.

15. Stuttgart and Augsburg, 1855. *Die Familie* had appeared somewhat earlier, but I have used the edition published in Stuttgart in 1861. *Musik im Leben des Volkes* dates from 1858 and was republished in an edition by J. Müller-Blattau, Cassel, 1936.

16. See *AMZ*, 1, 779; Riehl, *Geleitsbrief*; *AMZ*, ns, ii, 761.

17. For Kistler, see *Aufsätze über musikalische Tagesfragen*, 1880ff, passim. For Möbius, see 'Die Macht des deutschen Liedes' in *Musikalisches Wochenblatt*, ii, Leipzig, 1871, 273–7. The attitude surfaces again at the time of the First World War, for instance in E.L. Schellenberg's *Das deutsche Volkslied. Ein Hausschatz . . .*, 3 vols, Berlin, 1914–15.

18. *Neue Hausmusik* appeared in Leipzig, *c*. 1850, and contains twelve songs by each composer. Scholz was one of the adversaries of the 'New Music', by the way.

12
The Importance of Folksong

Folksong arrangements using existing melodies

Here Brahms is obviously the most famous example. The situation is complicated by the fact that not all the tunes selected by him were as genuine or as old as he thought.[1] Nor, indeed, was he greatly concerned about strict authenticity if the melody suited the text and sounded 'folkish'. And here his instinct was usually sure.

His accompaniments vary from the humblest chordal support to ingenious and elaborate piano figurations (but never taken to a point where they threaten to drown the voice or do violence to the spirit of the essentially 'popular' tunes). Where he employs a counter-melody in the treble of the piano part or some other contrapuntal device, this is always done fastidiously and unostentatiously. Hemiola, cross rhythms and unexpected harmonies add piquancy to many of these arrangements, but again are always matched to the character of the melody and the events or emotions of the poem. A striking example of Brahms's ability to do something quite unforeseeable which, on reflection, seems perfectly in keeping with his given material, comes in 'Du mein einzig Licht'. The song, which treats of the singer's hopeless love for a haughty beauty, has a rather foursquare melody in A major. Brahms asks for a pause on the singer's last note and gives a brief postlude in the relative minor. This twist of events (which always creates delighted surprise in performance) is exactly right, given the gloomy conclusion of the poem: the singer's exclusion from the joys of love. Some of the finest adaptations involve giving a different accompaniment to different stanzas or groups of stanzas. This may be no more than the straightforward elaboration of a simple chordal texture into decorative figures, but may also lead to the most exquisite and heartrending chromatic effects ('Gunhilde', 'Maria ging aus wandern').

In the Lied a perfect accord between text, vocal line and accompaniment is obviously of overriding importance. Where the composer takes over the tune readymade, the first two terms of the equation are already given (or should be). His task then consists of devising an accompaniment which realises and supports the melody and reflects both the general mood and the changing nuances of the poem. In this, Brahms seems to me triumphantly successful. Much as the question of 'authentic' versus 'synthetic' folk melodies may (properly) exercise both musicologists and folksong researchers, it is secondary as far as the essential musical experience is concerned. The fifteenth-century 'All mein Gedanken', a tune composed by Reichardt for Nicolai's *Almanach*[2] or one of Zuccalmaglio's synthetic productions (which may be a pastiche or even be cobbled together out of motifs from several folk melodies) — all are, in Brahms's arrangements, equally satisfying pieces of Hausmusik.

Many composers other than Brahms took up folk poems with their traditional tunes and provided accompaniments. O.H. Lange, in the Preface to his *Altdeutsche Lieder für eine Singstimme mit Pianoforte-Begleitung* (dating from the late 1870s) justifies the practice thus: old tunes, where given in the various anthologies of folksong, are almost invariably unaccompanied. But the modern ear needs some sort of harmonic support for the melody ('das moderne Ohr [kann] die ausfüllende Harmonie nicht gut entbehren'). Lange's accompaniments are technically much simpler than those of Brahms, although he sometimes commits errors of taste of which Brahms would never have been guilty, as in 'All mein Gedanken':

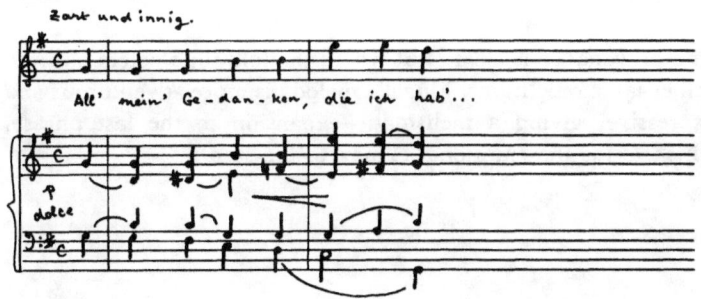

The Importance of Folksong

The piano figuration in Brahms may be more complex, but his basic harmonies are much more in keeping with the spirit of this noble old tune.

Lange's other technical shortcoming is his uncertainty concerning the treatment of long-held notes in some of the melodies he chooses to set. (These had come about because the earliest printed sources for many of these tunes were fifteenth- and sixteenth-century polyphonic versions, either 'a capella' or involving a solo voice with instruments.) The problem of accommodating these sustained notes — usually occurring at the end of a phrase — to a modern idiom of writing for voice and piano was a difficult one. However, most composers[3] managed to solve it better than Lange — or resolved the problem by changing the note-values.

The majority of folk tunes popular in the nineteenth and twentieth centuries are, of course, a good deal more recent than those taken up by Lange and Stade. They date in many cases from the eighteenth and nineteenth centuries, and represent a simplified version of the generally accepted musical idiom of the day. Some of the most interesting new versions are neither literal adaptions of the folk melody, as in Lange and Stade, nor original tunes; they are conscious or unconscious metamorphoses of the folk melody associated with that particular text. Here is the tune to which 'So viel Stern' am Himmel stehn' was sung from at least 1818 onwards:

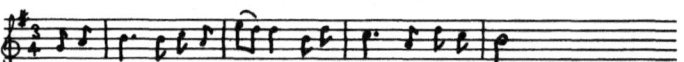

— and here is Gustav Flügel's variant:[4]

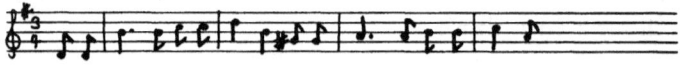

The provenance is clear. But where the folk tune peters out into rather lame repetitions, Flügel's melody is more adventurous and expressive, giving a melismatic expansion to the last phrase, which forms the emotional climax to the stanza:

The Importance of Folksong

A similar metamorphosis can be observed in settings of 'Mein Schatz ist auf die Wanderschaft hin', sometimes encountered as 'Ich weiß ja warum ich so traurig bin,/Mein Schatz ist gezogen nach England hin' — a reference to the enforced participation of German soldiers in England's campaign against the American colonists. A tune recorded by Zuccalmaglio is here compared to settings by Franz and Lammers:[5]

It may be added that while Franz contents himself — as often in his settings of folksong texts — with a fairly straightforward chordal accompaniment with no solo passages for the piano, Lammers has a plaintive little solo prelude which also serves as interlude between verses. Played with the required delicacy, it suggests a wisp of melody from a shepherd's pipe carried to the ear by the breeze and is exactly in keeping with the mournful text. I give it in the original key:

Such examples, adhering closely to the general style and structure of German folk melody, show quite clearly how 'Volksmusik' can be turned into 'Hausmusik' without in any way creating a sentimental or artificial effect.

Folksong texts to new melodies: the quest for the Volkston

Many composers elected to devise their own melodies, but consciously aimed at a Volkston. (It should be mentioned that *Lieder im Volkston* was a phrase still very common on title-pages throughout the nineteenth century.) One of the finest examples is Mendelssohn's setting of 'Es ist ein Schnitter, der heißt Tod', a song of the Grim Reaper, from whose sickle no flower can escape. Here is how Mendelssohn's version opens:

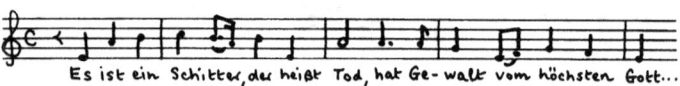

— and here is the traditional melody which goes back at least to a broadsheet of 1638:

Mendelssohn's austere, foursquare tune suits the text at least as well as the older melody; indeed, it paradoxically sounds the more 'old German' of the two.

As we have heard, Brahms stated in a letter that folksong was his stylistic ideal and that it was, moreover, the model which German song in general should emulate. So it is not surprising that, in addition to his arrangements of traditional tunes, he set many folk poems to his own melodies. Again, the result can seem

The Importance of Folksong

more 'folkish' than many an actual folksong:

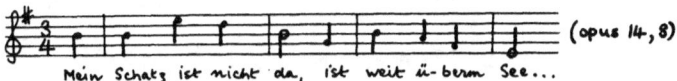

One could certainly apply Schulz's phrase, 'der Schein des Bekannten', to that example! But Brahms was never afraid to strike out beyond the limits of folk melody: by introducing long cantabile phrases, by means of modulations and harmonies which would be plainly impossible in unaccompanied or primitive 'a capella' folk music or by expressive subtleties in the accompaniment (see opus 7, 4–5 and opus 14, 2, 6 and 7).

No account, however brief, could omit Weber and Franz. Weber's most characteristic contribution seems to be in that territory where folksong and folk dance merge, in songs like 'I und mein junges Weib' or 'Mein Schatzerl is hübsch', where rustic dancing and merrymaking are clearly evoked in the music. Such examples are a salutory reminder that 'im Volkston' does not necessarily mean slow and sad. Franz, on the other hand, seems most successful in his settings of the more elegaic type of folk text (for instance, 'Könn'st du meine Äuglein seh'n', opus 23,6).

As we have noted in the case of Brahms, a composer, having once established the Volkston, will feel free to introduce whatever harmonic and rhythmic subtleties he wishes. Here is part of Ernst Streben's setting (opus 15,6, dating from 1854) of a folksong which appears to have had wide circulation in the Rhineland and which Heine had made famous by incorporating it in a trilogy of poems about ill-fated love:

The nearest equivalent I have been able to discover is a Rhenish melody recorded by Ludwig Erk:

The Importance of Folksong

It will be noted that Streben's setting is enriched both by rhythmical diversity and by little harmonic touches. The triplets bring out the rather languorous flow of the verse better than a straightforward 'dactylic' rhythm (♪ ♪ ♪) can do, while the dominant thirteenth on 'Reif' gives exactly the right doleful tone.

Some of the songs that contrive to evoke and transcend folk music at one and the same time are among the most beautiful of the simpler sort of Lied produced in the mid-nineteenth century. Attempts to reset folk poems in the Volkston are, of course, nearly always strophic, although the harmonisation may vary from stanza to stanza and, as in Brahms, differences in dramatic or emotional intensity can be brought out by setting the same melody against a changing piano texture. Less frequently, moving effects are achieved by small *melodic* variations from stanza to stanza, as in Lammers's setting of 'Mein Schatz, der ist auf die Wanderschaft hin'. 'Perhaps he is dead and lies at rest', sings the girl in the first stanza:

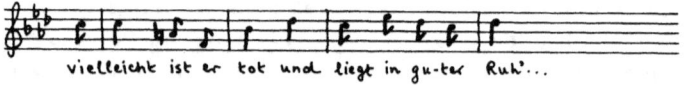

In the next stanza she accuses her parents of having married her off to a man whom she cannot love. The triplet figure on 'nimmermehr' here has the effect of a despairing cry from the heart:

Where, say, Franz is equally successful whether composing songs to folk poems or to texts by famous poets, some composers seem to do best when confronted with the former type; the comparative artlessness of the text restrains them. Thus Gustav Flügel's 'So viel Stern' am Himmel stehn', which has already been referred to, has a lyrical directness in marked contrast to some of the other songs in that same opus, which suffer from fussy modulations and ill-motivated changes of tempo and texture.

The Importance of Folksong

New melodies divorced from the Volkston

Many composers were drawn to folk poems and set them to new melodies without, apparently, any attempt at the Volkston. That is, they seem to have regarded the texts simply *as texts*, divorced from their association with folk culture, if such a thing was psychologically possible for a German in the nineteenth century. At least, that is the impression gained when one encounters Gustav Hasse's 'Der Wald hat sich entlaubet' (opus 23,1, 1876), with its romantic, shifting harmonies, or Carl Machts's 'Wenn du zu mein' Schätzerl kommst' (opus 29,4, 1874), with its exacting vocal line, added-note chords and general air of determined and self-conscious cheerfulness. Franz Bennat's *Altdeutsche Minnelieder* (1872) are a good deal more pleasing, although there is nothing in the least 'old German' or folkish about the music. Even where Bennat heads a song 'im Volkston', he cannot mean that it is intended to have Schulz's 'appearance of familiarity', only that it is to be *performed* simply and directly. But the songs themselves are nearer to *Winterreise* than to anything in the German folksong tradition. In the folksong settings of Reger and Richard Strauss we have moved yet further from the Volkston: these are well on the way to being virtuoso pieces, with complex vocal lines, 'advanced' chromatic harmonies and accompaniments which demand great skill and agility (see, for instance, Reger, opus 70, 6 and 10; 75, 12; 76, 11 and Strauss, opus 32,5; 36,3 and 49,6).

Settings of folk poetry which are beyond the abilities of reasonably competent amateurs seem incongruous — although it may be that this is a conditioned judgement brought about by very persistent propaganda to the effect that a folksong text newly set should retain some vestige of its origins and should belong to the realm of Hausmusik. The balance between imaginative and technical freedom on the one hand and faithfulness to the spirit of folk music on the other seems to have been struck with complete success by Mahler, whose settings of texts from *Des Knaben Wunderhorn* were composed in the last two decades of the century. Mahler always manages to evoke the atmosphere of German folk music without either resorting to pastiche or shackling his invention. His harmonic freedom and the atmospheric power of his accompaniments certainly contribute to the effect of the *Wunderhorn* songs, but it is the ingenuity of his vocal writing which is paramount, ranging from the varied refrains of 'Nicht Wiedersehen!' to the virtuoso ending of 'Wer hat dies Liedlein erdacht?'

and the adventurous leaps of 'Rheinlegendchen'. There can be few cases where the essential simplicity of the folk idiom coexists so happily with the technical variety and resourcefulness of late Romantic music.

The folksong vogue and its effect on poetry

Throughout the nineteenth century scores of affectionate imitations of folk poetry were produced. The poets often signalled their intention at the outset by adopting or varying an opening formula taken from the folk tradition:

Hoffmann von Fallersleben	*Folk tradition*
Es wollt ein Mädchen zur Kirche gehn . . .	Es wollt ein Mägdlein früh aufstehn . . .
Es steht ein Baum in jenem Tal . . .	Es steht ein Baum im Odenwald . . . Es steht ein Lind in jenem Tal . . .

Emanuel Geibel	*Folk tradition*
Der Mai ist gekommen . . .	Wohl kommt der Mai . . .
Wenn sich zwei Herzen scheiden . . .	Ach Gott! wie weh tut scheiden . . .

It should be stressed that such 'counterfeits' are neither parodies nor sentimental shams; they are the poets' tributes to the evocative power of folk poetry — and were recognised as such by composers such as G.F. Benkert, August Bungert, Constantin Decker, Mendelssohn, Riehl and Wilhelm Taubert. Feuchtersleben's 'Es ist bestimmt in Gottes Rat', as set by Mendelssohn in 1839, has virtually become an honorary folksong by virtue of its inclusion in song-book after song-book throughout the century.

More significantly, folk poetry captivated some of Germany's greatest poets and influenced their style of writing. Indeed, from the time of Herder's championship of 'die Lieder alter Völker' in the 1770s until at least the middle of the nineteenth century, there were few poets of note who escaped this influence. It may lead them to open variations on recognisable models, or it may take

The Importance of Folksong

less direct and hence less easily definable forms. But anyone with the slightest knowledge of the corpus of German folk poetry will find hosts of mostly short, structurally simple poems which are visibly related to the folk tradition through form, subject-matter, style, imagery, characteristic motifs and sometimes even syntax. I will take some of the poets and poetic movements in turn in order to illustrate this briefly.

Goethe

Here there is a clear progression from close imitation to cases where the influence can be more easily felt than defined. The following list is arranged not chronologically but according to the directness of the folksong influence:

'Heidenröslein': Goethe's variation on an existing song.
'Erlkönig': free and imaginative variant on a Danish folk ballad, known to Goethe in Herder's translation.
'Der König in Thule': an original work in close and loving imitation of the folk ballad.
'Der Fischer': draws on the world of the folk imagination where nature-spirits make contact with mortals in order to tempt and destroy them. Shows how the refrains and refrain-like repetitions of folk poetry can take on seductive tones in the hands of a master.
'Jägers Abendlied': here it is the simple structure and the identification of the hunter-figure with the lover that form the link. As in 'Der Fischer', Goethe's eloquent diction and restrained rhetorical skill show how far he transcends folk poetry even as he reveals his indebtedness to it.
'Gefunden': in its theme, a reversal of 'Heidenröslein'. The directness and concreteness in the style and the lack of moralising and abstract reflection form clear links with the folk tradition.

It is perhaps this virtue of concreteness, this tendency to let things speak for themselves without the intervention of the poet as commentator that chiefly characterises such poems. This seems to be the main lesson that Goethe learnt from folk poetry; its great merit, he says in the *Maximen und Reflexionen*, is that it takes its motifs directly from nature.[6] From Herder he had absorbed the

The Importance of Folksong

idea that true poetry is never the property of a literary clique, but the possession and heritage of the whole people. So well had he acted on this that Herder was able to include 'Der Fischer' in his anthology of folksongs, showing that the concept 'Volkslied' was now wide enough to include both folksong proper and recently composed poems which, it was felt, shared important characteristics with folksong and might come to rival it in broadness of appeal. The esteem enjoyed by 'Heidenröslein', 'Der König in Thule' and 'Der Fischer' proves this to be true, while the fact that generations of composers were drawn to these and similar poems show that they are true Lieder, that — like the folk poems and folk ballads that inspired them — they need to be complemented by melody.

The Romantics

The veneration of folk poetry was, if possible, even stronger among Germany's Romantic poets, enhanced as it was by a quasi-mystical notion of 'das Volk', by a rather dewy-eyed love of an ill-defined 'old Germany' which seemed to be epitomised in traditional folksongs and folk tales — and by nationalistic considerations which form a marked contrast to Herder's cosmopolitanism. Where his collection draws on many different folk cultures, the most famous anthology of the Romantic era, *Des Knaben Wunderhorn* by Arnim and Brentano, is essentially a German compilation. Uhland, when describing how the simplicity of folksong inspired his own work, talks of the 'truly German' poetic tradition ('unsre ältere Poesie . . . die wahrhaft deutsche' — letter of 13 March 1812). Uhland himself, Eichendorff, Brentano, Wilhelm Müller and others wrote many short lyrical poems and ballads in simple four-line stanzas, with a regular three or four beats to the line and (usually) an ABAB rhyme pattern. Millers, hunters, lovesick maidens, itinerant musicians and apprentices sing of the joys and sorrows of love and of wandering through nature with its beauties and its occasional menace. As in 'Erlkönig' and 'Der Fischer', nature spirits woo humans to destruction. The favourite motifs and images of folk poetry, drawn from nature or common daily experience are everywhere to be encountered, as are opening formulae which explicitly avow the poet's indebtedness to the folk tradition ('Da steht eine Burg überm Tale', 'Es ging Maria in den Morgen hinein', etc.). One poem of Eichendorff's, 'Das zerbrochene Ringlein', was set to music by Friedrich Glück in 1814 and became so popular that it has probably been sung by countless Germans who did not realise that it was not a 'genuine' and traditional folk poem. Its heritage becomes clear if we compare its opening with a fragment of folk poetry popular since the sixteenth century:

Eichendorff	*Folksong*
In einem kühlen Grunde	Dort hoch auf jenem Berge
Da geht ein Mühlenrad,	Da geht ein Mühlerad,
Meine Liebste ist verschwunden,	Das mahlet nichts denn Liebe
Die dort gewohnet hat.	Die Nacht bis an den Tag.

The traditional symbolic equation that sees love prospering as long as the mill-wheel turns is only implicit in Eichendorff; he assumes that the right associations will have been set up in the minds of his readers/listeners. Where the folksong develops the mill-wheel analogy to signal the end of love (Die Mühle ist zerbrochen,/Die Liebe hat ein End'), the Romantic poet picks up another traditional symbol, that of the broken ring: 'Sie hat die Treu gebrochen,/Mein Ringlein sprang entzwei'. It is at this point that Eichendorff departs from tradition. The folk poem ends with a conventional formula of parting ('So gsegn dich Gott, mein feines Lieb!/Jetz fahr ich ins Ellend'). But Eichendorff's forsaken lover loses himself in a series of daydreams: he would like to wander the world as a minstrel, turn soldier or, best of all, find peace in death. 'Das zerbrochene Ringlein' shows, as well as any single work could, how the Romantics were inspired by folk poetry but went beyond it, using it as a springboard for their own dreams and longings.

Heine

Heine's case was rather different from that of the Romantics. While the formative influence of folksong on his poetry was equally strong (see his letter to Wilhelm Müller of 7 June 1826), his complex disposition, in which romantic longings were at odds with disillusioned realism, meant that, for all his veneration of folk poetry, he was unable to surrender himself to its emotional world to the extent that the Romantics did. Indeed, his relationship to the Volkslied was as ambivalent as his feelings towards the Romantic movement or, indeed, towards Germany itself. When we hear echoes of folksongs in Heine's verse, we simultaneously detect a note of reserve — or of something more. The simple emotive themes of folk poetry are transformed, so that they sound complex and elusive: the love poetry takes on cynical overtones, the lover is exposed to malicious ridicule, the almost unbearable pain of separation is turned into open burlesque, incongruous words or images are introduced into 'innocent' contexts to set up calculated dissonances.[7]

It is instructive to examine one of Heine's most popular short narrative poems, 'Es war ein alter König', for its links with folk poetry. It tells a simple and stark tale of an old king with a young wife. She falls in love with a handsome young page, but this passion leads to their deaths. Heine deliberately makes it sound as if he were retelling an age-old story: he opens with a 'once-upon-a-time' formula and refers in the last stanza to 'das alte Liedchen'. The narrative is direct and swift, with gaps which the reader's or listener's imagination must fill. The style of story-telling depends on concrete details and simple antitheses. Thus far, Heine's poem evokes the world of the Volkslied. But the laconic ending, with its almost casual assumption that intense love automatically leads to destruction, produces a flavour wholly typical of the poet: 'Sie mußten beide sterben,/sie hatten sich viel zu lieb'.

More important even than such more or less direct evocations of folk poetry is the general effect on Heine's verse. It is incontrovertible that his constant use of the 'folksong stanza' and his liking for terse formulations depending on concrete motifs and images is a vital element of his poetry, especially in the *Buch der Lieder*, and a major factor which has assured his popularity among generations of song-composers. But the combination of apparent simplicity and artlessness in the external features of the verse and a complex, ambiguous and ironical tone also presented the composers with problems, since the sentiment is obviously easier to convey in music than the irony (see below, pp. 177f).

Mörike

Mörike was an extraordinarily versatile poet, so that the pieces in folksong style form only a tiny minority of his poems. However, their attraction for composers gives them an importance out of all

The Importance of Folksong

proportion to their numbers. Here I will deal briefly with two famous examples, both of which were set to music many scores of times, 'Das verlassene Mägdlein' ('Früh, wann die Hähne krähn') and 'Ein Stündlein wohl vor Tag' ('Derweil ich schlafend lag'). 'Das verlassene Mägdlein' is cast in the first person; the 'forsaken girl' of the title describes how she must rise at cock-crow to light the fire. As the flames leap upwards, she recalls that she dreamt of her faithless lover. Weeping, she longs for night to come again. The opening formula, as so often in these 'modern folksongs', is taken from the folk tradition, although the theme of the folksong is carefree and the tone lighter.[8] Like the other poets just discussed, Mörike evokes the world of folksong through the everyday setting, the strong visual and concrete elements and simple antitheses. The matter-of-fact bleakness of the opening, more expressive than any abstract description of the girl's mood could be, is particularly reminiscent of folk poetry. In Mörike, the girl has to get up *while the stars are still visible*; in a folk poem which goes back at least to the sixteenth century, the lover's way is barred and he is condemned to loneliness *because the snow has come too early*:

Mörike	*Folksong*
Früh, wann die Hähne krähn,	Es ist ein Schnee gefallen,
Eh die Sternlein verschwinden,	Wann es ist noch nit Zeit,
Muß ich am Herde stehn,	Ich wollt zu meinem Buhlen gan,
Muß Feuer zünden.	Der Weg ist mir verschneit.[9]

'Ein Stündlein wohl vor Tag', which again tells of a girl abandoned by a faithless lover, is a variant on a motif from the folk tradition. In the folksongs a bird may act as messenger between two lovers, or one of the pair may even be transformed into a bird. In Mörike the bird-messenger sings before the girl's window in order to *accuse* the lover ('Dein Schätzlein ich verklag'). The rapid alternation of narrative and dialogue is also characteristic of folk poetry as is, of course, the use of a refrain (here the cheerless 'ein Stündlein wohl vor Tag'). The diction is brought near to that of folk poems through its directness and simplicity, its touches of dialect ('singen tu'' for 'singe') and its ellipses ('nichts hören mag' instead of 'Ich mag nichts mehr hören'). But Mörike's five-line stanzas, with their metrical irregularity and sophisticated rhyme-scheme, are a far cry from the typical folksong quatrain, while certainly no folk poem could rise to the marvellously expressive device[10] which opens the third and final stanza: 'O weh! nicht weiter sag!/O still! nichts hören mag!' Other subtleties will be perceived by any attentive reader; suffice it to say that Mörike's poem is derived from a folksong tradition but transcends folksong almost infinitely by its artistry; we would have to go back to Goethe to find comparable instances.[11]

After Mörike, the influence of folksong on major German poets is less marked, although there is a superb pastiche, 'Meine Mutter hat's gewollt', by Theodor Storm. Since this occurs in his novella *Immensee*, following a conversation about folk poetry,[12] many readers will probably have been deceived. Both the theme (the girl's accusation that her mother has wished an unwelcome suitor on her) and the style are strongly reminiscent of the folk tradition. This poem too has been set to music very many times, the songs often being labelled 'im Volkston' by the composers.

The lyrics by Goethe, Heine, Mörike and the rest which we have been discussing, however similar they may be to folksongs in structure and various surface characteristics, are obviously many degrees subtler than any folksong and hence capable of provoking different responses from different readers. This combination of structural simplicity and inner subtlety endears them to composers, for the first of these features ensures that such texts lend themselves readily to musical treatment, while the second means that no one version can ever exhaust the meaning of the text or realise all its nuances, that — however often a particular poem may have been set to music before — new possibilities will always reveal themselves to a composer who is truly responsive to the verse. There is, of course, nothing to compel the composer to mirror the folksong element in the poem by setting it in the Volkston. But 'Heidenröslein', 'Der König in Thule' or Heine's 'Lorelei' certainly invite simple and direct musical treatment which, in turn, brings out important features of the text, features which may well be obscured in more elaborate through-composed settings (see Chapter 13).

It will have been seen that genuine folk poetry, 'pseudo-folksongs' and lyrics produced by great poets under the influence of folk poetry, have all been sought out and set to music by scores of composers and seem to have enjoyed great popularity in the drawing rooms of nineteenth-century Germany. 'Genuineness' does not seem to have been an overriding factor, any more than it was for Brahms when he came to select tunes to arrange: if the text seemed to express some universal emotion or experience, if it had at least something of the form and tone of the folk poetry that formed part of the cultural inheritance of nineteenth-century Germans, if it was set simply and melodiously with some echo or suggestion of folk melody — it would have its appeal among amateur lovers of song.

Notes

1. See Siegmund Helms, 'Die Melodiebildung in den Liedern von Johannes Brahms . . .,' Diss. (Berlin), 1968; Max Kalbeck, *Johannes Brahms*, i, Vienna, 1904, p. 192; W. Morik, 'Johannes Brahms und sein Verhältnis zum deutschen Volkslied', Diss. (Göttingen), 1953, especially pp. 103ff.

2. See Bibliography, section 6. A collection of folksongs with tunes, some old, some newly provided by Reichardt and by Nicolai himself. Intended as a parody and an attack on the cult of folksong in the 1770s, the collection indirectly came to provide Brahms with material. In particular, the tunes supplied by Reichardt are far from parody; he was too sensitive and too much in harmony with German folk melodies to descend to that. For Zuccalmaglio, see below, note 5.

3. E.g. W. Stade, 1855.

4. The poem exists in a number of variants. Flügel's version is that given in *Des Knaben Wunderhorn*, of which a brief account is given on p. 166. The folk melody seems first to have been published in *Deutsche Lieder für Jung und Alt*, Berlin, 1818, p. 19 and was reprinted in many anthologies of folksong. Flügel's version is no. 4 of his opus 3, 1842. I have transcribed it down a semitone to make comparison easier.

5. See Kretschmer/Zuccalmaglio, i, no. 198; Franz, opus 23,4; J. Lammers, opus 8,4. Zuccalmaglio has been much criticised for altering melodies, inventing sources and otherwise troubling the waters of folksong research. But the above melody seems genuine enough. Keys and, in the case of Franz, note-values have been changed for easier comparison.

6. *Werke*, Wegner, Hamburg, 1953, xii, p. 498.

7. See 'Wenn zwei voneinander scheiden'; 'Da droben auf jenem Berge'; 'Ich steh auf des Berges Spitze'. See too the account of 'Gekommen ist der Maie', p. 186.

8. See J.W. Smeed, 'The texts of "volkstümliche Lieder" . . .', *MLR*, lxxxi, 1986, p. 129.

9. Or one could cite a folksong about an unwilling novice in a nunnery, who complains about the austere fare and the early rising.

10. This is obviously linked to the rhetorical figure known as isocolon, but does not qualify from a strictly technical point of view.

11. For more details on Mörike and folk poetry, see Jessie H. Kneisel,

Mörike and Musik, n.p. (New York?), 1949, pp. 130ff.
    12. *Immensee* was published in 1851. See the chapter headed 'Meine Mutter hat's gewollt'.

13
A General Assessment

By now I hope that a pattern will have become discernible, in which a handful of famous composers — innovators in widely differing ways — made the pace and urged song into ever more complex and difficult forms. But at the same time, a host of minor composers wrote their songs in more traditional and technically simpler styles. Influential music critics, working mainly in and through the periodicals of the day, strove to check the development towards complexity, helped by those who made propaganda in the cause of Hausmusik. Active and admiring pursuit of the Volkston, both on the part of poets and composers, was a major — perhaps the main — factor in the persistence of the drawing room song as a cultural activity easily accessible to amateurs. In the following pages I will try to give some idea of how the song-composers, both famous and obscure, set their most famous poets. It is not easy to do this without slipping into an anthology of snippets, but I have tried to choose representative examples of the various trends.

The impact of folk poetry on Goethe, the Romantics, Heine and Mörike has been discussed. But the influence goes much further than the specific examples cited. The simple structure and direct, concrete diction of German folk poetry coloured the attitude of most German poets towards their art. If German poetry from about the 1770s to 1900 contains a much greater number of simply constructed, obviously 'singable' lyrics than we find in either England or France in the same period, this is in large part due to the vogue of folk poetry and 'das Volkstümliche'. Before we examine further the question of how composers responded to this invitation, it is necessary to know a little more about which poets and which texts were favoured and why.

A General Assessment

A number of poets who had been very popular with the late eighteenth-century composers lost much of this popularity after 1800: Klopstock, Claudius, Voß, Hölty and others. Hölty, particularly, came to seem dated both as to sentiment and style. This is clear from a review of J.F. Kittl's opus 23, in which the anonymous writer affects mild but gratified surprise that the composer has chosen a text by Hölty, since it contains 'patriarchal' archaisms, together with phrases and images which would probably provoke a smile in fashionable salons.[1] Kittl had, in fact, already set a text by Hölty with great fastidiousness and eloquence as his opus 16,2. But not all nineteenth-century settings of Hölty reveal so sure a touch. Often the result seems too lush and emotive, as if a certain innocence had been lost. This applies, I feel, even to such beautiful songs as Brahms's 'Mainacht' and 'Minnelied' (opus 43,2 and 71,5). Schubert's simpler treatments (D194 and D429), still very obviously linked to the strophic Affektlied of the previous century, seem more appropriate. So, for that matter, does Kittl's opus 16,2.[2]

But at least Hölty was still set from time to time. By contrast, Hölderlin was hardly set at all in the nineteenth century, partly because his work was little known, but also because of his difficult imagery and the metrical complexities of his verse. By a perverse historical chance, these demanding poems had to wait until the twentieth century to find composers, by which time music had ventured into regions of such esoteric complexity that most of the resultant settings made the texts virtually impossible to comprehend when sung.[3]

Needless to say, Goethe's lyrical poems and shorter ballads remained popular with the composers, as did a number of Schiller's poems ('Das Mädchen aus der Fremde', 'Des Mädchens Klage', 'An die Freude', etc.). The Romantics, cultivating as they did the forms and style of their native folk poetry, were much set, together with Heine and Mörike. Other important sources for the song-composers include the shorter and simpler poems by Storm, Keller, Lenau, Meyer, Platen and Rückert. In addition, of course, one encounters a host of texts by obscurer authors, some of them no more than sentimental versifiers.[4] There were a few composers who were their own poets and poets who dabbled in composition: Cornelius provided many of his own texts, Annette von Droste-Hülshoff and Nietzsche tried their hands at composing songs and Mahler wrote the poems as well as the music to the *Lieder eines fahrenden Gesellen*. But Annette and Nietzsche would

A General Assessment

have been better advised to leave composing to the professionals, while Mahler's poems are like pale copies of Wilhelm Müller. Cornelius was a little more successful in combining the two activities, but not until this century, with Ernst Krenek's *Reisebuch aus den österreichischen Alpen* of 1929, do we find anything like a genuine matching of musical and poetic talent in one person's work. Nineteenth-century German song has no Thomas Campion, no composer-poet equally skilled in both fields.

What determines the composer's choice? There are cases where he shows the most sensitive awareness not only of what has songlike potential, but also of what is good poetry. Wolf set very little that is not of high standard as verse; even the most lighthearted trifles in the *Italienisches Liederbuch* are able, witty and elegant *jeux d'esprit*. Schumann too picks a high proportion of good poems (together with some that are merely arch or sentimental, it must be admitted). Less famous composers who were usually meticulous in their choice of texts include Franz, Fröhlich, A. von Goldschmidt, Krazeisen and Riehl. At the other extreme is Reger, who openly preferred second-rate poems as raw material for song. Goethe has been done to death ('auskomponiert'), says Reger; moreover, a Goethe poem says so much in itself that there is little left for the composer to add.[5] And it is notorious that, apart from folk poems, Brahms set comparatively little of merit. The most that can be said of the chosen texts from Daumer, Halm, Klaus Groth and the rest is that they usually express a strongly defined mood which lends itself well to musical treatment. It is not difficult to find minor composers who seldom went beyond the trivial in their choice of texts — whether from poor aesthetic judgement or whether they too felt that Goethe, Heine, etc. were 'auskomponiert' is impossible to say. A list of such composers would include C.F. Hille and Alex Ritter. Rudolf Louis, in *Die deutsche Musik der Gegenwart* of 1909 (see note 5), sees two main lines of development in German song from Schubert on. One, which leads naturally to Brahms, regards the text as raw material for the music which is of paramount importance for the composer. The other line, leading via Schumann to Wolf, pays the most fastidious regard to everything which is in and behind the words of the poem and employs all possible means to express the poet's nuances (p. 212). Louis concedes that this is a generalisation, but there is obviously some substance in it. A division of song-composers according to this criterion is arguably as important as any distinction in purely musical terms between 'traditionalists' and 'innovators', although there must clearly be some overlapping. Brahms, who belongs to Louis's first category, is relatively traditional in style; Wolf, the prime representative of the second line of development, *had* to experiment with the technical language of song if he was to bring out all that he sensed in his chosen texts.

The great majority of composers seem to have had no dogmatic views and to have been guided by no fixed aesthetic criteria. If a poem was fairly simple and 'singable' and if it contained something that set the composer's imagination working, that was sufficient. The 'something' could be a mood or emotion; it could be a story so told as to invite — or positively demand — musical treatment; it could be a concrete object or natural event mentioned in the text in such a way that a musical motif suggested itself to the composer.

The reasons for the popularity of Goethe's most-set poems ('Heidenröslein', 'Der Fischer', 'Der König in Thule', the *Wilheim Meister* songs, the two *Wandrers Nachtlieder* and so on) are so obvious as to need no expounding. The circumstances surrounding Heine and Mörike as providers of song-texts are more complex.

For Heine, says J.L. Sammons,[6] poetry was 'lyrical melody in relatively simple forms'. This definition undoubtedly holds the key to Heine's immense popularity among the composers. The title which Heine himself gave to his first book of verse, *Buch der Lieder*, signals that these (or most of them) are poems to be sung as well as read or recited. The references in the *Buch der Lieder* to the poet's sentiments winging their way to the beloved *as songs* are thus not mere poetic conceits. The simplicity of form referred to by Sammons is very much that of most German folk poetry — a four-line stanza, usually of three or four beats and with a regular rhyme-pattern. Although Heine's poems are full of tiny metrical subtleties and variations, these are not such as would present difficulties to nineteenth-century composers with their sophisticated notions of how to accommodate poetic metre to musical rhythm.

But within this formal simplicity — and sometimes partially masked by it — Heine commands great variety of tone and mood; many of his most characteristic poems veer between sentiment and irony, set up a romantic mood only to explode it in the last couplet or play in various other ways on the strange conflicts that beset the poet. Understandably enough, it was the lyrics that express one dominant emotion (whether of love, grief or loneliness) in comparatively unified and unalloyed form which attracted song-composers most: 'Ich will meine Seele tauchen', 'Im wunderschönen Monat Mai', 'Leise zieht durch mein Gemüt' and so on.[7] Texts which establish a mood — usually of longing for the assurance of reciprocated love — but go on to introduce a note of doubt and insecurity at the end are also well suited: 'Du bist wie eine Blume', with its note of melancholy as the poet is confronted by beauty and innocence, as if to suggest that these qualities are too fragile to last, or 'Wenn ich in deine Augen seh', with its extraordinary reversal of mood in the last couplet:

Wenn ich in deine Augen seh,
so schwindet all mein Leid und Weh;
doch wenn ich küsse deinen Mund,
so werd ich ganz und gar gesund.

Wenn ich mich lehn an deine Brust,
kommts über mich wie Himmelslust;
doch wenn du sprichst: Ich liebe dich!
so muß ich weinen bitterlich.

(When I look into your eyes, all my sufferings and pain vanish; when I kiss your lips, I am completely restored to health. When I lean against your breast, heavenly bliss comes over me; but when you say, 'I love you!', I must weep bitterly.)

But Heine's irony has tested composers severely. In poems where the sentiment is only lightly tinged with irony, we may sometimes suspect that the composer responded to the emotional power of the text, while failing to notice the irony at all. Mendelssohn's setting of 'Auf Flügeln des Gesanges' is seductive and mellifluous throughout, well conveying the poet's longing for the exotic kingdom into which he hopes to transport his beloved by means of song. But was not Heine simultaneously mocking his own romanticism? There is something ambivalent about this realm: the violets *titter* ('kichern') and the gazelles ('fromm und klug') seem to combine innocence with that knowingness which is the loss of innocence. Wilhelm Berger (opus 16,3) seems as unaware as Mendelssohn of any ambivalence in the poem.

Music has no language in which to convey irony, says a reviewer in the *NZfM*.[8] Few people today would go that far, but equally few would deny that irony is the most difficult mood to convey in music. More than one contemporary reviewer remarked on Heine's typical combination of profound feeling, sharpness and irony, adding that this made the composer's task exceptionally difficult.[9] Other critics were more hostile, describing his verse as unhealthy, tasteless, even sly ('schielig'). A favourite word is the untranslatable 'zerrissen', meaning torn by opposite and irreconcilable impulses. A reviewer of Otto Tiehsen's opus 7 advises the composer, with his naturally healthy disposition, to steer clear of Heine's 'sickly' texts.[10] This is not far distant from the attitude taken by many nineteenth-century literary critics who distanced themselves from Heine's *Zerrissenheit* and compared him unfavourably with the healthy and truly German Eichendorff. Ferdinand Gumbert, C.G. Reissiger and some other composers certainly made a stylistic distinction between their Heine and Eichendorff settings which suggests that they felt this difference.

The uncertainties and ambiguities in Heine's verse have constantly given rise to disagreements among his readers. As a consequence, there is no other poet where judgements of the merits and demerits of musical settings are so much bound up with the listener's reading of, and reaction to, the poetic text. Perhaps, even, our age — encouraged by its literary critics — is obsessed with irony and sees it where Heine intended none, and certainly where his early composers saw none. Let us, however, take a few examples where the irony is manifest and see how composers responded to it. In 'Ein Jüngling liebt ein Mädchen', Heine tells the story of a rejected girl who, on the rebound, marries a young man whom she does not love and who is made miserable. The irony resides in the laconic detachment with which the poet tells the story and his curt reminder in the last stanza that this old tale is constantly renewing itself, breaking a heart each time. His formulation ('Es ist eine alte Geschichte,/doch bleibt sie immer neu') is not far from Mephistopheles' mordant comment to Faust that Gretchen is not the first to find ruin in love ('Sie ist die erste nicht'). As C.S. Brauner points out,[11] Schumann's answer is to provide Heine's verses with a jaunty melody and a swashbuckling accompaniment, thus underlining the ironic element within the poem (disasters related in such a way that we hardly know whether to side with the unhappy protagonists or the worldly-wise commentator).

Johann Vesque von Püttlingen, that eccentric nobleman who published his songs under the pseudonym of 'J. Hoven', was described by one contemporary reviewer as the 'successful composer of texts which cannot be set to music' ('glücklicher

Componist uncomponirbarer Lieder').[12] He certainly ventured where no other composer before him had dared to go, his chief weapon being a broadly comic but effective use of musical pastiche by which he brings out the incongruities in the texts. 'Die Jahre kommen und gehen' is a strange poem, even for Heine. He sets the permanence of his love against a long perspective of years and generations:

> Die Jahre kommen und gehen,
> Geschlechter steigen ins Grab,
> Doch nimmer vergeht die Liebe,
> Die ich im Herzen hab.

Once more he would like to see the object of his love in order to make his dying protestation:

> Nur einmal noch möcht ich dich sehen
> Und sinken vor dir aufs Knie
> Und sterbend zu dir sprechen:
> Madam, ich liebe Sie!

The formal address and the return to 'Sie' after the intimate 'du' produce a grotesquely incongruous effect which Püttlingen matches with a mock-operatic cadence:

The humour in 'Der deutsche Professor' is broader. After complaining of the 'fragmentary' nature of life, the poet resolves to visit a professor who will patch together a philosophical doctrine to 'plug the holes in the world-system'. After an opening in 'quasi-recitativo' style which effectively expresses the poet's uncertainty, the composer sets the latter part of the poem to a mock-fugue. The idea is brilliant, the execution unfortunately less so.

Another composer who was attracted by the satirical strain in Heine was Louis Ehlert. 'Philister in Sonntagsröcklein', which Ehlert set as no. 4 of his opus 14, describes how the 'philistines' dress up and sally forth into woods and fields, dutifully admiring the beauties of nature. There are many such descriptions in Heine, implying that the German bourgeoisie had been infected by the Romantic adulation of the countryside without, however, possessing the aesthetic sensibility to appreciate it. Love of nature had become a duty and an affectation. The incongruity between the natural scene and the philistinism of those who pay homage to it is conveyed in Heine's poem by the mention of the Sunday coats, by an impossibly frisky choice of words ('jauchzen und springen') and by the reference to the long ears with which, ass-like, the walkers take in the song of birds. Ehlert provides a further dimension, that of musical incongruity, by setting this part of the poem in the form of a rather pompous march:

What should ideally be a rapt saunter through the beauties of nature has turned into a relentless trudge. Heine's verses go on to show a contrast between the philistines and the poet, who sits at home behind drawn curtains brooding over his lost love. Ehlert sets these lines in mournfully romantic, rather Schumannesque tones. The contrast between the two halves of the poem is thus exactly matched in the music.

A wide spectrum of moods, then, from fairly straightforward expressions of sentiment, through poems only touched with irony to examples of broad humour or bitter satire. Even the genuinely eerie strain that we sometimes encounter in Heine attracted composers. Schubert's setting of 'Der Doppelgänger' is familiar to all lovers of song, but six other composers were to set that text by the end of the century. Nor was Schumann by any means the only composer to set that disquieting little poem, 'Lieb Liebchen, leg's Händchen aufs Herze mein'. Even Heine's bleak poem about the suicide's grave ('Am Kreuzweg wird begraben') and his account of a spectral love-affair ('Sie liebten sich beide') had found twenty and twenty-four composers respectively by 1900. The poems which composers passed by were on the whole those in free verse together with those that dealt with political and social themes.

Until Wolf, the most popular Mörike poems (as far as song was concerned) were the structurally simple ones which visibly derived from elements in folk poetry. These, as we have seen, were by their nature capable of drawing a wide variety of different responses from different composers. But it was Wolf who, more than anyone else, encouraged the notion that a much wider *range* of poems by Mörike might be successfully turned into song. He set many poems in free and irregular forms as well as a good deal of ironic and humorous verse, together with a number of the most dramatic and eerie ballads. Some of these had already been set to music, but in a very tame manner. Unlike, say, 'Das verlassene Mägdlein', 'Die Geister am Mummelsee' needed a Wolf to do it justice. One of the lesser-known *Mörike-Lieder*, 'Frage und Antwort' (no. 35), may serve to illustrate how the mysterious and emotionally ambivalent elements often present in Mörike benefit from the technical — especially the harmonic — resources at Wolf's command.

The poem starts by evoking the anguish and bitterness of love: 'do you ask me why I do not abjure love rather than suffer its pangs?' (This is the 'Frage' of the title.) In the middle stanza, the power of love is likened to natural forces. And so to the 'Antwort': one might as well try to control wind and water as achieve mastery over the feelings unleashed by love. Perceiving that the first part of the poem is dominated by the notion of the suffering and uncertainties of love and the second by its irresistible power, Wolf sets out to provide a clear and dramatic contrast, while still maintaining unity. The unity is provided by the shape of the vocal phrases, especially by the leaps of sixths and sevenths common to both parts of the song; the contrast is achieved mainly by harmonic means. In the first part of the song everything is shifting and uncertain. We start with an ambiguous succession of chords, the inner parts full of chromatic progressions. Only in the fourth bar can the ear orientate itself, as Wolf moves on to the dominant seventh of the home key of the song, A flat. Here is that little prelude, puzzling to the ear however logical a harmonic analysis may show it to be:

Even the opening chord is ambiguous, for the G in the tenor is oddly like a passing-note that came from nowhere. Then, no sooner do we appear to be in D flat (bar 3) than the inner parts, through their chromatic movements, shift into further uncertainties. The harmonic disorientation is reflected in the notation: in the implied enharmonic change in the last beat of the first bar (as the D flat in the bass 'becomes' a C sharp and the F flat in the treble an E natural) and in the fact that these four bars of music require twenty accidentals. The music continues as it started, with bold semitonal clashes, more chromatic passing-notes and augmented chords. Nowhere are we allowed to feel at rest until the confident 'Banne du' of bar 25, with its drumming common chords in the piano. This is in fact the first time that a common chord has been held for more than one beat in the entire song! From now on, as befits the new mood, the accompaniment is assertive, chordal, less swiftly changing in its harmonies and devoid of the chromatic passing-notes that created such an unstable atmosphere in earlier measures. Other examples of the expressiveness made possible by Wolf's chromatic language are 'In der Frühe' (*Mörike-Lieder*, no. 24) — again with a much more tranquil and harmonically stable second part — and 'Seufzer' (no. 22). In this last case the mood is one of bitter self-recrimination on the part of a sinner; and again the impression of anguish is achieved through constantly shifting harmonies which create the bewildering impression that the music could move towards almost any harmonic centre at almost any point. Only for four bars when the voice first enters and during the postlude is the listener allowed any relatively secure awareness of where he is, harmonically speaking.

Hence, Wolf encouraged composers to set their sights on some of Mörike's less obvious poems — and this at a time when technical developments in the musical language of the late Romantic era began to hold out hopes of matching the poet's nervous intensity and emotional confusion in music. In the last two decades of the century the range of Mörike poems which were set to music continued to expand. Something similar can be observed in Goethe settings, where many texts had to wait until quite late in the century for a setting, or, at least, a satisfactory setting. 'Als ich auf dem Euphrat schiffte', included by Wolf in his Goethe-Lieder, was set only twice more by 1900; 'Dies zu deuten', which should logically be regarded as an indispensable companion-piece to the previous poem, was set only once in the

A General Assessment

nineteenth century; 'Ein Wunder, ist der arme Mensch geboren' had to wait until the turn of the century. Examples could be multiplied. It would seem that earlier composers were wary of the elusive irony of many of Goethe's later poems, while the lyrics of the *Westöstlicher Divan* were too remote from the mainstream of the German poetic tradition to be tempting. Other poems may have had too much of what the Germans call *Gedankenlyrik* about them (that is, philosophical poetry) to commend themselves to composers still inclined to think of song as basically an expression of a lyrical mood. A breakdown of Goethe-settings, showing not only how many times each poem was set but also in what decades, would undoubtedly reveal much regarding both changing tastes in poetry and changing notions of what could and should be attempted in song.[13]

Familiar and well-loved poems were set to music time and time again. Hence, the pleasures of discovering a new song are often allied to the pleasures of comparison. (And it must be stressed that this act of comparison is not a scholarly exercise in reading music, but an experience made possible only through and during performance). Since a very famous song by Schubert or Schumann may lead us to assume that a particular text is the private property of a particular composer, these new discoveries are a salutary experience, a demonstration that different approaches may be equally legitimate. Not everybody has taken this view, however; some nineteenth-century reviewers seemed to think that the existence of an outstandingly good setting should preclude further attempts.[14] There are a few cases where one setting seems 'definitive' (Schubert's dynamic realisation of 'An Schwager Kronos' is the obvious example). But the austere views just mentioned would, if applied to song-texts in general and widely accepted, mean that the field of German poetry would be littered with 'Keep Out' signs. Most composers have ignored such views — and rightly so. Since the most popular texts are often the best texts, it is barely likely that any one setting, however good, will exhaust the nuances and possibilities. One of the most stimulating of musical experiences is to come across an unfamiliar setting of a famous poem, a setting so different from the better known version or versions that we are forced to re-examine the poem in order to see how two composers can possibly have experienced it so differently. Given the scope of the present volume, I will have to content myself with a few illustrations of this complex question, beginning with a number of famous texts which face the composer with a choice between the strophic and the through-composed methods.

The debate as to the relative merits of strophic and through-composed song had already begun in the eighteenth century. The issue became critical with the enormous popularity of simple, folksong-*like* poems by Goethe, Heine and the rest. Goethe's 'Der Fischer', a short ballad of four very regular eight-line stanzas, provides a good example. The poem tells how an angler is tempted to his destruction by a water sprite whose description of her underwater kingdom draws him half involuntarily into the water. The rippling of the stream runs through the poem and seems to merge with the tones of the water sprite, whose words are as hypnotically musical and repetitive as the sound of the rivulet. Much of the effect of this poem depends on echoes and near-echoes, on half-lines, lines and couplets which answer and balance each other, flowing and rippling like the water itself. All this can be brought out admirably in a strophic setting, especially if the accompaniment suggests the movement of the water, as it does in many versions, including that by Schubert. Exactly the same musical phrase will tell of the rippling of the water (stanza 1) and of the water sprite's song; it will introduce the seductive account of her realm (stanza 3) and will become the sound of the water again in the final stanza:

1. Das Wasser rauscht', das Wasser schwoll . . .
2. Sie sang zu ihm, sie sprach zu ihm . . .
3. Labt sich die liebe Sonne nicht . . .
4. Das Wasser rauscht', das Wasser schwoll . . .

A strophic version will thus be able to suggest how the words of temptation emerge from, and merge back into, the sounds of the water, how nature and nature-spirit are one. No elaborate through-composed setting could do this as effectively. (In fact, a reviewer in the *AMZ* states roundly that 'Der Fischer' should not be through-composed (xxxiv, 503).)

But, as always with strophic settings, a price must be paid. The most eloquent passages in Goethe's poem, especially in the third stanza where the water sprite tempts the angler, will receive the same musical treatment, note for note, as much less emotionally charged parts of Goethe's ballad. By contrast, a through-composed setting can give the most expressive words and phrases the most expressive treatment, as happens in Loewe's version,

A General Assessment

opus 34,1. The opening is a neutral parlando against a gently rippling accompaniment. But the third stanza is set in luscious, almost operatic style against a sensuous counter-melody in the treble of the accompaniment.[15] Heine's 'Lorelei' forces a similar choice on the composer. A strophic setting in the Volkston, such as the famous version by Friedrich Silcher, is in keeping with the suggestion that this is an ancient tale ('ein Märchen aus alten Zeiten') which arises unbidden out of distant recollections in the poet's mind. But such a setting leaves it to the singer to make what he can of the colour, the power of the Lorelei's song ('gewaltig'), the calamitous effect this has on the boatman, and so on. By preferring a through-composed setting, Liszt and others can give due stress and variety to the different stages in the story — but only at the cost of the strict, almost tangible unity of a strophic version.

'Heidenröslein' lends itself less well to a through-composed treatment; most settings of this poem known to me are in fact either in strophic form or close derivations from it. Eichendorff's 'Das zerbrochene Ringlein' is a slightly more complex case, for as we have seen, it opens with the closest possible echoes of folk poetry, but goes it own way in the middle stanzas. Although simple strophic settings are not inappropriate, given the poem's heritage, the middle section seems to demand something more elaborate if it is to make its full effect. Alexis Holländer's version (opus 6,5, 1864) gets the best of both worlds. The opening is like a mournful little folksong and is given the simplest possible accompaniment:

The middle stanzas, in which the singer gives expression to his longings, are set in a restless and agitated fashion, with more varied harmonies and somewhat more adventurous piano-writing. At the end, as the poet returns from dreams of escape to his starting-point ('Hör ich das Mühlrad gehen'), Holländer reverts to his opening melody. The form of Eichendorff's poem has thus found its exact equivalent in a ternary setting, while the impression of the Volkston, because recalled in the recapitulation, remains dominant in the listener's mind.

This last example makes it clear that the choice is by no means between absolute simplicity and the complexities of a through-composed version. Many composers manage to create a Volkston, keep to relatively simple musical forms and textures and yet inject something of their own musical personality without an impossible stylistic wrench. (Franz would be another example.)

In fact, comparatively few composers are content to evoke the Volkston and leave it at that. Song had become more ambitious since Schulz had popularised the notion, with the consequence that the claim for parity as between music and poetry was seen as applying to 'Lieder im Volkston' too. It must be recalled that folk melodies, on which the concept of the Lied im Volkston is based, must be simple enough to be easily memorised and must also be capable of being sung unaccompanied. Many of the eighteenth-century composers had indeed stipulated that their songs might be performed without the accompaniment; some had even prided themselves on the fact that their works were sung in the fields and streets. But for most nineteenth-century composers, to adopt such attitudes would have seemed like putting the clock back.

Nor should we forget that we are no longer considering settings of folksongs, but of short lyrics by some of Germany's greatest poets which, while recalling the world of folk poetry in a number of ways, transcend it in richness of vocabulary, rhythmic variety and the ability to hint at complex, elusive or ambivalent psychological states. When composers evoke the tones of folk music but quickly go beyond this, they are only following the poets' lead. Robert Schwalm, in his setting of Heine's 'Gekommen ist der Maie' (opus 3,2, 1874) matches music to poetic mood with great exactitude. The poem talks of the joys of spring much in the manner of traditional *Frühlingslieder*: 'Gekommen ist der Maie,/die Blumen und Bäume blühn'. Compare the old folksong: 'Wohl kommt der Mai mit mancherlei/Der Blümlein zart nach seiner Art'. But where conventional spring songs show the singer to be at one with the mood of nature, Heine characteristically excludes himself from the joy around him:

A General Assessment

Ich kann nicht singen und springen,
ich liege krank im Gras;
ich höre fernes Klingen,
mir träumt, ich weiß nicht was.

If we turn to Schwalm's setting, we find that the vocal line opens with a cheerful, rather folkish phrase:

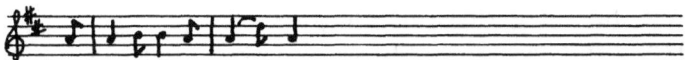

Compare:

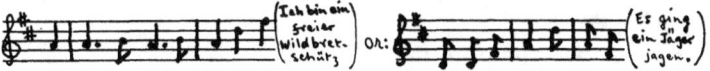

Yet Schwalm's extrovert opening for the singer has been preceded by a curiously hesitant little piano solo, which seems at first sight an incongruous lead-in to a song which begins with the words 'May has come':

The final stanza tells us why; now this motif reappears, perfectly in keeping with the poet's lugubrious mood. This seems a very apt setting, for not only are poet and composer in complete accord; each stands in a similar relationship to a folk tradition, in poetry and music respectively.

We cannot leave the question of how the nineteenth-century *Kunstlied* related to popular forms without a word on the chorale. Its influence is by no means as great as that of folksong, but is nevertheless potent, given its deeply emotive associations for Germans. A chorale-like style continues to be used, of course, in settings of sacred texts: by Beethoven and Schubert, by Schumann (more rarely), by Bernhard Klein (Novalis songs, opus 40) and by F.E. Fesca in his setting of Fouqué's 'Lied' ('Aus der Tiefen rufe ich'). This last song is exactly like a church chorale arranged for

A General Assessment

solo voice and piano.[16]

But as in the eighteenth century, the 'secularised' chorale is also met with, taking on considerable importance because of its association with one of Goethe's noblest short poems, 'Wandrers Nachtlied', 2 ('Der du von dem Himmel bist'). The poem is a prayer to peace:

Der du von dem Himmel bist,
Alles Leid und Schmerzen stillest,
Den, der doppelt elend ist,
Doppelt mit Erquickung füllest,
Ach, ich bin des Treibens müde!
Was soll all der Schmerz und Lust?
Süßer Friede,
Komm, ach komm in meine Brust!

(You who come from Heaven and calm all sorrow and pain, filling those who are doubly wretched with double consolation — Oh, I am weary of this bustle! What is the point of all this pain and joy? — Sweet peace, come, oh come into my breast!)

The hymnlike quality has often been recognised by composers and expressed in their settings; Mikuli even heads his version 'Andante religioso'.[17] It will be noted that the parenthesis in lines 5-6 momentarily interrupts the prayer, introducing at the same time a greater note of personal urgency. For this reason some of the most effective settings are those in which a chorale-like atmosphere is established, interrupted by a contrasting section, then recaptured for 'Süßer Friede . . .'. This is what Wolfrum does in his beautiful setting of 1885 (opus 16,5), achieving his contrast through a modulation to a remote key, an increased tempo, a crescendo to the one and only forte of the song and a broken bass line (again for the one and only time).[18]

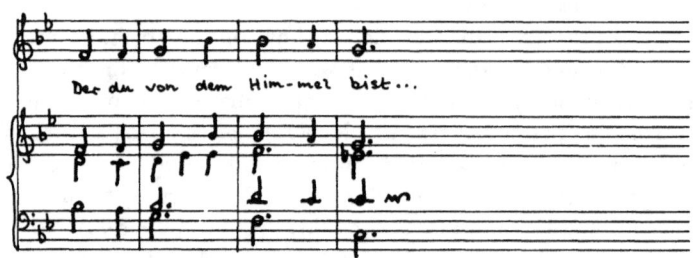

A General Assessment

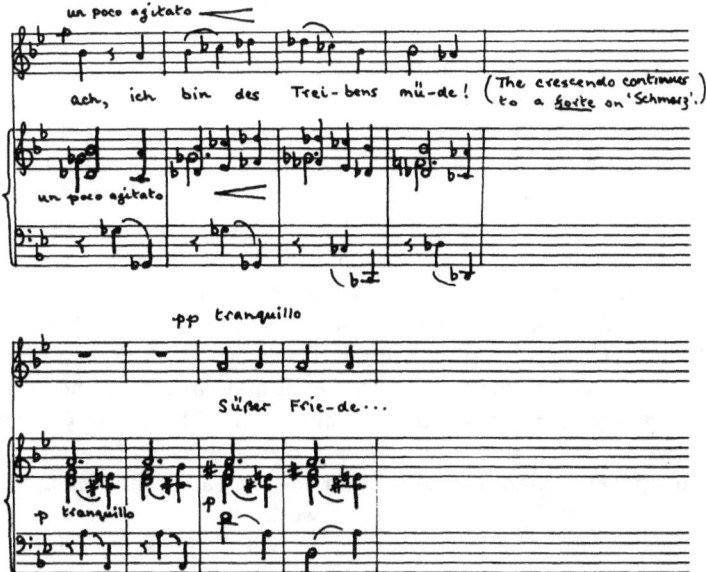

For a more straightforward example, where the song progresses from an agitated movement to a calmer, chorale-like texture at the moment where the poet utters a prayer to the beloved ('and I pray, I implore: lovely eyes, lights of grace, fill my soul with bliss'), see Franz's setting of 'Auf dem Meere' ('An die blaue Himmelsdecke') by Heine, opus 6,3.

The nineteenth century, then, was not only a period in German music which seemed to offer the song-composer greatly expanded possibilities of subtle and technically advanced expression; it also faced him with a choice of *policy*, one might almost say. This, as has been implied, was acutest in the case of poems which were simple in their external features but full of subtleties and nuances. Should he set such texts in the Volkston or with a high and demanding degree of technical sophistication? Was he aiming at the amateur in the drawing room or the professional or near-professional of salon or concert platform? Different settings of a given poem will often range from the most unassuming strophic versions to pieces of great complexity and, occasionally, even virtuosity.

Mörike presents an interesting case. For most music-lovers, *Mörike-Lieder* will inevitably suggest Wolf. But poems like 'Das verlassene Mägdlein', 'Ein Stündlein wohl vor Tag' and 'Denk es, o Seele!' were all set many times before Wolf, often in the Volkston. As we have seen, Mörike is able to take up folksong

A General Assessment

models and inject a degree of emotional intensity or ambiguity into them which would be quite unthinkable in a folk poem. 'Das verlassene Mägdlein' appears simply to offer escape into renewed dreaming — but even as she promises herself this, the girl must know that a reawakening into harsh reality will inevitably follow. This is quite different from the uncomplicated situation in those folksongs where the abandoned girl looks forward to death as a *lasting* release. In 'Ein Stündlein wohl vor Tag' the singer branches out from her own predicament in order to voice a mood of general scepticism and pessimism about human behaviour ('Ach, Lieb und Treu ist wie ein Traum'). 'Denk es, o Seele!' employs the directness, concrete detail and simple antitheses of folk poetry to express a morbid obsession with mortality: who knows in what garden the rose is growing that will blossom on your grave; perhaps the horses that you see gaily cantering today will draw your coffin before many weeks are past.

In his settings of these, as of other Mörike texts, Wolf brings out the emotional intensity and almost neurotic melancholy by all manner of musical devices: plaintive chromatic touches, broken phrases and dramatic leaps in the vocal line, by harsh clashes of seconds and sevenths, by that most 'uneasy' of chords, the augmented fifth (often in succession, unresolved), by passing-notes in the inner parts which give rise to a restless and unstable effect, by abrupt and unexpected modulations and by dynamic contrasts of near brutal intensity. That is to say, he always tends to bring out the individual aspect of these and similar poems in his settings. By contrast, settings 'im Volkston'[19] implicitly relate the poem to a realm of shared experience by evoking a common heritage of simple but potent melodiousness — a heritage which, as we have seen, was imbued with intense nostalgic power for any German possessing the least musical sense. It is worth stressing that both approaches are perfectly legitimate; the external similarities that exist between Mörike's poems and folksong proper indicate the shared experience (for we have all felt the pangs of love or the fear of death), while the subtleties and nuances show that these are the works of a great and intensely individual poet.

As an example of a simple strophic setting which seems to stress the folkish elements in the text, one might take Wilhelm Speidel's 'Ein Stündlein wohl vor Tag' (opus 9,3, 1854). One might truly be listening to an untutored girl pouring her feelings into song:

A General Assessment

A composer, once he has established the Volkston, feels free, of course, to respond to the emotional climaxes of the poem by means of contrasting, agitato passages.[20] In Otto Scherzer's eloquent setting of 'Ein Stündlein' (xxv Lieder, no. 15), the muted sadness explodes into a dramatic outburst at the singer's realisation that love and faithfulness are but a dream:

In such cases the composer usually returns to the gentler strains of the opening at the end of the song, thus ensuring that the overriding impression carried away is of the same realm of folk art which Mörike evokes, even if he too does not feel himself circumscribed by it. That particular combination of the individual and the generic that comes about when a highly sensitive poet exploits and simultaneously transcends folk poetry, finds its musical equivalent in such compositions. We may thus be confronted by simple settings reminiscent of folk music, by sophisticated compositions which respond to every nuance and change of pace or mood in the text (Wolf, 'Denk es, o Seele!'), or by songs which occupy all manner of positions between those extremes. Which type we prefer is a matter of taste or may even depend on the mood of the moment. To speak personally, I sometimes relish a penny-plain song like Speidel's 'Ein Stündlein' as an emotional respite after Wolf's more highly charged responses to Mörike.

Similarly, Holstein's direct and lyrical reading of 'Frage und Antwort' (opus 24,1, 1870) makes a refreshing contrast to Wolf's almost neurotic interpretation, discussed above. Here is part of Holstein:

This brief discussion of different ways of setting Mörike will have proved — if proof be needed — that great complexity does not necessarily mean better songs, merely different songs. To turn to Goethe: Wolf's 'Grenzen der Menschheit' is undoubtedly more complex and dramatic than Schubert's setting of the same poem, but the huge leaps in Wolf's voice part may sound forced to some listeners, where Schubert's falling phrases through the notes of the diminished seventh chord are a precisely judged way of conveying a sense of insecurity at this stage of Goethe's argument ('his uncertain feet can find no hold').[21]

In the case of Klärchen's song from *Egmont* ('Freudvoll und leidvoll'), the settings range from perfectly unassuming strophic versions, such as that by Reichardt, to highly elaborate through-composed songs, such as the second of Liszt's three settings, with its vocal leaps, rhythmical intricacies and enharmonic changes. Each approach can be justified; preference is again a matter of taste. If we know the dramatic context, our judgement *may* be affected by what we know of Klärchen and her situation. This question, the importance of which is not always given due attention in discussions of song, will be considered further when we come to the much more famous example of Mignon's songs from *Wilhelm Meisters Lehrjahre*.

There are certainly cases where a text has been over-composed. Some composers, in their settings of 'Heidenröslein' and Walther von der Vogelweide's 'Unter den Linden', fall into the trap of setting what should be a fairly artless refrain in an absurdly ornate fashion. A reviewer in the *AMZ* roundly accused Liszt of overwhelming his chosen texts by the sheer weight of his imaginative power (xlvii, 85). It is at least possible to argue that Wolf, through an almost too fastidious attention to detail, falls short in his settings of the more direct and unaffected texts which he chose. And certainly, when we reach Reger and Strauss, the music is often too rich for the text. Reger seems to have reacted against his own tortuosities towards the end of his life and composed a substantial number of much simpler songs (*Schlichte Weisen*), much as one who indulged himself extravagantly in youth might embrace an ascetic old age.

To demonstrate that an obscure composer can sometimes serve a text at least as well as a more famous man and that the aesthetic worth of a song need not have much to do with complex or 'advanced' styles of composition, I would like to consider three of the many settings of Mignon's song, 'Kennst du das Land'. Here, Mignon expresses her longing for the half-remembered land of her childhood. Each stanza paints a picture — of the sun-drenched Italian landscape, of the house, of dramatic mountainous scenery — and each ends with a refrain. This structure clearly invites strophic composition and, in fact, most composers have responded to the invitation.

Schubert's version, which is in slightly modified strophic form, nevertheless does something very strange to Goethe's text. The refrain ('Dahin! Dahin/Möcht' ich mit dir, o mein Geliebter, ziehn') is set in such a way that 'Dahin . . . ziehn' is sung twice and the single word 'dahin' another seven times. Goethe's ten words have come to occupy twenty-two bars, whereas the five lines which form the verse — the description of the land 'where the lemons blossom' — take up only eighteen bars. If we read the poem, we will be struck by the colourful description and the nostalgic evocation of a southern landscape. To demote all this to a position of secondary importance seems a barely excusable distortion of the natural proportions of the stanza. In Schubert's version, the opulent motifs of lines 1–4 are almost forgotten in the onward surge which characterises the setting of 'dahin', with its quicker tempo and the rush of triplets in the accompaniment. (The point applies to all stanzas of the poem.)

But when we consider settings of 'Kennst du das Land', we need also to bear in mind the relationship of the song to the (original) singer. The piece is not quite in the same category as the 'Wandrers Nachtlieder' or 'Gefunden', for it is firmly associated with a character and a situation in a novel. Although Goethe gives a (for him) fairly detailed account of how Mignon renders the song, there is, of course, no reason why a composer should follow this. (To my knowledge, only one came near to attempting any such thing.) Indeed, if one took the passage in the novel *au pied de la lettre*, one would have to translate the verse into Italian and provide an accompaniment on the zither! But in the case of a figure from one of Germany's most famous novels, there may well be some constraint on the composer to devise a setting more or less in keeping with Mignon's general character.

Mignon is a girl of twelve or thirteen years of age who first makes her appearance as an unwilling performer in a rather disorderly band of tightrope-walkers, conjurors and dancers, where she is exploited and ill-treated. Rescued by Wilhelm, she attaches herself passionately to him, as to a second father. She is a pathetic but affectionate little waif, consumed with longing for that lost Italian home. She is also simple, naïve and uneducated. It is hardly possible for a composer to set 'Kennst du das Land' and other songs of hers without having — and revealing — some notion of her personality. Wolf evidently discerned passionate longing, mystery and a mood almost of wildness in the text when he made his tempestuous song out of 'Kennst du das Land'. But this, with its violent dynamic contrasts, chromatic harmonies, changes of tempo, passionate counter-melodies and syncopations in the accompaniment, together with a vocal line which spans nearly two octaves, seems to have little to do with, as Jack Stein puts it, the 'timid, curious, puzzling and intriguing' character of Mignon herself.[22] If the composer is guided by this character, he will set the poem in a fairly simple, direct and lyrical manner, however poignant an atmosphere he may create. Nor will the accompaniment be rich or complex. This simple approach is well illustrated by Moritz Hauptmann.

Hauptmann's setting (from his opus 37, dating from *c.* 1852) starts with a delicate little prelude of four bars, just sufficient to establish key and mood. The vocal writing is virtually syllabic, beginning with a hymnlike phrase:

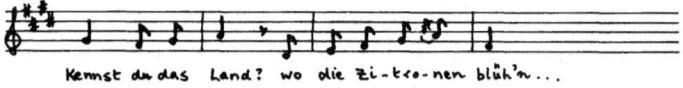

The climax, which arrives in due course on 'dahin', is again characterised by simplicity and a sort of inevitability, as the voice ascends the scale:

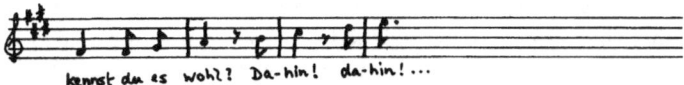

The accompaniment veers between simple chords and gently flowing broken chords in semiquavers, with only two brief solo passages which wistfully echo the singer's phrases. And unlike Schubert, Hauptmann maintains a proper proportion between verse and refrain. I do not think that it is pedantic to prefer this unassuming but intensely lyrical version to the more famous settings just mentioned. For any German listener, Mignon's songs are as intimately bound up with her character as, say, Ophelia's are with hers for an English listener. Read attentively, 'Kennst du das Land' reveals Mignon's childlike submissiveness to Wilhelm: he is beloved, protector and father in one ('Geliebter, Beschützer, Vater'). This comes through well in Hauptmann's wistful ending:

By contrast, Wolf's treatment of the refrain, with its marking 'leidenschaftlich hingebend', suggests rather that Wilhelm is to be dragged off willy-nilly by the scruff of the neck. And Schubert's treatment is at this point not far from involuntary comedy:

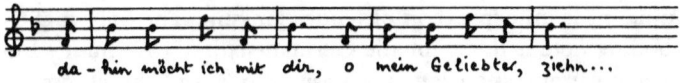

Schubert's song raises a further issue: should the composer maintain the basic structure of the text or is he free to destroy its proportions? Traditional theories of song in Germany have insisted on the former; if song is to be a true meeting of poetic and musical values, they have been right to do so.

It may be, then, that an obscure setting can be better — or at least truer to the form and spirit of the poem even if not as exciting in purely musical terms — than the more famous versions. More commonly, however, the new or unfamiliar settings will simply be *different*; they will provoke thought as to possible interpretations of the text without raising what are often unanswerable questions of value-judgement. The way in which a poem by Mörike can be made to reveal its nuances and its highly individual character or,

A General Assessment

through a composition in the Volkston, will suggest its general validity, has already been touched on. Something similar can be observed if one compares settings of various of the *Winterreise* poems, in which minor composers may again elect to stress the folkish element, where Schubert had been concerned with the bleak and morbid atmosphere.

Heine's verses — for reasons already sufficiently hinted at — have provoked widely differing responses from different composers. 'Du bist wie eine Blume' veers between adoration of beauty and innocence and the fear that these may not long survive:

> Du bist wie eine Blume
> so hold und schön und rein;
> ich schau dich an und Wehmut
> schleicht mir ins Herz hinein.
>
> Mir ist, als ob ich die Hände
> aufs Haupt dir legen sollt,
> betend, daß Gott dich erhalte
> so rein und schön und hold.

(You are like a flower, so sweet and beautiful and pure; I look at you and melancholy steals into my heart. I feel as if I ought to lay my hands upon your head, praying that God may preserve you so pure and beautiful and sweet.) The most famous setting, that by Schumann, is an expression of tender longing. The only slightly foreboding note is the emphatic German sixth at 'Wehmut'. But the general impression left is a positive one and the chromatic harmonies in the little postlude are luscious rather than disquieting. The implications of Püttlingen's setting (opus 11) are, I believe, rather different. Like Schumann, he begins in a tender and lyrical strain:

Püttlingen too picks on 'Wehmut' (here by modulating briefly into C minor) and, again like Schumann, returns to a serene mood in his setting of the second stanza. The significant difference comes in the postlude, where the opening phrase is repeated, but with minor colouring:

A General Assessment

Perhaps there is some doubt as to whether the poet's prayer will be granted.[23]

One short poem by Heine has called forth sharply contrasting reactions on account of the violent contrast which the poem itself contains within its eight lines:

Lehn deine Wang an meine Wang,
dann fließen die Tränen zusammen;
und an mein Herz drück fest dein Herz,
dann schlagen zusammen die Flammen!

Und wenn in die große Flamme fließt
der Strom von unsern Tränen,
und wenn dich mein Arm gewaltig umschließt —
sterb ich vor Liebessehnen!

(Place your cheek against mine, then our tears will mingle; press your heart against mine, then the flames will join as one. And when the flood of our tears flows into the great flame and when my arm clasps you powerfully, I shall die of longing!) As the poem is so brief, it would not lend itself very readily to a musical treatment which would mirror the change from the wistful beginning to the turbulent ending. Two of the composers whose settings are known to me certainly decided to treat the text as an emotional unity, but read it in startlingly different ways. Schumann (opus 142,3) begins at the end, so to speak, and interprets the whole as an outburst of wild longing. Adolf Jensen (opus 1,1), on the other hand, responds to the wistful opening and ignores the invitation to a more passionate treatment contained in the last line. Having decided on this approach, Jensen finds himself obliged to repeat 'Lehn deine Wang an meine Wang' at the end of the song, taking up the musical material of the opening bars note for note and thus stressing what he regards as the ruling mood of the poem. Each composer makes a choice (and rejects an equally inviting and valid alternative). This can best be illustrated by citing the beginning of the one setting and the middle section of the other:

A General Assessment

Schumann's setting makes perfect sense provided that we detect latent passion in the comparatively muted opening words; Jensen's version invites us to see the possibility that the 'Liebestod' is not much more than a sentimental dream. There is room for both interpretations.[24] Certainly we cannot listen to these songs without going back to look at Heine's poem very intently.

A closely similar example is afforded by 'Und wüßten's die Blumen', made famous by Schumann (*Dichterliebe*, no. 8). Heine's first three stanzas play on the possibility of a sympathy between the poet and the natural world: if flowers, birds and stars knew of his wounded heart, they would comfort him. But the final stanza, as often, reveals the sting: the only one who knows of his grief is she who caused it. The ending is violent: she has *rent* or *torn* his heart (Heine's 'zerrissen' is stronger than merely 'broken'). Schumann's setting ends with a tempestuous postlude, hinting at the depths of the poet's grief. This version is so well known that it comes as a great surprise when one encounters that by W.H. Veit (opus 21,1, *c.* 1844), which is characterised by an unvaried mood of gentle melancholy. 'Sie hat es selbst zerrissen' is sung to a phrase barely more passionate (if that is a word that can be applied to this song at all) than the opening. Once one has got over the initial surprise, however, Veit's setting seems perfectly admissible; the poet *may* be dying of a broken heart — but he may merely be posing and dramatising his predicament. Again, a salutory 'second opinion'.

In a much lighter vein, one might take Goethe's 'Gutmann und Gutweib'. This is a free rendering of a Scottish folk-ballad. The couple are lying in bed, the door has been left ajar and the wind causes it to rattle. Since neither Gutmann nor Gutweib wants to leave the warmth of the bed, they make a wager: the one who speaks the first word must get up and close the door. Time passes. Two benighted wanderers pass that way, find the door open and take shelter. They discover the food that Gutweib has prepared for Martinmas and devour it, watched in obstinate — if furious — silence by the couple in bed. Only when they light on Gutmann's schnaps does he finally break his silence and hence lose the bet. Loewe's setting (opus 9) is genial and lighthearted throughout, as readers of the ballad might expect. If one is familiar with this version, it comes as something of a shock to hear Wolf's. This has its jocose element, but also contains two thunderous climaxes with drumming triplet chords, rapid scale passages and near-glissando effects. Gutweib's outburst at the end ('You spoke first. Now go and bar the door!') seems an expression of almost grotesque and sadistic triumph in Wolf's setting — and the wild postlude only strengthens this impression.

Can this latter reading be justified? It would certainly be a rash spirit who decided without careful scrutiny that Wolf got a Goethe text wrong. I am inclined to think that he sensed beneath the trivial and comic events some hint of the animus that can blow up trivial marital squabbles into something a good deal more serious — even where there is love, as is explicitly stated by Goethe in his first stanza. Perhaps the ballad is not merely about a banging door or even a conflict of wills, but about latent hostilities. So, where Loewe responds to the lighthearted surface texture of the narrative, Wolf gives expression to the obstinacy and the unwillingness to lose face that are just hinted at in the text: if it banged for a hundred years, I wouldn't close it, says Gutweib defiantly. This reading is supported by the ending of the poem; their property has been violated and their provisions have been taken, but Gutweib thinks only of the wager that she has won and crows over her husband. Again the disparity of mood between the musical versions sends us back to the text in search of an explanation.

Examples could be multiplied indefinitely. To see what different composers have made of the same text is one of the most

A General Assessment

fascinating results of studying Lieder in more than the most casual way of enjoyment.[25] Leaving the question of intrinsic beauty aside for the moment, the 'validity' of an interpretation does not necessarily stand in any close relation to the fame or obscurity of the composer and, as said, often has little to do with questions of complexity or degrees of purely musical experimentation. But in addition, many of the forgotten composers have produced songs of great intrinsic attractiveness. The sheer number of composers and mass of material necessarily means that most of the songs produced are either conventional or derivative. But a minority are very good — and even a small minority of such a huge total means a considerable amount of unjustly neglected material. To give an adequate idea of this would require an anthology far beyond the scope of the present brief survey, but I hope that some of the extracts given will at least afford hints of what awaits rediscovery.

No one of these forgotten *Kleinmeister* consistently turned out first-rate songs (posterity is not as fickle as that), but very many were capable of producing a small-scale masterpiece from time to time. This should not surprise us. Song was a very well established *petit genre* whose main stylistic and formal problems were more or less solved by the time of, say, Schubert and Loewe, whatever developments were still to come. It depends in about equal measure on musical qualities and the composer's response to the text. If a minor composer found his imagination fired by a poem and a particularly felicitous tune came into his mind, he would seldom find any difficulty in developing it, mastering any formal or harmonic problems it posed and providing an appropriate and technically adept accompaniment. It may be that composers who would not be equal to the almost architectural problems posed in the construction of a symphony or full-scale chamber work could occasionally excel within the smaller compass of the Lied.

One reservation is necessary: among the minor composers we will seldom encounter that genuinely eerie strain which is sometimes to be found in Schubert and Schumann — the sense of mystery in 'Der Doppelgänger' or the almost neurotic wildness of Schumann's Hans Andersen songs, the cheerlessness of some of *Winterreise* or of Schumann's 'Auf einer Burg'. But even in the works of the greatest masters, such songs are the exceptions. They could never form the regular diet of a singer or a music-lover. What the many *petits maîtres* offer is a wide variety of less emotionally disturbing, but beautiful songs.

As we have seen, an unknown composer may produce perceptive

A General Assessment

and challenging songs to familiar and much-set texts without going beyond the conventional musical idiom of his day. No minor composer expanded the range of song as Schubert did, no one rivalled Schumann in advancing the role of the accompaniment into realms seemingly beyond words, no one developed such hitherto undreamt-of complexities in the relationship of vocal line to accompaniment as we find in Wolf. But the question of originality or innovation is not as important as it might seem. Since a song is a response to a poem and not 'pure' music, it can make a fresh and novel, even exciting, effect even if it is not novel in any strictly musical sense, that is, formally or harmonically innovative. We have seen how fairly conventional harmonic progressions, which would almost pass unnoticed in a piano piece of the day, can contribute notably to our perception of the poem. The best of the minor composers, even if they never did anything technically startling, are far from merely aping their predecessors; they are their own men and their songs, in those cases where a congenial poem triggered off their imaginations and allowed them to realise their highest potential, have a flavour of their own.

A more general point suggests itself here. In nineteenth-century song, as in all periods and branches of musical composition, there was in any given generation a tiny group of innovators and revolutionaries who pushed back the technical and expressive frontiers of their art and revealed unsuspected possibilities to fellow-composers, performers and listeners. (Whether such innovations were always understood or welcomed is another matter, as we have seen.) But the great majority of composers were content to work within the conventional idiom of their age or even to employ the style of a generation or so before. This coexistence of 'innovators' and 'traditionalists' has always been present in the music of Western Europe and seems no bad thing. For, at the same time as dynamic and often unnerving changes are being achieved by the few, the many continue to provide more conventional fare for the ordinary music-lover or amateur performer to enjoy. It would be an impossibly purist attitude if one were to complain of, say, Alexis Holländer's 'Gefunden'[26] on the grounds that it was behind the times or written in a 'conventional' idiom:

Notes

1. *AMZ* xlv, 215. A poem which had been popular with composers between 1790 and about 1820 and which declined in favour thereafter is the lachrymose 'Das Grab' by J.G. von Salis-Seewis.

2. For minor composers who fell into the error of 'over-composing' Hölty, see Louis Ehlert (opus 30,2, 1864) and Heinrich Schnell (opus 6,2, 1880). Anton Urspruch's settings of Wieland and Klopstock (opus 23, nos. 2 and 7, 1885) are displeasing for the same reason.

3. For more on this, see Chapter 14. It is not insularity if I say that Britten's are among the best of Hölderlin settings — but Britten chose short and relatively simple texts.

4. No apology seems necessary for having concentrated on settings of the best poems; poor verse set by minor composers is often depressing.

5. See Adalbert Lindner, *Max Reger. Ein Bild seines Jugendlebens und künstlerischen Werdens*, Stuttgart, 1923, p. 281. Rudolf Louis (*Die deutsche*

A General Assessment

Musik der Gegenwart, Munich and Leipzig, 1909, p. 232) flatly denies Reger any feeling for poetry at all.

6. *Heinrich Heine. A critical biography*, Manchester, 1979, p. 60.

7. It goes without saying that the short narrative ballads were popular as song-texts too.

8. Oswald Lorenz, *NZfM*, ix, 1838, 136.

9. *AMZ*, xxxvi, 533 and xlv, 565.

10. *AMZ*, xliii, 493; see too xxxiv, 64 and xxxvii, 471f.

11. 'Irony in the Heine Lieder of Schubert and Schumann', in *The Musical Quarterly*, lxvii, 1981, 272. Brauner's other examples are not so well chosen, however. For a discussion of the final song in *Dichterliebe*, see above, pp. 120f.

12. *NtMZ*, iv, 1856, 204.

13. Unfortunately, a detailed survey would be beyond the scope of the present study. Indeed, if it were to be more than a catalogue, it would require a book of its own.

14. See *AMZ*, xxxi, 667f; xxxviii, 204; xliii, 1036. This is only a selection.

15. Richard Strauss, in a youthful setting dating from *c.* 1877, achieves a similar contrast, although his song is intrinsically much inferior to Loewe's.

16. For a quotation from a chorale in the course of a long ballad, see Loewe's 'Jungfrau Lorenz' (opus 33,1) at the words: 'Doch wie die Sinnen ihr vergehn'.

17. Mikuli, opus 27,4 (1880).

18. M. Siering achieves a similar contrast: see *Des Mägdleins Liederwald*, ed. Graben-Hoffman, 2nd edn, vol. 2, Dresden, n.d., pp. 41f. Some settings of 'Über allen Gipfeln' (e.g. that by Schleinitz, opus 3,5) have pronounced hymnlike qualities.

19. The phrase often appears as an instruction to the performers at the beginning of a song, where we might expect an indication of tempo.

20. E.g. at 'Plötzlich, da kommt es mir' ('Das verlassene Mägdlein') or 'O weh! nicht weiter sag!' ('Ein Stündlein wohl vor Tag'). See L. Hetsch's and Max Zenger's settings of the first poem and A. Fesca's version of the second.

21. Schubert, 'Grenzen der Menschheit', bars 64-7. Contrast Wolf's treatment of the words 'und viele Geschlechter reihen sich dauernd' in his setting.

22. Stein, 1971, p. 180. Settings which include florid, quasi-operatic phrases for the singer also seem wrong for Mignon. Examples: Abeille and Häußler. Reviewers in the *AMZ* paid much attention to this point.

23. Many settings of this poem are, however, no more than sentimental.

24. Fritz Becker's setting (opus 5,3) also dies away to a muted close and is, in general, an oddly languorous realisation of Heine's text.

25. See the settings of Heine's 'Mein Wagen rollet langsam' by Schumann and Richard Strauss; they are so different that they hardly seem to have been prompted by the same poem!

26. Opus 6,6. First published in 1864.

14

Paths into the Twentieth Century

Although I am not expert enough to pursue the history of song into this century in any great detail, a word or two must be said. The most obviously striking factor is the sudden proliferation of idioms, as shown in an almost comically extreme form by the anthology *Das moderne Lied. Eine Sammlung von 50 Gesängen*, edited by Josef Wöß and published in Vienna in 1914. 'Modern' on the title-page relates to the composers' dates of birth (1860s to 1880s), with the result that the anthology ranges from the innocent and rather sentimental charm of songs by Eugen d'Albert and Leo Blech, through the harmonic and technical complexities of Reger to the vastly more experimental idioms of Paul von Klenau and the early work of Schönberg.

There are almost as many styles as composers in Wöß's collection and, despite the near-contemporaneity just mentioned, some of these styles are light-years apart. By about 1910 the difference between traditionalists and innovators has become so wide that they do not speak the same musical language and hardly address the same audience. At the one extreme are composers who still champion the values of Hausmusik (see above, p. 153), and those who continue to set folk poems in a manner not yet completely divorced from traditional notions of the Volkston (for example, Alfred Stier and E.J. Wolff). At the other extreme are those who, in their different ways, try to adapt song to various experimental idioms, including atonal and twelve-note music.[1] Even within the work of a single composer we may find a variety of styles. Apart from obvious examples such as Berg's passage from lush late Romanticism to the rigours of serial composition, one could cite Heinz Tiessen, who can range from the fantastic strains of the *Galgenlieder* (opus 24), through the astringency of his setting of

Heine's 'Weltlauf' (opus 55,1), to the limpid Volkston of Storm's 'Als ich dich kaum gesehn' (*Für dich! Drei Lieder*, no. 1). It is probably true to say that the majority of twentieth-century German song-composers have written in a fairly accessible and even traditional manner. But in song, as in other aspects of modern music, it is the experimenters who have set the pace and received most of the critical attention.

Where composers write in an advanced idiom, tension may well arise between text and music. Of course, many poems that had traditionally served song-composers as texts were rightly rejected; a modernistic composition of Eichendorff's 'Das zerbrochene Ringlein' would be about as aesthetically acceptable as a jazz setting of a Milton sonnet. In fact, where twentieth-century composers have gone to the eighteenth- and nineteenth-century poets in search of inspiration, there has sometimes been a clash between the two elements in the resultant song, as in the second (1925) of Berg's settings of Storm's gentle little poem, 'Schließe mir die Augen beide'. 'Close my eyes with your dear hands', says the poet. Berg:

A similar disharmony between the two ingredients of the song can be seen in Webern's treatment of folk poetry and in some twentieth-century settings of Eichendorff. Or, to return to Storm, Ernst Krenek set the innocent 'Musikanten wollen wandern' in wild strains that would certainly have amazed the poet, had he been alive to hear them (*Fiedellieder*, opus 64,2, 1930).

Many composers, while attracted by Germany's famous poets, tried to avoid the obvious texts. Some chosen items from the comparatively neglected pages of Goethe's *Westöstlicher Divan*, Hanns Eisler explores some of the byways of Mörike's poetry, many composers gave belated recognition to Hölderlin. But such choices — rejecting as they do the conspicuously 'singable' part of Germany's poetic legacy — can create great difficulties for the hearer. These are acute in many of the Hölderlin songs, where it can be very hard to comprehend the text as it is sung. But the Lied is not a form that has traditionally demanded detailed 'homework' on the part of the listener; it is difficult to see why he should need to know the poem virtually off by heart if he is to have any hope of understanding the song.

To show the difficulties that may arise, let us take the second of Webern's Stefan George settings which make up his opus 4. The poem opens thus:

Noch zwingt mich Treue über dir zu wachen
und deines Duldens Schönheit daß ich weile,
mein heilig Streben ist mich traurig machen,
damit ich wahrer deine Trauer teile.

(My fidelity compels me still to wake over you and the beauty of your fortitude [compels me] to stay. My sacred endeavour is to make myself sad so that I shall the more truly share your grief.) These verses are made difficult by their concentration, by the fact that a repetition of 'zwingt mich' has to be understood in the second line. The ear, having taken in 'deines Duldens Schönheit', is surprised by the conjunction 'daß' and needs time to make the necessary connection with the 'zwingt' of the opening line. Moreover, the meaning and function of the 'mich' after 'Streben' become apparent only when we reach 'machen' — and this is precisely the point at which Webern elects to put in a pause!

This example shows clearly enough that when both music and poetry are written in a difficult idiom,[2] the Lied is in deep water indeed. Moreover, such a song virtually demands performers of professional standard, so that the old amateur status of the Lied (and with it the possibility for music-lovers gradually to work their way into an unfamiliar song in the most practical and effective way) is lost.

Fischer-Dieskau, surveying the history of song, cautiously asks whether there are possibilities for any fruitful new developments.[3] I think there may be. A good deal of Brecht's poetry, relatively simple in form and language but often astringent in tone, is eminently suitable for song and has been admirably realised by Hanns Eisler and others. On a lighter note, there are many witty settings of Morgenstern's *Galgenlieder*. Or for those who have the courage to follow such a path, the austere simplicity of Kilpinen's song style might be a temptation and an invitation.[4]

Paths into the Twentieth Century

That is to say: where modern poets eschew 'difficulty' and composers can find a style which does not place too great a burden on the listener, but is nevertheless not backward-looking or artificially maintained on a simple level, there are possibilities enough. Composers of this century who have written tuneful and reasonably accessible songs without in any way sacrificing their musical integrity and who have chosen — or, in one case, written — texts which exactly suit their style include Wolfgang Fortner, Kurt Hessenberg, Ernst Krenek (for much of the time), Ernst Pepping, Schoeck and Pfitzner, whose setting of Eichendorff's 'In Danzig' (opus 22,1) can, in its beauty and atmospheric power, stand comparison with any song by Wolf. Armin Knab, about whose songs opinions differ radically, probably stands on the very borderline between a respectful traditionalism and slightly sentimental nostalgia.

The above remarks are intended as no more than a collection of hints as to how the traditional criteria which have governed the Lied may yet survive in a century of unparalleled musical experimentation. If I have seemed to place emphasis on the demands made on the listener, this is partly because discussion of modern music appears to me to lean heavily towards the analytical[5] and thus to underestimate the problems posed for the ear at the moment of performance, but also because the difficulties of appreciating Lieder are themselves often underestimated. Even for those experienced in listening to Lieder, the first hearing of an unfamiliar Wolf song can be a testing experience — and many songs written in this century will place near-impossible demands on the poetic and musical understanding.

There is another factor which has helped to remove song further and further from its origins as a relatively popular art-form. For a century at least melody was regarded as primary. It carried and expressed the meaning of the poem; other aspects of the Lied were subservient to it and determined by it. With Wolf we already find a radical change: the voice may be demoted to a sort of sung commentary on the accompaniment, a counterpoint to the essential melodic ideas sounded in the piano part.

But in the twentieth century the decline of melody within the Lied has become more acute. This is not simply or even mainly a result of yet greater intricacy in the relationship between voice and accompaniment; indeed, it is difficult to see how this particular aspect of song could be taken much further than in Wolf's most subtle and elaborate efforts. No, the melodic aspect of song has been threatened by a rejection — defiant in some cases, slightly shamefaced in others — of the 'good tune'. Even where there is nothing in the least avant-garde about his idiom, a composer may resort to angular leaps in the vocal line, as if afraid to sound too lyrical:[6]

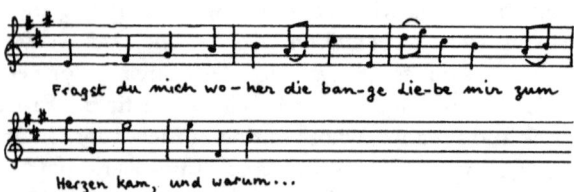

Or a tune which is in itself manifestly linked to a lyrical tradition in German song may be, as it were, negated and rendered slightly acid by harsh clashes in the accompaniment:[7]

The astringencies and austerities of much twentieth-century song are understandable enough. Many Lieder of the 1890s in which the harmonic idiom of Liszt or Wagner was debased and made to express a thoroughly sentimental reading of the text, are displeasing, and were bound to provoke a reaction. But a less embarrassed attitude towards melodiousness and lyricism may have to come about if art-song is not to become a hopelessly esoteric genre. But even if this happens, the barriers erected by the poets are at least as formidable. For a century and a half most of Germany's best poets wrote at least part of their work in styles and forms which both invited musical setting and were conceptually accessible to an educated but middlebrow public. The situation has changed drastically, to a point where most contemporary poetry is too difficult to find a large popular following and far removed from 'songlike' rhythms. Whether contemporary composers can find inspiration in what is being written — or find older texts which seem appropriate to them — may turn out to be as critical a question as any purely musical consideration.

Notes

1. Here, as Fischer-Dieskau notes, the form of the poem comes to the aid of the music — but at the listener's cost (*Töne sprechen, Worte klingen*, p. 172).
2. Webern would no doubt disagree, believing that, if music possessed organic unity, it must be comprehensible: see *The Path to the New Music*, especially Lecture 3. But this would not affect my point about the word-setting in the case of what itself is a difficult text. The same point, by the way, would apply to many songs based on poems by Rilke.
3. *Töne sprechen*, pp. 184f.
4. See Willy Burkhard's late setting of Morgenstern's 'Erster Schnee', opus 70, 4, and some of Schoeck's late songs.
5. It seems significant that Hans Redlich's long commentary in his edition of Berg's 1925 Storm-setting contains an elaborate analysis of the composer's serial technique, but not a word on how this relates to Storm's poem (Vienna, U.E. 12241).
6. Metzner/Mörike, no. 8. The point would not apply to all of Metzner's Mörike settings, however.
7. From Krenek's setting of Klopstock's 'Die frühen Gräber', opus 19, 5.

Select Bibliography

For greater convenience, this has been subdivided as follows:

Section 1: Modern editions and collections of source-material involving two or more composers
Section 2: Nineteenth-century anthologies of song
Section 3: Alphabetical list of composers
Section 4: Cycles of *Wanderlieder* (see above, p. 114)
Section 5: Songs with accompaniment for piano and/or guitar
Section 6: Books on music

In the case of eighteenth-century song, locations are given in the *Répertoire international des sources musicales* (*RISM*), International Musicological Society, 1960 ff. In the absence of anything similar for the nineteenth century, I have given locations for all but the most easily accessible works, following the abbreviations used in the *RISM*, namely:

B	State Library, West Berlin
Bc	Library of the Royal Conservatory, Brussels
Bds	State Library, East Berlin
BNu	University Library, Bonn
Bu	University Library, Basle
DS	*Hessische Landes- und Hochschulbibliothek*
DÜk	Library of the Goethe Museum, Düsseldorf
Gs	*Niedersächsische Staats- und Universitätsbibliothek*, Göttingen
Hmb	City Library, Hamburg
Hs	University Library, Hamburg
Kl	*Landesbibliothek*, Cassel
KNmi	*Musikwissenschaftliches Institut*, University of Cologne
Lbl	British Library, London
Lcml	Central Music Library, London
LÜh	Municipal Library, Lübeck
Mbs	Bavarian State Library, Munich
Sl	*Württembergische Landesbibliothek*, Stuttgart
Wgm	Library of the *Gesellschaft der Musikfreunde*, Vienna
Wn	Austrian National Library, Vienna
Wst	*Stadtbibliothek*, Vienna

By the time we reach twentieth-century song, the situation is easier: here, I have given locations for very obscure works only. In view of the 'internationalisation' of music publishing, it has sometimes seemed more sensible to name the publisher rather than the place of publication.

Not all the composers given in the Bibliography are specifically mentioned in the text; brief comments, details of poems set, etc. are given in the Bibliography where it seemed appropriate. I have dated the items as exactly as possible, relying on A. Hofmeister/C.F. Whistling,

Select Bibliography

Musikalisch-literarische Monatsberichte, Leipzig, 1852 ff (running lists of music publications), contemporary reviews, publishers' lists and advertisements. In a limited number of cases, a work can be dated precisely from the publisher's plate-number; here I am above all indebted to O.E. Deutsch, *Musikverlagsnummern* . . ., *1710–1900*, 2nd edn Berlin, 1961, together with articles by Rudolf Elvers on Berlin publishers in *Festschrift Walter Gerstenberg* . . ., Wolfenbüttel, 1964, 37–44 and *Festschrift O.E. Deutsch* . . ., Cassel, 1963, 291–5. Alexander Weinmann has produced a series of catalogues of eighteenth and early nineteenth-century Viennese music publishers (1960 ff). *Musik in Geschichte und Gegenwart*, Grove, and other encyclopedias occasionally give dates. See too Bibliography, Section 6, for monographs on individual composers. Since nineteenth-century sheet music hardly ever carried a date, it seemed a waste of space to put virtually all the entries in the form 'n.d. (*c*. 1810)'. I have reserved 'n.d.' for those cases where no date can be established and surmise seems pointless. In ordering entries which carry no composer's name, I have gone by the first word, disregarding articles: thus, *Musikalische Monatsschrift* comes after *Die Muse*.

In Section 6 I had to be highly selective. Since bibliographical data regarding the famous song-composers are quite easy to come by, I have omitted these, except in cases of major indebtedness. Secondary material, to which reference is made once only in the body of the work and where my indebtedness is confined to that particular point, is covered in the Notes and does not appear in the Bibliography.

Section 1

(Note that modern editions of, and selections from, individual composers are given under the composer's name in Section 3.)

Alte Meister des deutschen Liedes, ed. H.J. Moser, Peters, 1914 (repr. 1931). Begins in the 1620s and carries through to Reichardt and Zelter.

Balladen von G.A. Bürger . . ., ed. D. Manicke, Mainz, 1970 (= *Das Erbe deutscher Musik*, xlv–xlvi). Includes settings by Johann André, F.L.A. Kunzen, Reichardt, Tomasek and Zumsteeg.

Gedichte von Goethe in Compositionen seiner Zeitgenossen, ed. Max Friedlaender, Weimar, 1896 (= *Schriften der Goethe-Gesellschaft*, xi).

Gedichte von Goethe in Kompositionen, 2 vols, ed. Friedlaender, Weimar, 1916 (= *Schriften der Goethe-Gesellschaft*, xxxi).

Das Wiener Lied von 1778 bis Mozarts Tod, ed. M. Ansion and I. Schlaffenberg, Graz, 1960 (= *DTÖ* liv).

Das Wiener Lied von 1792 bis 1815, ed. H. Maschek and H. Kraus, Graz, 1960 (= *DTÖ* lxxix).

Select Bibliography

Section 2

Arion. Sammlung auserlesener Gesangstücke . . ., Brunswick, 1829 ff (Kl)
Arnold, F.W. *Pfennig-Magazin für Gesang und Guitarre. Herausgegeben von einem Verein rheinländischer Tonkünstler* . . ., Cologne, 1834–5. (Mbs) Schubert, Mozart and Beethoven rub shoulders with lesser masters and the unknown authors of folksongs.
Erk, Ludwig *Deutscher Liederschatz* . . ., Leipzig and Berlin. Many editions. A book once to be found in most German homes with any pretence to musical interest.
―――― and Böhme, F.M. *Deutscher Liederhort*, 2 vols, Leipzig, 1893–4. Mainly folksongs and 'volkstümliche Lieder'; texts and melodies.
Fink, G.W. *Musikalischer Hausschatz der Deutschen. Eine Sammlung von 1000 Liedern und Gesängen* . . ., Leipzig, 1843.
Graben-Hoffmann, G. *Des Mägdleins Liederwald. 80 . . . Lieder*, 2 vols, 10th edn, Hannover, 1860. (Mbs) A typical mid-nineteenth-century anthology ranging from J.S. Bach to the editor and his contemporaries.
Lieder-Album, no. 2, first published late 1840s. Edition seen: Berlin and Posen, 1880. (Bu)
Lieder für eine Singstimme . . ., Vienna, Diabelli, n.d. A running collection of songs and small groups of songs. Items numbered individually. (Sl)
Lieder-Tempel. Album für Gesang . . ., Berlin, n.d. (1840s). Contributions from over a dozen composers.
Musikalische Gartenlaube. Hausmusik für Pianoforte und Gesang, ed. Hermann Langer, Leipzig, 1870–3. Most numbers conclude with a song. Many composers represented. (Sl)
Orpheon. Album für Gesang mit Pianoforte, ed. T. Täglichsbeck, 7 vols Stuttgart, 1842. (Sl)

Section 3

Abeille, L. *Acht Lieder*, Leipzig, c. 1797. No. 1 = 'Kennst du das Land?'
―――― *Gedichte von L.H.C. Hölty*, Stuttgart, c. 1800 (Sl)
―――― *Der Jüngling am Bache*, Leipzig, 1812 (Mbs)
Abenheim, J. *Sechs Göthe Lieder*, Stuttgart, n.d. (Sl)
―――― *Sechs Lieder*, opus 2, Leipzig, 1830 (Sl)
―――― *Dein Bild* (= Heine's 'Wenn ich auf dem Lager liege'), first published in *Europa* in 1836. Edition used: *Orpheon*, no. 169 (Sl)
Abt, F.W. *Abt-Album* . . ., vols 1/2, Leipzig, 1878. (Bu) A typical example of a rather sentimental and derivative kind of composer who abounded at the time. Many of his songs sound like watered-down Mendelssohn.
d'Albert, Eugen *Zehn Lieder*, opus 3, Berlin and Posen, c. 1886 (Lbl)
―――― *Sechs Lieder*, opus 19, Berlin, 1899 (Sl)
André, Jean Baptiste *Acht Lieder*, opus 14, Offenbach, 1853 (Mbs)
―――― *Acht Lieder*, opus 15, Offenbach, 1853 (Mbs)

Select Bibliography

―――― *Sechs Lieder im Volkston*, opus 41, Offenbach, *c.* 1871 (B)
André, Johann *Lieder, Arien und Duette beym Klavier*, 2 parts, Berlin, 1780–2
―――― *Neue Sammlung von Liedern* . . ., 2 parts, Berlin, 1783–4
―――― *Lieder am Clavier*, Berlin, *c.* 1800
Arlberg, F. *Vier Lieder*, opus 14. Copenhagen, n.d. (Bds) Clearly shows Liszt's influence.
Assmuss, J.K.G. *Lieder für Gesellschaft und Einsamkeit*, Riga, *c.* 1795
Auserlesene geistliche Lieder von Kloppstock (sic!), Cramer, Lavater und anderen berühmten Dichtern . . ., Zürich, 1775
Auserlesene moralische Lieder von den neusten und besten Dichtern . . ., Zürich, 1776. See too under *Fortsetzung*.
Bach, C.P.E. *Herrn Professor Gellerts Geistliche Oden und Lieder* . . ., 1758. I have used the 4th edn, Berlin, 1771.
―――― *Herrn Doctor Cramers übersetzte Psalmen* . . ., Leipzig, 1774. There are many Lieder by Bach in the various early compilations of Berlin song and in the *Göttinger Musenalmanach*. There is a modern selection by Herman Roth (Peters, 1921).
Bach, J.C.F. *Musikalische Nebenstunden*, 3 parts, Rinteln, 1787. I have seen part 1 only.
Bach, J.E. *Sammlung auserlesener Fabeln*, 1749 (= *DDT* i, 42)
Bachmann, Gottlob *Des Mädchen's Klage* (Schiller's 'Der Eichwald brauset'), Augsburg, 1799. A very competently written early through-composed song. By contrast, his setting of Bürger's *Lenardo und Blandine* (opus 37, *c.* 1803) lacks all unity. (copy in Gs)
Baehr, Otto *Sechs Lieder* (no opus), Leipzig, 1841. (B) No. 6 is to the same text as the opening song of Schubert's *Die schöne Müllerin* and is unabashed plagiarism.
Bagge, S. *Vier Lieder* (= 2. Folge der Lieder-Sammlung), Mainz, 1859 No. 4 = Heine's 'Fichtenbaum' (Bu)
―――― *Sechs Gedichte von Goethe*, opus 18, Leipzig and Brussels, *c.* 1885. (Lbl) Seems deliberately to have avoided the obvious texts.
Banck, Carl *Deutsche Volkslieder*, 2 Hefte, Leipzig, 1836 (Bds)
―――― *Des Leiermanns Liederbuch*, opus 21, Leipzig, *c.* 1837. (Bds) No. 1 = Wilhelm Müller's 'Leiermann', another plagiarism of Schubert.
―――― *24 Lieder und Gesänge*, opus 70, Leipzig, *c.* 1860. Includes several Mörike-settings. (Bds)
Bauer, G.C. *Zwölf Lieder* . . ., Hof, 1785. Theologian and amateur composer.
Baum, Catharine *Hör' ich das Liedchen klingen* (no opus), Berlin, 1869 (B)
―――― *Zwei Lieder*, opus 7, Berlin, 1874. (B) Texts by Goethe.
―――― *Fünf deutsche Lieder* (no opus), Berlin and Posen, mid '70s. (B) A celebrated singer, but not very skilful at matching musical stresses and poetic accents.
Baumbach, F.A. *Lyrische Gedichte vermischten Inhalts mit Melodien*, Leipzig, 1792. Contains a setting of 'Die Forelle' with the moralising final stanza which Schubert omitted.
Baumgartner, W. *Eine Frühlingsliebe. Liederkreis* . . ., 2 Hefte, opus 12, Leipzig, 1853. (Bu) The harmonies are sometimes too lush for the texts.
Becher, A.J. *Acht Gedichte*, opus 1, Elberfeld, *c.* 1834 (Lbl)

Select Bibliography

Beck, F.A. *Sammlung schöner Lieder mit Melodien*, Frankfurt, Hanau and Leipzig, 1775
Becker, Albert *Sechs Lieder*, opus 7, Leipzig, 1877. (Lbl) The best is no. 4, a setting of Heine's creepy little poem, 'Am Kreuzweg wird begraben'.
Becker, Fritz, *Fünf Gesänge*, opus 5, Schwerin, c. 1878 (Hmb)
Beethoven, L. van *Werke. Vollständige kritisch durchgesehene Ausgabe*, Breitkopf & Härtel, photo reprint, 1949. The songs are in *Serie* 23.
Behn, Hermann *Fünf Gesänge*, opus 2, Leipzig, 1892. (Bds) Best when he writes 'im Volkston'; otherwise tends to 'over-compose'.
Bellermann, H. *Sechs Lieder*, opus 10, Berlin, 1866. (Lbl). Technically accomplished songs without much originality.
Benda, Georg *Sammlung Vermischter Clavier- und Gesangstücke für geübte und ungeübte Spieler*, 6 parts, Leipzig, 1780 ff. There are also many songs by Benda in the *Göttinger Musenalmanach*.
Benecken, F.B. *Lieder und Gesänge für fühlende Seelen*, Hannover, 1787
Benkert, G.F. *Drei deutsche Lieder*, opus 1, Stuttgart and New York, 1855 (Bds)
——— *Zwei deutsche Lieder*, opus 9, Stuttgart and New York, 1855 (Sl)
——— *Drei Bariton-Lieder*, opus 13, Stuttgart and New York, 1855 (Sl)
——— *Sechs kleine Lieder*, opus 26, Berlin and New York, c. 1857. (Bds)
Like Behn, best when composing in a simple Volkston.
Bennat, F. *Altdeutsche Minnelieder*, 3 Hefte, Vienna, 1872 (Mbs)
Berg, Alban *Zwei Lieder*, UE 12241, Vienna, 1955. The 1900 and 1925 versions of Storm's 'Schliesse mir die Augen beide'.
Berger, Ludwig *Gesänge aus einem gesellschaftlichen Liederspiele 'Die schöne Müllerin'* . . ., opus 11, 1819. Edition used: Leipzig, c. 1841 (Mbs)
——— *Deutsche Gesaenge mit Begleitung des Fortepiano*, Karlsruhe, 1823. (Sl) No. 3 is a simple, ballad-like version of 'Kennst du das Land?'
——— *Zehn Lieder*, opus 27 (= *Sämmtliche Lieder, Gesänge und Balladen, 1. Lieferung*). Edition: Leipzig, c. 1840 (Lbl)
——— *Dreizehn Lieder* (= *Sämmtliche Lieder* . . ., *5. Lieferung*), Leipzig, 1841. (Bu) Contains opus 13 and 35. See too Bibliography, Section 5.
Berger, Wilhelm *Lieder und Gesänge*, opus 16, Bremen, 1885 (Hmb)
Berls, J.R. *Neue Volkslieder fürs Klavier*, Leipzig, 1797
Bischoff, Hermann *25 neue Weisen zu alten Liedern*, opus 15, Leipzig, 1903. A good example of how folk poems were re-composed to provide Hausmusik.
Blasser, G. *Lieder und Gesänge*, opus 70, Offenbach, c. 1890. (B) Includes Heine's 'Fichtenbaum' set in a way reminiscent of Liszt's treatment.
Blumenlese: see Boßler.
Bode, J.J.C. *Zärtliche und Schertzhaffte Lieder* . . ., 2 parts, Leipzig, 1754-7
Bolck, O. *Sechs Lieder*, opus 5, Leipzig, 1866. (Bds) No. 1 is 'Nur wer die Sehnsucht kennt'; Bolck captures the atmosphere of longing well.
Boßler, H.P. (ed.) *Blumenlese für Klavierliebhaber* . . ., 4 Jahrgänge, Speier, 1782-4 and 1787. A mixture of piano solos and songs, mostly by South German composers, some of whom show a striking awareness of the dynamic possibilities of the new fortepiano.
Brahms, J. *Sämtliche Werke*, Breitkopf & Härtel, repr. Michigan, 1949. The songs are in vols 23-6.

Select Bibliography

Brambach, C.J. *Sechs Lieder*, opus 4, Leipzig, 1861. (KNmi) No. 3 is a setting of Eichendorff's 'Dein Bildnis wunderselig', also set by Schumann (opus 39,2).

Brandl, J. *Sechs Lieder von Schubart und anderen Dichtern. Zum Singen beym Klavier durchaus in Musik gesetzt*, Heilbronn, 1793

Brede, S.F. *Lieder und Gesänge am Klavier zu singen*, Offenbach, 1786

Breidenstein, H.K. *Romanzen und Lieder*, 2 Hefte, Frankfurt a/M, 1833. (KNmi) Includes settings of Goethe and Wilhelm Müller.

Breitkopf, B.T. *Neue Lieder in Melodien gesetzt*, Leipzig, 1770. Some of the earliest Goethe-settings.

Bronsart, Ingeborg v. *Die Loreley* . . ., Mainz, 1865. (Mbs) A through-composed setting, not unlike Liszt's in its general form.

Bruch, Max His songs do not form an important part of his output. Some are to be found in *66 Lieder neuerer Meister*, Leipzig, c. 1880.

Bruyck, Carl v. *3 Lieder Gretchens aus Goethes Faust*, Leipzig, 1900 (Mbs)

Bülow, Hans v. *Fünf Lieder*, opus 5, Munich, 1865 (Mbs)

────── *Der König von Thule. Gedicht von Göthe, im Volkstone*, Munich, 1925. To be sung either unaccompanied on stage or to the piano. Composed and first published in 1869.

Bürde, Jeanette *Gesaenge*, opus 7, Magdeburg, c. 1850 (B)

────── *Gesaenge*, opus 9, Magdeburg, c. 1850. (B) One of those who wrote agitated and complex accompaniments which mask a nondescript vocal line.

Bungert, A. *Bungert-Album. Lieder und Gesänge*, Leipzig and Berlin, 1892 (KNmi)

────── *Lieder. Auswahl*, 3 vols, Dresden, 1903 (Sl)

────── *Lieder*, 3 vols. Freiburg, 1981

Burgmüller, N. *6 Gesänge*, opus 3, Leipzig, 1837 (Mbs)

────── *5 Deutsche Lieder*, opus 6, Leipzig, 1838 (Mbs)

────── *Fünf Gesänge*, opus 10, Leipzig, 1840 (Lbl)

────── *Ausgewählte Lieder*, ed. Willi Kahl, Mönchengladbach, 1927. Burgmüller died at the age of 26 in 1836; most of his songs were published posthumously. He was of a melancholy disposition and was drawn to gloomy texts. A very interesting minor composer.

Burkhard, Willy *Neun Lieder nach Gedichten von Christian Morgenstern*, opus 70, Bärenreiter, 1947

Burmann, G.W. *Monatliche Clavier-Unterhaltungen*, Berlin, 1779

Cläpius, W. *Fünf Gesänge*, opus 6, Berlin, c. 1838. (Mbs) Agreeable, undemanding drawing-room songs.

Claudius, G.C. *Lieder für Kinder*, Frankfurt, a/M, 1780

Clemens, C.G. *Lieder fürs Clavier*, Berlin, 1790. One of the more amateurish of the amateur composers of the day.

Commer, Franz *Vier Gesänge*, n.p. 1843. (BNu) No. 2 is one of the best settings of Goethe's 'Heiß mich nicht reden' known to me. Commer also set poems by Heine. The best is 'Ich stand gelehnet an den Mast', opus 25,2, first published in 1852. Copy used: *Orpheon*, no. 167. (Sl)

Cornelius, Peter *Musikalische Werke*. Gesamtausgabe von Max Hasse, repr. 1971

Curschmann, F. *Curschmann-Album* . . ., Leipzig, c. 1872. Curschmann, who died in 1841, published most of his songs 1832–40. An able composer who set, among other things, texts by Goethe, Heine and Wilhelm Müller. The best single song that I have come across is 'Danksagung', opus 5,1 (1833). This poem also provides the text for no. 4 of *Die schöne Müllerin*.

Damcke, B. *Sechs Gesänge*, opus 9, Bonn, *c.* 1838 (Bds)

——— *Sechs Gesänge*, opus 11, Bonn, *c.* 1838. (Bds) A genuine melodic gift combined with expressive piano-writing and occasional harmonic piquancies make him a very pleasing song-composer. The Heine-settings are especially good.

Danzi, F. *Sechs Deutsche Lieder*, opus 14, Munich, *c.* 1803 (Mbs)

——— *vi Deutsche Lieder*, opus 19, Munich, *c.* (Mbs) These collections include some good Goethe-settings in a simple, slightly folkish style.

Decker, C. *Drei Gedichte von E. Geibel*, opus 28, Leipzig, *c.* 1850 (Bds)

Degele, E. *Der Fischer*, opus 11, Leipzig, *c.* 1874. (Bds) One of the better of the through-composed settings of this Goethe ballad.

Deprosse, A. *Drei Lieder im Volkston*, opus 9, Leipzig, *c.* 1865. (Bds) No. 2 is a wistful setting of Mörike's 'Ein Stündlein wohl vor Tag', unusual in that it is in the Phrygian mode.

Deurer, E. *Drei Lieder*, opus 11, Leipzig and Weimar, 1871 (Lbl)

Dietrich, Albert *Fünf Lieder von Göthe*, opus 12, Winterthur, *c.* 1860. (Bds) No. 1 ('März') shows how well Goethe's simpler poems lend themselves to composition 'im Volkston'.

Dietrichstein, M. v *xvi Lieder von Göthe*, Vienna, *c.* 1810. (Mbs) Some are simple to the point of banality. Best: nos. 8 ('Wechsel') and 11 ('Der du von dem Himmel bist').

'Dilettant aus Schwaben', *Unterhaltungen beym Clavier* . . ., Leipzig and Winterthur, 1778. Good texts, hopeless settings.

Dorn, Heinrich *Sechs deutsche Lieder*, opus 9, Leipzig, *c.* 1831. (Mbs) No. 5 is an eloquent setting of Heine's 'Wenn ich in deine Augen seh'.

Draeseke, F. *Vier Lieder*, opus 81, Dresden, 1906. (KNmi) Contains a very forceful setting of Mörike's 'Denk' es, o Seele'.

Dressler, E.C. *Freundschaft und Liebe in Melodischen Liedern*, Nuremberg, 1774

Droste-Hülshoff, Annette v. *Lieder und Gesänge*, ed. K.G. Fellerer, Münster, 1954. Germany's greatest poetess — but an amateurish composer.

Eberl, Anton *Gesaenge mit Begleitung des Pianoforte*, opus 23, Vienna *c.* 1810. (Wgm) Two, including Goethe's 'Der Fischer', in *DTÖ*, 79.

Eberwein, Carl *Lieder aus Goethe's West-oestlichen* (sic!) *Divan*, 2 Hefte, Hamburg, *c.* 1821. (Mbs) One of the very few early nineteenth-century attempts at these poems.

Eggers, Gustav *Zwei Lieder*, opus 3, Hamburg, 1858. (Mbs) No. 2 is an exciting setting of Heine's 'Mit schwarzen Segeln . . .'

——— *Sechs Lieder im Volkston*, opus 10, Leipzig and Wintertur, 1861 (Bds)

Egli, J.H. *Singcompositionen* . . ., 2 parts, Zürich, 1785–6. Includes some songs by J.J. Walder.

——— *Musicalische Blumenlese* . . ., Zürich, 1786. An anthology of songs by *German* composers.

——— *Schweizerlieder* . . ., Zürich, 1787

Select Bibliography

Ehlers, Wilhelm 'Schäfers Klage', 1801. This setting of Goethe's poem became so famous that it figures in virtually all the anthologies of German song throughout the nineteenth century.

Ehlert, L. *Fünf Lieder*, opus 2, Berlin, 1847. (Mbs) No. 4 is Mörike's 'Das verlassene Mägdlein', here entitled 'Am Feuer'.

──── *Sechs Lieder*, opus 14, Leipzig, 1850 (Mbs)

──── *Fünf Lieder*, opus 30, Leipzig, *c.* 1864 (Mbs)

Eicken *Lieder für das Klavier*, Mannheim, 1793. One of the less successful imitators of Schulz.

Eidenbenz (ed.) *Musikalischer Potpourri* . . ., 5 Hefte, Stuttgart, 1790–1. Each volume contains a mixture of piano solos and songs. Contributors include Abeille, Eidenbenz himself, Schubart and Zumsteeg.

Eisler, Hanns *Ausgewählte Lieder*, 5 vols. Leipzig, 1975

Endter, C.F. *Lieder zum Scherz und Zeitvertreib*, Hamburg, 1757

Engel, Carl, *Drei Lieder*, opus 5, Berlin, *c.* 1843. Nos. 2 and 3 are settings of Wilhelm Müller texts which also figure in *Die schöne Müllerin* (nos. 9 and 3 respectively). (B)

Esser, Heinrich *Des Saengers Fluch*, opus 8, Mainz, *c.* 1843. A very able through-composed setting of Uhland's ballad.

Eunike, I.F. *Sechs Deutsche Lieder*, Berlin, *c.* 1810 (Bu)

Evers, Carl *Gedichte von Lenau*, opus 11, Vienna, *c.* 1841. (Mbs) No. 1 is a setting of the very popular text, 'Bitte'.

Fesca, Alexander *Fesca-Album. 48 Lieder und Gesänge*, Brunswick, *c.* 1853. (Mbs) Contains some good Heine and Mörike-settings. A posthumous collection; Fesca had died in 1849.

Fesca, F.E. *Sechs deutsche Lieder*, Bonn and Cologne, 1822. (Bu) This is Alexander's father.

Fielitz, Alexander v. *Lieder und Gesänge*, 4 vols, Leipzig, 1899 (first published 1893). (Hmb) This collection shows that Fielitz was slow to find his own style . . .

──── *Sechs Gedichte*, opus 67, Magdeburg, 1897. (Mbs) . . . and this reveals that he had found it. No. 3 is one of the best of the many settings of Heine's 'Fichtenbaum'.

Fink, Christian *Fünf Lieder*, opus 7, Leipzig, *c.* 1866 (Sl)

──── *Fünf Lieder*, opus 12, Leipzig, *c.* 1866. (Sl) Some good settings of texts by Goethe and Heine. Apparently no relative of the more famous G.W.F.

Fischer, G.E. *Zwölf Lieder von Goethe, Tiek* (sic!), *Klopstock und Matthison*, Berlin, 1820. (DÜk) No. 2 is Klopstock's 'Cidli, du weinest'.

Flaschner, G.B. *Zwanzig Lieder vermischten Inhalts*, Zittau and Leipzig, 1789

Fleischer, F.G. *Oden und Lieder mit Melodien*, 2 parts, Leipzig, 1756–7. I have used the second (1762) edition of Part 1.

──── *Sammlung größerer und kleinerer Singstücke* . . ., Brunswick, 1788

Flörke, F.J. *Oden und Lieder von verschiedenen Dichtern*, Bützow and Wismar, 1779. An amateur composer of very uneven talent.

Flügel, Gustav *Acht Lieder*, opus 3, Stettin, 1842 (Wn)

Foerster, E.A. *12 neue deutsche Lieder*, Vienna, *c.* 1791

Forkel, J.N. *Herr Gleims neue Lieder* . . ., Göttingen, 1773. Forkel was

Select Bibliography

more eminent as scholar than as composer; many of these songs are unappealing and 'unvocal'.

Fortner, W. *Vier Gesänge nach Worten von Hölderlin*, Mainz, 1940

Fortsetzung Auserlesener moralischer Lieder . . ., Zürich, 1780

Franz, Robert There is no collected edition, but various selections were published in the late nineteenth and early twentieth centuries. I have therefore simply given opus-numbers.

Freystädter, F.J. *Sechs Lieder der besten deutschen Dichter*, Vienna, 1795

Friberth, Karl and Hofmann, Leopold *Sammlung Deutscher Lieder für das Klavier*, Vienna, 1780. Many in *DTÖ*, 54.

Fröhlich, Th. *Acht deutsche Canzonetten*, opus 3, Berlin, *c.* 1828 (Bu)

—— *Sechs Lieder für eine Altstimme*, opus 8, Leipzig, 1830. (Bu) A composer of tempestuous and melancholy disposition who died in 1836 at the age of 33. Criticised for reckless harmonic experimentation in his day.

Fuß, Johann *Gesänge*, opus 16, Leipzig, 1813. (Wgm) One given in *DTÖ*, 79.

Gabler, C.A. *vi Lieder mit Begleitung des Piano-Forte*, opus 14, Leipzig, 1795

—— *Deutsche Gesänge, 6. Sammlung*, opus 36, Leipzig, 1816 (Wgm)

—— *Deutsche Gesänge, 7. Sammlung*, opus 37, Leipzig, *c.* 1818. (Wgm) Melodious songs with very idiomatic accompaniments.

Gernsheim, F. *Sechs Lieder*, opus 3, Leipzig, 1865. (Mbs) Uneven, but no. 6 (Uhland's 'Heimkehr') is very good.

Gluck, C.W. *Klopstock's Oden und Lieder*, composed early 1770s. Some were published in the *Göttinger Musenalmanach* in 1774–5, the rest *c.* 1780. Edition used: *Lieder und Oden mit Begleitung des Pianoforte*, Berlin, 1840.

Glück, J.L.F. (Friedrich) *Lieder für eine Singstimme*, Munich, *c.* 1814. (Bds) No. 7 is Eichendorff's 'Das zerbrochene Ringlein' which achieved huge popularity.

Görner, J.V. *Sammlung neuer Oden und Lieder*, 3 parts, 1742–52. Modern edition: *DDT*, i, 57, One of the liveliest and most individual of the early song-composers.

Göttinger Musenalmanach, Göttingen, 1770–1804. Contains many songs by C.P.E. Bach, Benda, Gluck, F.W. Weis and others of poems by Bürger, Hölty, Klopstock, Voß, etc. Modern reprint: Hildesheim, 1979.

Göttsching, R. *Fürs Haus. Lieder mit Pianofortebegleitung*, Leipzig, 1913 (B)

Goetz, Hermann Many editions and selections. Among the best songs are settings of Mörike's 'Das verlassene Mägdlein' (opus 12,5) and Goethe's 'Der du von dem Himmel bist' (opus 19,6): 1876 and 1879 respectively.

Goldschmidt, A. v. *Lieder für eine Singstimme mit Klavierbegleitung* (no opus), Berlin, n.d. (Hmb)

Graedener, C.G.P. *Herbstklänge. Sieben Lieder*, opus 50, Leipzig and Winterthur, 1867. (Bds) See too Bibliography, Section 4.

Gräfe, J.F. (ed.) *Samlung* (sic!) *verschiedener und auserlesener Oden* . . ., 4 parts, Halle, 1737–43. Songs by C.P.E. Bach, Gräfe himself, Graun and others.

—— *Fünfzig Psalmen* . . ., Brunswick and Leipzig, 1760

Select Bibliography

Graener, Paul *Sieben Galgenlieder* . . ., Berlin, 1917
―― *Neue Galgenlieder* . . ., 1922. Repr. Wiesbaden, 1959. One of several composers who have tried to match Morgenstern's *Galgenhumor* in song.
Gräser, T.C.G. *Gesänge mit Clavier-Begleitung für Frauenzimmer*, Leipzig, 1785
Graun, C.H. (ed.) *Auserlesene Oden zum Singen beym Clavier* . . ., 1. und 2. Sammlung, Berlin, 1764. Songs by Benda, Graun himself, Quantz and others. Typical collection of early strophic songs. Some still have figured bass.
Greith, Carl *Acht Lieder*, opus 41, Munich, 1888. (Bds) No. 3 = Eichendorff's 'Dein Bildnis wunderselig', an original setting with irregular phrase-lengths. Posthumous publication: Greith had died in 1887.
Grönland, P. *Lieder, Balladen und Romanzen von Göthe*, Leipzig, 1817. (Wgm) Still visibly influenced by Schulz's Volkston.
Grosheim, G.C. *Sammlung teutscher Gedichte*, opus 4, Mainz, 1787
―― *Sammlung teutscher Gedichte* (2nd part), Mainz, *c.* 1792
―― *Sammlung teutscher Gedichte* (4th part), Cassel, *c.* 1805
―― *Sammlung teutscher Gedichte* (5th part), Cassel (before 1810)
―― *Sammlung teutscher Gedichte* (6th part), Brunswick (before 1813). (All LÜh)
Gruber, G.W. *Des Herrn Bürgers Gedichte für das Klavier und die Singstimme gesezt* (sic!), 2 parts, Nuremberg, 1780
Grund, F.W. *Sechs Lieder von Goethe*, Hamburg, *c.* 1820. (Lbl) No. 4 ('Am Flusse') is very good.
Grünwald, J.J. *Erste Sammlung Zwölf deutscher Lieder für das Klavier oder Fortepiano*, Vienna, 1785. Seven in *DTÖ*, 54.
Gumbert, F. *Drei Lieder für eine Baßstimme*, opus 3, Berlin, 1843 (Bu)
―― *Drei Lieder*, opus 13, Vienna, *c.* 1846 (B)
―― *Fünf Lieder*, opus 67, Breslau, 1855 (Bds)
―― *Gumbert-Album. Ausgewählte Lieder*, Leipzig, *c.* 1897. (Bu) Contains various opus numbers. Some of Gumbert's Heine-settings are intensely atmospheric.
Hackel, J.C. *Sammlung Achtzehn Deutscher Lieder*, Vienna, 1786. 3 in *DTÖ*, 54.
Häßler, J.W. *Clavier- und Singstücke verschiedener Art*, 2 parts, Erfurt and Leipzig, 1782-6
Häußler, E. *vi Gedichte von Friedrich Matthison*, Zürich, 1793
―― *xii Lieder beym Clavier zu singen*, Zürich, 1793
―― *vi Gedichte von J.G. von Salis*, Zürich, 1796
―― *Sechs Gedichte von Carl Witte*, Zürich, 1798
―― *Gedicht Kennst du das Land* . . . ? *aus Wilhelm Meisters Lehr-Jahren von Goethe* . . ., Augsburg, n.d.
Hartmann, L. *Lieder und Gesänge*, 3 Hefte, Dresden, *c.* 1860. (B) Many Heine-settings.
Hasse, Gustav An interesting composer who set many folk poems and much Heine. Edition seen: opus 6-21 and 22-31 bound into 2 vols, Berlin, 1877. (Bds)
Hauptmann, Moritz *Sechs deutsche Lieder*, opus 22, Leipzig, 1834 (Mbs)

Select Bibliography

―――― *Kennst du das Land?* opus 37, c. 1852. Edition used: *Beliebte Lieder und Arien*, Cologne, n.d. (KNmi) A graceful song-composer, some of whose Goethe-settings are very good in their simple lyrical vein.
Hausius, C.G. *Frohe und gesellige Lieder für das Clavier*, Leipzig, 1794
Haydn, Josef *Werke*, Munich-Duisburg, 1960. The songs are in series xxix, vol. 1.
Heinemann, Karl *Zwölf Lieder von Geibel*, opus 8, Bremen, 1846. (Bds) No. 7 is a good setting of the very popular 'Wenn sich zwei Herzen scheiden'.
Hemmleb, R. *Feldblumen. Dreißig Lieder im Volkston*, opus 8, 6 Hefte, Langensalza, 1913 (Bds)
Hensel, Fanny (née Mendelssohn-Bartholdy) *Sechs Lieder*, opus 7, Berlin and Breslau, 1847. (DÜk) No. 5 = Lenau's 'Bitte'.
―――― *Sechs Lieder*, opus 9, Leipzig, n.d. (posth. c. 1850?). (Bds) No. 5 = 'Die frühen Gräber'.
Herbing, A.B.V. *Musikalische Belustigungen*, Leipzig, 1758
―――― *Musikalischer Versuch in Fabeln* . . ., 1759. Modern edition: *DDT* i, 42.
Hertel, J.W. *Musik zu Vier und zwanzig neuen Oden und Liedern* . . ., Rostock, 1760
Hertz, Hedwig *Zwölf Lieder von Heinrich Heine*, Berlin, c. 1867. (B) Some originality, but also some harmonic miscalculations.
Herzog, S. *Vier Lieder* (no opus), Berlin and Posen, c. 1885 (B)
Herzogenberg, H.v. *Fünf Lieder*, opus 29, Leipzig and Winterthur, 1881. (Bu) Includes beautiful and sombre compositions to texts by Lenau and Mörike.
―――― *Fünf Lieder*, opus 30, Leipzig and Winterthur, 1881 (Bu)
Hesse, J.H. *Lieder zum unschuldigen Vergnügen*, Lübeck, 1757
Hessenberg, Kurt *Wunderhorn-Lieder* . . . 2 Hefte, Vienna and Leipzig, 1924
Hetsch, L. 'Das verlassene Mägdlein' in *Musikbeilage zu Maler Nolten*, Stuttgart, 1832. (Sl) The first of innumerable settings.
―――― 'Hör' ich das Liedchen klingen': *Musikbeilage* to Lewald's periodical *Europa* (1840). (Mbs) A gentle and muted setting.
Heubner, K. *Fünf Lieder*, opus 4, Leipzig, 1885 (Bds)
Heymann-Rheineck, C. *Sechs Lieder*, opus 2, Berlin, 1882. (Hmb) Nos. 2 and 6 are Goethe-settings: 'Nur wer die Sehnsucht kennt' and 'Am Fluße'.
―――― *Vier Lieder*, opus 7, Berlin, 1877. (Hmb) No. 2 is Mörike's 'Das verlassene Mädchen' (sic!).
Hille, C.F. The complete songs can be found in two volumes in Gs, together with the composer's handwritten catalogue. The songs date mostly from 1850–70. Texts in the main are trivial.
Hiller, Ferdinand *Neuer Frühling* . . ., opus 16, Leipzig, 1833. (Hmb) Heine-settings.
―――― *Neue Gesänge*, opus 100, 3 Hefte, Leipzig, 1879. (Mbs) Heft ii, 5 = Mörike's 'Um Mitternacht'. First published c. 1866.
―――― *Sechs Lieder*, opus 204, Leipzig, 1885. (Lbl) No. 1 = Goethe's 'An den Mond'.
―――― *Hiller-Album*, Bremen, n.d. (Bu) No. 15 = 'Nur wer die

Select Bibliography

Sehnsucht kennt'; no. 23 = 'Über allen Gipfeln'. A different — and fussier — version of the latter poem is given by Friedlaender from a manuscript copy in Weimar: *Gedichte von Goethe*, ii, no. 62.

Hiller, Johann Adam *Lieder für Kinder*, Leipzig, 1769
—— *Lieder mit Melodien*, Leipzig, 1772
—— *Lieder und Arien aus Sophiens Reise* . . ., Leipzig, 1779
—— *Religiöse Oden und Lieder* . . ., Hamburg, 1790
—— *Letztes Opfer in einigen Lieder-Melodien* . . . Leipzig, 1790

Hillmer, G.F. *Oden und Lieder Moralischen Inhalts* . . ., Frankfurt an der Oder, 1781

Himmel, F.H. *Sechs Lieder von Göthe*, opus 21, Leipzig, *c*. 1807 (DÜk)
—— *Drey Lieder*, opus 36, Leipzig, 1810. (Sl) Pretty, but rather characterless songs.

Hinrichs, F. *Lieder*, opus 7, 2 Hefte, Leipzig, *c*. 1879. (Hmb) Contains Goethe, Mörike and folk poems.

Hitzelberg, M.J. *Für fülende* (sic!) *Seelen am Klavier*, 1. Sammlung, Vienna, 1784

Hobein, J.F. *Lieder mit Melodien für das Clavier*. 1. und 2. Sammlung, Wolfenbüttel, 1778-9. Prominent piano part with liberal use of expression marks for that age.

Hoffmann, Adolf *Zehn Gesänge*, opus 5, Leipzig, 1884. (Lbl) No. 3 is a beautiful setting of Lenau's 'Bitte' (here called 'Gebet').

Hoffmann, H.A. *Gesänge beim Klavier* . . ., opus 4, Offenbach, 1799. A pleasing collection which seems to occupy a position halfway between Schulz and the simpler kind of Schubert song.

Hofmann, Leopold See under Friberth.

Holländer, A. *Sechs Lieder im Volkston*, opus 6, 1864. Edition used: Leipzig, 1882. (Bds)

Holstein, F. v. *Vier Lieder*, opus 24, Leipzig, 1870. (Bu) No. 1 = Mörike's 'Frage und Antwort', a much more serene reading of the poem than Wolf's.
—— *Fünf Romanzen*, opus 29, Leipzig, 1872 (Bu)
—— *Fünf Lieder*, opus 31, Leipzig, 1872 (Bu)
—— *Fünf Lieder*, opus 37, Leipzig, 1877 (Bu)
—— *39 Lieder und Gesänge*, Leipzig, *c*. 1902 (Hmb)

Holzer, J. *Lieder mit Begleitung des Fortepiano*, Leipzig, 1779
—— *xii deutsche Lieder*, Vienna, 1787. Several songs in *DTÖ* 54.

Hoven See under Püttlingen.

Huber, Joseph *Zwei Lieder*, opus 13, Stuttgart, 1879. No. 2 = Heine's 'Wenn zwei von einander scheiden'.
—— *Zwei Lieder*, opus 14, Stuttgart, 1879. No. 1 = Heine's 'Am fernen Horizonte'.
—— *Drei Lieder*, opus 17, Stuttgart, 1885
—— *Vier Lieder* (no opus), Leipzig, 1865. Nos. 1 and 3 are to texts by Heine. In general, the most imaginative of Huber's songs are the Heine-settings. (all Sl)

Hummel, Ferdinand *Vier Lieder*, opus 6, Berlin, *c*. 1875 (Bds)

Hummel, J.B. *Zwölf deutsche lieder* . . ., 2. Auflage, Berlin, *c*. 1880

Hurka, F.F. *Scherz und Ernst in xii Liedern*, Dresden, 1789
—— *15 deutsche Lieder* . . ., Berlin, 1797

Select Bibliography

———— *Neu-Jahrs Geschenk in Sechs Liedern* . . ., Oranienburg, 1799. The piano accompaniments are often quite elaborate.

Jansen, Gustav *Musikalisches Goethe-Album*, 6 Hefte, Magdeburg, 1863. (Bds) Very uneven. The best is ii, 2 ('An die Türen will ich schleichen').

Jensen, Adolf *Sechs Lieder*, opus 23, Leipzig, *c.* 1863. (KNmi) Includes 'Der König in Thule' (pp. 21-3).

———— *Alt Heidelberg, du feine! Konzertlied*, opus 34, Leipzig, *c.* 1876 (KNmi)

———— *Sechs Lieder* (no opus), Berlin, 1882. (Mbs) No. 6 = Goethe's 'Kennst du das Land?'. There are, in addition, various selections of Jensen's songs, including one by Friedlaender, Leipzig, n.d.

Jensen, W.G.M. *Fünfzehn Deutsche Lieder* . . ., *Neue Auflage*, Königsberg, 1799

Käsermann, N. *Geistliche Oden und Lieder von C.F. Gellert*, Bern, 1804

Kahn, Robert *Kahn-Album* . . ., Leipzig, 1901. (Bu) The songs contained here were originally published in the 1880s and 90s. Some Mörike and Uhland.

Kallenbach, G.E.C. *Oden und Lieder zum Singen beym Klavier* . . ., Magdeburg, 1796

Kauffmann, E.F. *Lieder und Gesänge*, 6 Hefte, Stuttgart, 1857-68. (Sl) Good taste in poetry, uneven touch as a composer. The setting of Lenau's 'Bitte' (Heft v, 3) is simple and very beautiful.

Kayser, P.C. *Vermischte Lieder mit Melodien*, Winterthur, 1775

———— *Gesänge mit Begleitung des Claviers*, Leipzig and Winterthur. 1777. Includes some of the earliest Goethe-settings.

———— 'Um Friede' (= Goethe's 'Der du von dem Himmel bist'), first published in 1780. Appeared in almost all the popular anthologies of song throughout the nineteenth century.

Keller, J.G. *Lieder einiger neuer deutscher Dichter*, Dessau, 1782

Kempe, Fr. *Drei Deutsche Lieder*, opus 12, Paris and Leipzig, 1863 (Lbl)

Kienlen, J.C. *Zwölf Lieder von Göthe*, Leipzig, 1810. (Wgm) The best are nos. 1 and 9 ('Heidenröslein' and 'Freudvoll und leidvoll').

Kinkel, Johanna *Sechs Lieder*, opus 6, Leipzig, *c.* 1837 (Bu)

———— *Sechs Lieder*, opus 7, Berlin, *c.* 1838 (Bu)

Kirchner, Th. *Zehn Lieder*, opus 1, 2 Hefte, Leipzig, *c.* 1843 (Bu)

———— *Sechs Lieder*, opus 81, Leipzig, *c.* 1887. (Hmb) Contains interesting settings of Goethe's 'Am Flusse' and Heine's 'Fichtenbaum' (nos. 3 and 4).

Kirnberger, J.P. *Oden mit Melodien*, Danzig, 1773

———— *Gesänge am Klavier*, Berlin and Leipzig, 1780. I have not seen this; Friedlaender gives two songs from it.

Kirsten, F. *Lieder für gesellige und einsame Freuden*, Leipzig, 1797. Observes a clear stylistic distinction between 'social' and 'private' song.

Kittl, J.F. *Drei Gesänge*, opus 16, Berlin, *c.* 1844. (Bds) I have not been able to locate a copy of his opus 23, referred to on p. 174.

Klein, Bernhard *Gesänge mit Begleitung des Pianoforte*, Leipzig, *c.* 1820

———— *viii Gedichte von Göthe*, Leipzig, *c.* 1820

———— *Neun Lieder von Göthe*, opus 15, Berlin, *c.* 1832

———— *Drei Nachtlieder von J. von Eichendorff*, opus 16, Berlin, n.d.

———— *Geistliche Lieder von Novalis*, opus 40, Berlin, n.d. All Lbl except

Select Bibliography

opus 15. (Bds) One of the ablest and in his day most respected of the early nineteenth-century song-composers.
Knab, Armin *Wunderhorn-Lieder*, Breitkopf & Härtel, 1921
———— *George-Lieder*, UE, 1925
———— *An eine Rose. Vier Lieder* . . ., Litolff, 1948.
Kozeluch, L. *xv Lieder* . . ., Mannheim and Munich, *c*. 1795
———— *xii Lieder mit Melodien* . . ., Vienna, *c*. 1798. *DTÖ* 54 has six of his songs.
Kraus, Joseph *Airs et Chansons pour le Clavecin*, Stockholm and Leipzig, *c*. 1785. Contains 15 Geman songs.
Krause, C.G. See under Ramler.
Krazeisen, Carl *Zehn Lieder*, opus 1, Munich, 1877 (Mbs)
Krenek, Ernst *Neun Lieder*, UE, 1924. Contains the Klopstock-setting referred to on p. 208.
———— *Fiedellieder* . . ., opus 64, UE, 1930. See too Bibliography. Section 4.
Kreutzer, Conradin *Sechs Lieder von Uhland*, opus 23, Berlin, by 1822 (KNmi)
———— *Zwölf Lieder und Romanzen*, 2 Hefte, opus 75, Leipzig, *c*. 1827 (Wgm)
———— 'Der Pilgrim. Gedicht von Schiller', in *Orpheon*, no. 88. (Sl) Greatly admired in his age, unjustly neglected today. See too Bibliography, Section 4.
Kriegel, C.F.W. (ed.) *xxxvi Lieder beym Clavier zu singen* . . ., 1. Sammlung, Dresden, 1790
———— *xxxviii Lieder beym Clavier zu singen* . . ., 2. Sammlung, Dresden, 1792. Songs by Naumann, Seydelmann and others.
Krufft, N. v. *Sammlung deutscher Lieder mit Begleitung des Claviers*, Vienna, 1812. (Wgm) 3 in *DTÖ* 79.
Kücken, F. *Zwei Gesänge*, opus 31, Leipzig, *c*. 1840 (Sl)
Kuntzen, A.C. *Lieder zum unschuldigen Zeitvertreib*, 3 parts: Hamburg, 1748; Lübeck, 1754; London, 1756
Kunzen, F.L.A. *Weisen und lyrische Gesänge*, Flensburg and Leipzig, 1788
———— *Hymne auf die Harmonie*, Zürich, 1795. An accomplished through-composed song. His setting of 'Lenore' is contained in *Balladen von G.A. Bürger*: see Bibliography, Section 1.
Lachner, Franz *Sängerfahrt*, 1–3. Lieferung, Vienna, *c*. 1830 (Mbs)
———— *Zwölf deutsche Gesänge*, 2 Hefte, opus 35, Vienna, *c*. 1833 (Bu)
———— *Deutsche Gesänge*, opus 49, Mainz, *c*. 1834 (Hmb)
Lammers, J. *25 Lieder und Gesänge*, Leipzig, mid-1870s. (Wn) Contains various opus numbers. Opus 8 dates from *c*. 1860.
Lang, E.J.B. *Einige Gedichte des Herrn G.A. Bürgers* . . ., Nuremberg, *c*. 1779
Lange, O.H. *Altdeutsche Lieder* . . ., Brunswick, n.d. (after 1877) (Mbs)
Lecerf, J.A. *Sechs Gesänge*, Leipzig, *c*. 1819. (Wgm) No. 3 is a graceful and flowing version of Goethe's 'An den Mond'.
————*Neun Gesänge zu Goethe's Faust*, Berlin, *c*. 1839. (Wgm) Some unusual choices, including part of Faust's soliloquy, lines 1178–85 and 1194–1201.
Lenz, Leopold *vii Gesaenge für eine Baßstimme*, opus 5, Munich, *c*. 1827

Select Bibliography

—— *Sechs Gesaenge*, opus 11, Munich, 1832
—— *Gesaenge und Lieder aus der Tragödie Faust von Goethe*, opus 14, 2 Hefte, Mainz, *c*. 1833. More expected choice of texts than Lecerf's.
—— *Deutsche Lieder und Gesaenge*, opus 21, Munich, *c*. 1837
—— *Lieder*, opus 26, Munich, *c*. 1840. (all Mbs) See too Bibliography, Section 4. At his best, Lenz is very good: see opus 5,1: 11,2; 26,2.
Leyding, J.D. *Oden und Lieder*, Altona, 1757
Lieder für den Landmann . . ., Zürich, 1773. Settings of Gleim.
Lieder, mit neuen Melodien, Anspach, 1756
Liszt, Franz *Musikalische Werke*, Leipzig and Berlin, repr. Gregg Press, 1966. For the songs, see section vii, vols 1–3.
Loewe, Karl *Balladen, Legenden, Lieder und Gesänge. Gesamtausgabe in 17 Bänden*, ed. Runze, Breitkopf & Härtel, 1899–1904
Lührss, Carl *Sechs Lieder* (no opus), Bonn, 1845. (B) Lührss was attacked in his day because of the difficulty and dominance of his accompaniments. I find the criticism somewhat exaggerated.
Machts, Carl *Vier Lieder*, opus 29, Leipzig, 1874 (Bds)
Mahler, Gustav There are so many editions of the *Wunderhorn* songs and the *Lieder eines fahrenden Gesellen* that it seems pointless to specify one.
Mangold, C.A. *Vier Lieder von Göthe*, opus 1, n.p., 1835
—— *Das Fischermaedchen*, opus 9, Darmstadt, 1839
—— *Liederkranz. Zwölf Lieder*, opus 26, Berlin, 1856
—— *5 Göthelieder*, opus 71, Darmstadt, 1878
—— *Sechs Lieder*, opus 74, Darmstadt, 1883. All DS except opus 26 (= B).
Marpurg, F.W. *Berlinische Oden und Lieder*, 1–3, Leipzig, 1756–63. Texts mainly light and playful; composers include C.P.E. Bach, Kirnberger, Krause, Marpurg himself and Nichelmann. Important for the early history of Berlin song.
—— *Geistliche, moralische und weltliche Oden* . . ., Berlin, 1758. Again, songs by Marpurg and others.
Marschner, Franz *Ausgewählte Lieder*, 7 Hefte, Vienna, *c*. 1900. (Wgm) Heft 2 contains the two 'Wandrers Nachtlieder', Heft 3 has 'Heidenröslein'.
Marschner, Heinrich *Lyra. Ein Liederkranz*, opus 8, Leipzig, *c*. 1817 (Bu)
—— *Vier Gesänge für eine Baritonstimme*, opus 160, Leipzig, *c*. 1850 (Lbl)
—— *Balladen in 4 Bänden*, ed. Hirschberg, Hildburghausen, 1912
Mathieux, Johanna. See under Kinkel. Mathieux was her first married name. Songs and reviews may be found under both names.
Mattheson, Johann *Odeon Morale* . . ., Nuremberg, 1751. Texts and music by Mattheson.
Mayr, J.S. *Lieder beim Klavier zu singen*, Regensburg, 1786. Another disciple of Schulz.
Mendelssohn-Bartholdy, Felix *Werke*, ed. Rietz, Breitkopf & Härtel, repr. Gregg Press, 1968. The songs are Serie 19.
Methfessel, Albert *Liederkranz*, iii. Heft, Rudolstadt, *c*. 1829 (Mbs)
Metzner, L. *Lieder* . . . *nach Gedichten von Eduard Mörike*, Landsberg/Lech, n.d. (= *c*. 1930?)
Mikuli, Carl *Sieben Lieder*, opus 27, Leipzig, 1880 (Bds)
Moritz, C.T. *Dreizehn Lieder und Gesaenge*, opus 5, Leipzig, *c*. 1813. (Wgm) No. 3 is an effective setting of 'Meine Ruh' ist hin', with broken

Select Bibliography

figures in the accompaniment which well convey Gretchen's restlessness.

Moses, J.G. *Versuch einiger Oden und Lieder* . . ., Leipzig, 1781

Mottl, Felix *Acht Lieder deutscher Minnesinger*, Vienna, 1904. (Mbs) No. 4 is an absurdly ornate setting of Walther von der Vogelweide's graceful 'Unter der Linden'.

Mozart, W.A. The songs are in Series iii, vol. 8 of the *Neue Ausgabe sämtlicher Werke*, ed. E.A. Ballin.

Muck, F. *Lieder* . . ., Leipzig, 1793

Müller, G.F. *Angenehme und zärtliche Lieder*, Dessau, 1760

Müthel, J.G. *Auserlesene Oden und Lieder* . . ., Hamburg, 1759

Die Muse, 2 parts, Leipzig, 1776. Songs by C.P.E. Bach, Hiller, Neefe, Rust and others.

Musenalmanach, 5 vols. Neustrelitz, 1796–1800, edited by Schiller. Important collection of poems by Goethe, Schiller, A.W. Schlegel and others. Song-composers represented include Reichardt and Zelter.

Musikalische Monatsschrift für Gesang und Klavier, Stuttgart, *c.* 1786. Songs and piano pieces by South German composers, including Zumsteeg.

Musikalisch-wöchentliche Belustigungen . . ., Zürich, 1775

Nägeli, H.G. *Lieder in Musik gesezt*, 3 parts, Zürich, 1795–9. Facsimile repr. by G. Walter, Zürich and Leipzig, 1943.

Naubert, A. *Sechs Lieder*, opus 14, Cassel and Leipzig, *c.* 1880. (Bds) No. 1 is a very good setting of 'Ein Stündlein wohl vor Tag'.

Nauert, G.E. *Oden und Lieder* . . . 2 parts, Nuremberg, 1758–64. Most of the texts belong to the Arcadian world. The accompaniment has an unusually important role, considering the early date of the songs.

Naumann, J.G. *Vierzig Freymäurerlieder*, 1782. Edition used is the 2nd, Berlin, 1784.

——— *Sammlung von Liedern* . . ., Pförten, 1784

Neefe, C.G. *Oden von Klopstock* . . ., Flensburg and Leipzig, 1776

——— *Serenaten beym Klavier zu singen*, Leipzig, 1777

——— *Vademecum für Liebhaber des Gesangs und Klaviers*, Leipzig, 1780

——— *Bilder und Träume von Herder*, Leipzig, 1798

Nessler, V.E. *Vier volksthümliche Lieder*, opus 41, Leipzig, *c.* 1871 (B)

——— *Vier Lieder von Heinrich Heine*, opus 43, Leipzig, *c.* 1871 (B) Very dramatic — arguably overdramatic — readings of Heine.

Neubauer, F.C. *Gesaenge mit Begleitung des Claviers*, Zürich, 1788

Nevin, E. *Album*, Mainz and London, 1893. (Hmb) An example of the lush sentimentality of the late Romantic idiom.

Niggli, F. *Sechs Lieder*, opus 3, Leipzig and Zürich, *c.* 1890. (Mbs) A rather uneven talent. No. 1 (Heine's 'Am Kreuzweg') creates a genuinely eerie atmosphere.

Overbeck, C.A. *Lieder und Gesänge* . . ., Hamburg, 1781. An amateur composer who was unequal to his chosen texts (Goethe, Hölty, Klopstock, Voß).

'P', C.J. *Lieder zum Gesang und Klavier* . . ., Nuremberg, 1782

Paradis, Maria T. *12 Lieder auf ihrer Reise* . . ., Leipzig, 1786

——— *Lenore*, Vienna, 1790

Paulsen, C.F.F. *Lieder mit Melodien* . . ., 2. Sammlung, Flensburg and Hamburg, 1798

Select Bibliography

Pepping, Ernst *Haus- und Trostbuch*, Bärenreiter, 1949
Perfall, K. *Lieder für eine Singstimme* . . ., Leipzig, 1859. (Bds) No. 4 = 'Das verlassene Mädchen' [sic!], in which the composer skilfully conveys the bleakness of the poem.
Pfitzner, Hans *Sämtliche Lieder*, 2 vols, Mainz, 1978–83
Pilz, K.P.E. *Acht gefühlvolle Lieder*, Leipzig, 1794. Popular in its day. One song, 'Die Tabakspfeife', appears in innumerable nineteenth-century anthologies of song.
Pohl, Wilhelm *Lieder mit Melodien fürs Clavier* . . ., Breslau, 1785
Preu, F. *Lieder fürs Clavier*, Leipzig, 1785
Preuß, Carl *Vermischte Oden und Lieder*, Hannover, 1783
Püttlingen, J. Vesque v. Published many songs between 1830 and the mid-1850s under the pseudonym of 'J. Hoven'. Set much Heine. There is a modern selection, edited by H. Schultz, Vienna, 1932. See too *Ironische Lieder von Heinrich Heine*, opus 41, Berlin, *c*. 1850 (Wgm) and *Die Heimkehr*, Vienna, 1851 (88 Heine-settings). (Bc)
Quantz, J.J. *Neue Kirchen-Melodien zu denen geistlichen Liedern des Herrn Professor Gellerts* . . ., Berlin, 1760. Other songs by Quantz are to be found in the Berlin anthologies of the day.
Queck, J.C. *Singstücke am Klavier*, Göttingen, 1790
―――― *Klavier- und Singstücke, zwote Sammlung*, Göttingen, 1792
Ramler, C.W. and Krause, C.G. *Oden mit Melodien*, 1. Theil, Berlin, 1753. Ramler collected and edited the texts; Krause, together with C.P.E. Bach, Benda, Nichelmann, Quantz and Telemann, provided the music. The collection, with its strophic settings of light and playful texts, set the tone for the early years of Berlin song.
―――― *Lieder der Deutschen mit Melodien*, parts 1–4, Berlin, 1767–8. A much larger, but broadly similar, collection.
Reger, Max The songs form vols 30–4 of the *Sämtliche Werke*, Breitkopf & Härtel, 1958ff.
Reichardt, J.F. *Oden und Lieder*, 3 parts, Berlin, 1779–81
―――― *Lieder von Gleim und Jacobi*, Gotha, 1784
―――― *Deutsche Gesänge mit Clavier-Begleitung*, Leipzig, 1788
―――― *Geistliche Lieder von Lavater* . . ., Winterthur, *c*. 1790
―――― *Lieder geselliger Freude*, 1–2, Leipzig, 1796–7: many composers represented.
―――― *Gesänge der Klage und des Trostes*, Berlin, 1797
―――― *Schillers lyrische Gedichte* . . ., 2 vols Leipzig, n.d. There is a modern edition by W. Salmen of the Goethe settings: 2 vols, 1964 = *Das Erbe deutscher Musik*, 58–9.
Reichardt, Luise (1780–1826, daughter of J.F.R.) Wrote many songs which were published from the turn of the century onwards in various collections. A selection, *Ausgewählte Lieder und Gesänge*, was edited by G. Rheinhardt, Munich, 1922.
Reinecke, Carl A prolific but rather superficial song-composer. The songs were published as single opus numbers between about 1844 and 1895. Some can be found in *66 Lieder neuerer Meister* (details under Bruch).
Reissiger, C.G. *Deutsche Lieder von Wolfgang von Göthe*, opus 48, Leipzig, 1828. (Mbs) Best are nos. 1–2 ('Trost in Tränen' and 'Der Fischer').
―――― *Lieder und Gesänge*, opus 53, Dresden, 1829. (Mbs) No. 3 is

Select Bibliography

Wilhelm Müller's 'Der Neugierige', no. 6 in *Die schöne Müllerin*.
—— *Gesänge und Lieder* . . . opus 79, Leipzig, 1832. (DÜk) Nos. 1-3 are Goethe-settings and all very good.
—— *Lieder und Gesänge*, opus 89, Dresden, 1834. (Mbs) No. 4 = Heine's 'Fischermädchen'.
Reiter, Josef *Der Pilgrim vor St Just*, opus 18,3: single edition, Leipzig, 1900. (Mbs) A dramatic setting of a ballad also treated in an oddly muted but equally effective way by Loewe.
Rheineck, C. *Lieder mit Clavier Melodien* . . ., Nuremberg, *c*. 1779
—— *Lieder-Sammlung*, parts 2-5, Memmingen, 1780-90
Riehl, W.H. *Hausmusik. Fünfzig Lieder deutscher Dichter* . . ., Stuttgart and Augsburg, 1855 (Mbs)
Ries, Franz *Sechs Lieder*, opus 8, Bielefeld, *c*. 1865. (Bds) No. 4 is a very imaginative setting of Heine's 'Lieb' Liebchen, leg's Händchen . . .'
—— *Tragödie*, opus 42, Berlin, 1899. (Mbs) Texts by Heine.
Ritter, Alex *Belsazar von Heinrich Heine* . . ., opus 8, Würzburg, *c*. 1890. (Mbs) In general, however, he showed no great poetic taste in his choice of texts.
Romberg, Andreas *Oden und Lieder* . . ., Bonn, 1793. Texts: Goethe, Herder, Klopstock.
Rosenbaum, C.E. *Scherzhafte Lieder mit Melodien*, 1760. I have used the 2nd edn, Altona, 1772.
—— *Lieder mit Melodien. Zweeter Theil*, Altona and Lübeck, 1762
Roth, W.A.T. *Lieder aus der Wochenschrift: Der Freund* . . ., Berlin, 1757
Rubinstein, Anton *Die Gedichte . . . aus Goethe's 'Wilhelm Meister's Lehrjahre'*, opus 91, Leipzig, *c*. 1872. (Sl) Very imaginative settings. Having been over-praised in his day, Rubinstein is unjustly neglected today. There are various collections and anthologies dating from the late nineteenth century and the 1900s, including *Gesang-Compositionen mit Clavierbegleitung*, 8 vols, Leipzig, *c*. 1884. The solo songs are in vols 1-3.
Rudorff, E. *Sechs Gedichte von J. von Eichendorff*, opus 3, Leipzig, 1864. No. 1 = 'Auf einer Burg', also set by Schumann. (Mbs)
Ruprecht, M. *6 Lieder für das Pianoforte*, Vienna, *c*. 1785. 3 in *DTÖ* 54.
Rust, F.W. *Oden und Lieder aus den besten deutschen Dichtern* . . ., 2 parts, Dessau and Leipzig, 1784-96
Sahr, Heinrich v. *Sechs Lieder*, opus 9, Leipzig, *c*. 1867 (Bds)
—— *Sechs Lieder*, opus 11, Leipzig, *c*. 1877 (Mbs)
—— *Acht Gesänge und Lieder*, opus 13, Leipzig, *c*. 1878. (Mbs) Does not always rise above the conventional; best in his Eichendorff-settings: opus 9,3; 11,2; 13,1; 14,2.
Saupe, C.G. *Deutsche Gesänge* . . ., Leipzig, 1791
Scharwenka, X. *Vier Lieder*, opus 10, Leipzig, *c*. 1873 (Lbl)
Scherzer, Otto *xxv Lieder*, Nördlingen, *c*. 1860. (Mbs) Poets include Goethe (15 texts), Mörike (3) and Uhland (4).
Schleinitz, Alexandra v. *Herbstblumen. Zehn Lieder*, opus 3, Berlin and Posen, *c*. 1864. (B)
Schmidlin, J. *Singendes und spielendes Vergnügen* . . ., 3rd edn, Zürich, 1767
—— *Schweizerlieder*, first published 1769. I have used the posthumous edition, Zürich, 1786.

Select Bibliography

Schmitt, Aloys *Liedersammlung*, opus 28, Mainz, *c.* 1822. (Lbl) No. 2 = Goethe's 'Geistesgruß'.

Schmügel, J.C. *Sing- und Spieloden vor (= für) musikalische Freunde componirt* . . ., Leipzig, 1762

Schnell, Heinrich *Drei Lieder*, opus 6, Berlin, 1880 (Lbl)

Schnyder v. Wartensee, X. *Acht deutsche Gesänge*, Bonn and Cologne, *c.* 1823. (DÜk) Contains two versions of 'Heidenröslein'. One (no. 2) is very pretty; the other (no. 3) banal.

Schoeck, Othmar *Das holde Bescheiden. Lieder und Gesänge nach Gedichten von Eduard Mörike*, opus 62, 2 Hefte, UE, 1956

Schönberg, Arnold *Sechs Lieder*, opus 3, 1903. No. 1 is a folksong setting in which Schönberg out-Regers Reger.

—— *15 gedichte aus 'das buch der hängenden gärten' von stefan george* (sic!), 1914 (Many editions of both collections.)

Scholze, J.S. See under 'Sperontes'.

Schröter, Corona, *Fünf und Zwanzig Lieder*, Weimar, 1786

Schubart, C.F.D. 'An die Tonkunst' in *Etwas für Clavier und Gesang* . . . Winterthur, 1782

—— *Musikalische Rhapsodien*, 2 Hefte, Stuttgart, 1786

Schubert, Franz The songs occupy vols 13–17 of the Complete Edition published in Leipzig by Breitkopf & Härtel, repr. New York (Dover), 1965–9. The seven-volume Peters edition is extremely valuable, but manages to exclude some gems.

Schulz, J.A.P. *Gesänge am Klavier*, Berlin and Leipzig, 1779

—— *Lieder im Volkston*, 3 parts, Berlin, 1782–90. I have used the 2nd edn of Part 1 (Berlin, 1785).

—— *Johann Peter Uzens lyrische Gedichte religiösen Innhalts* . . ., Hamburg, 1784

—— *Religiöse Oden und Lieder* . . ., Hamburg, 1786. The *Göttinger Musenalmanach* for 1802 contains several settings of poems by Voß.

Schumann, Clara *Sechs Lieder*, opus 13 (Breitkopf & Härtel, *Deutscher Liederkatalog*, no. 303, n.d.) Nos. 1–2 to texts by Heine. First published 1844.

Schumann, Robert *Werke*, ed. Clara Schumann, Leipzig (Breitkopf & Härtel). Repr. Gregg Press, 1968. Songs: Series xiii, vols 1–4.

Schwalm, R. *Drei Lieder*, opus 3, Breslau, 1874

Seckendorff, S. v. *Volks- und andere Lieder* . . ., 3 parts, Weimar and Dessau, 1779–82

—— *Zwölf Lieder*, Leipzig, 1819. (DÜk) No. 12 = 'Meine Ruh ist hin', entitled 'Gretchens Klage'.

Siebmann, F. *Sechs Lieder*, opus 60, Leipzig, *c.* 1880 (Bds)

Silcher, Fr. Main importance is as editor and arranger of folksongs. His setting of Heine's 'Lorelei' (1837) appeared in almost all popular anthologies of song for a century and has virtually become an 'honorary folksong'.

Spazier, K.G. *Lieder und Gesänge am Klavier*, Halle, 1781

—— *Lieder und andere Gesänge für Freunde einfacher Natur*, Neuwied and Leipzig, 1792

—— *Lieder am Klavier*, Leipzig, 1799

Speidel, W. *Vier Lieder*, opus 9, Munich, 1854 (Mbs)

Select Bibliography

'Sperontes' *Singende Muse an der Pleiße* . . ., 1736–45. Modern edition by Edward Buhle, 1909, repr. 1958: *DDT* i, 35–6.

Spohr, Ludwig *Sechs deutsche Lieder*, opus 94, Bonn, *c.* 1834. (Bds) No. 4 = 'Ungeduld' (also the text of no. 7 in *Die schöne Müllerin*). Individual songs by Spohr figure in various modern selections. 'Meine Ruh ist hin' (opus 25,2) is in Friedlaender, *Gedichte von Goethe*, i, no. 33.

Stade, W. *Lieder*, Heft 1, Leipzig, *c.* 1842. (Bds) No. 3 = 'Aus Wilhelm Meister' ('Wer nie sein Brot . . .').

—— *Deutsche Lieder aus dem 15. und 16. Jahrhundert*, 3 Hefte, Leipzig, 1855. (Bds) Old tunes, new accompaniments.

Stange, Max *Zwei Lieder im Volkston*, opus 13, Berlin, 1888 (Lbl)

—— *In Danzig. Gedicht von Joseph von Eichendorff*, Berlin, 1911. (B) A good setting, but overshadowed by Pfitzner's.

Steffan, J.A. *Sammlung Deutscher Lieder für das Klavier*, parts 1–2 and 4. (Wn) Many in *DTÖ* 54. Part 3 = Friberth and Hofmann (qv).

Sterkel, J.F.X. *xii Lieder mit Melodien* . . ., Vienna, *c.* 1785

Stier, Alfred *Moderne Liedermappe* . . . *16 Lieder und Gesänge nach Texten Deutscher Volkslieder*, opus 10, Darmstadt, 1910 (B)

Strauss, Richard *Lieder. Gesamtausgabe*, ed. Trenner, 3 vols, Boosey & Hawkes, 1964

Streben, Ernst *Zehn Lieder*, opus 15, Vienna, 1854 (Bds)

Tag, C.G. *Lieder beym Klavier zu singen*, i, Leipzig, 1783

Taubert, W. A prolific composer who seldom rose above conventional prettiness. The best songs that I have found are: 'In der Fremde' ('Es steht ein Baum in jenem Tal'), opus 67,2, first published *c.* 1846. Source: *Sammlung ausgewählter Lieder und Gesänge*, Berlin, n.d. no. 55 (Bu) and 'Der König in Thule' no. 6 in *Sechs Gesänge*, opus 151, Leipzig and Winterthur, *c.* 1862. (Bds)

Telemann, G.P. *Vier und zwanzig . . . Oden* . . ., 1741. Modern edition: *DDT*, i, 57.

Teumer, C.F. *6 Oden von Klopstock*, Leipzig, 1797

Thonus, P.J.v. *xxv leichte Lieder beym Klavier* . . ., Leipzig, 1792

Tiehsen, Otto *Frühlingslied* (= Heine's 'Gekommen ist der Maie'), opus 6,2 is in *Liederspende. Sammlung ausgewählter Gesänge*, Berlin, n.d., no. 46. (B) I have not seen his opus 7, referred to on p. 178.

Tiessen, Heinz *Galgenlieder*, opus 24, Essen, 1923

—— *Drei Lieder*, opus 55, Dresden, n.d.

—— *Für Dich! Drei Lieder*, Leipzig, n.d. (all Hmb)

Tomasek, W.J. A very able song-composer who set much Goethe. *Gedichte von Goethe*, ops 57–9, Prague, 1815. (DÜk) Some additional Goethe-settings given by Friedlaender.

Türck, D.G. *Lieder und Gedichte aus dem Siegwart*, Leipzig and Halle, 1780

Urspruch, Anton *Acht Lieder*, opus 23, Hamburg, 1885 (Hmb)

Veit, W.H. *Sechs Gesänge*, opus 21, Leipzig, *c.* 1844 (B)

Vierling, Georg *Fünf Gedichte*, opus 21, Breslau, *c.* 1858. (Wn) No. 2 is a tempestuous setting of Heine's 'Mit schwarzen Segeln . . .'

Volkmann, Robert *Die Bekehrte von Göthe*, opus 54, Mainz, 1879 (Lbl)

Wagner, Richard Set two of the songs from Goethe's *Faust*. Dating from 1832, they were published posthumously. Given by Friedlaender,

Select Bibliography

Gedichte von Goethe, ii, nos. 66–7.

Walder, J.J. *Lieder zum gesellschaftlichen Vergnügen* . . ., Zürich, 1804. See too under Egli.

Warneke, G.H. *Lieder mit Melodien* . . ., Gotha, 1780

Weber, Carl Maria v. There are many editions and selections, but no complete modern critical edition. See too Bibliography, Section 5 and 6 (under Jähns).

Webern, Anton v. *Eight Early Songs*, Boosey & Hawkes, n.d. Written between 1901 and 1904.

────── *Songs*, opus 12, UE, 1925. No. 1 = 'Der Tag ist vergangen (Volkslied)'.

────── *Fünf Lieder nach Gedichten von Stefan George*, opus 4, UE, 1923

Weingartner, Felix *Drei Lieder*, opus 14, Berlin, 1894. (Hmb) No. 1 = Lenau's 'Bitte'.

────── *12 Poems by Gottfried Keller*, opus 22, London, 1898 (Lcml)

────── *Frühlings- und Liebeslieder. Gedichte von Eduard Mörike*, opus 41, Leipzig, 1906 (Hmb)

Weis, F.W. *Lieder mit Melodien*, 1–3, Lübeck and Leipzig, 1775–9. Weis also published songs in the *Göttinger Musenalmanach*.

Wenckel, J.F.W. *Clavierstücke für Frauenzimmer*, 1–2, Leipzig and Hamburg, 1768–71. (Songs as well as piano pieces.)

Werner, Heinrich Chiefly remembered for his setting of 'Heidenröslein', first published in *Arion*, 17. Heft, no. 128, 1830. (Sl) Reappears, with inessential variants, in numerous anthologies of song.

Widemann, Paul *Aus des Herzens Nacht. Vier Gesänge*, opus 1, Leipzig, 1875 (Bu)

Wiedebein, J.M. *Oden und Lieder* . . ., Brunswick, 1779

Winterberger, A. *20 Gesänge*, opus 10, Leipzig, 1863 (Bds)

Witthauer, J.G. *Sammlung vermischter Clavier- und Singstücke*, Hamburg, 1785

Wöhler, G. *Drei Balladen von Heinrich Heine*, opus 1, Leipzig, n.d. (B) No. 3 ('Lorelei') shows the futility of trying to enliven a drab tune with a 'fancy' accompaniment.

Wolf, Ernst Wilhelm *Wiegenliederchen für deutsche Ammen*, 1772. Edition used: Riga, 1775.

Wolf, Hugo The mature songs are easily available in Peters, arranged according to poets: *Mörike-Lieder, Goethe-Lieder, Italienisches Liederbuch* and so forth. For the early works and all posthumous publications, see: *Nachgelassene Werke* . . ., 4 Hefte, Leipzig, 1936 and *Sämtliche Werke*, vii/3: *Nachgelassene Lieder*, iii, ed. Jancik, Vienna, 1976.

Wolff, C.M. *Sammlung verschiedener Oden und Lieder*, Stettin, 1777

Wolff, Erich J. *Gesammelte Lieder aus dem Nachlaß*, 3 vols, Berlin, 1913–4. Many settings of folk poems.

Wolfrum, Philipp *Lieder und Gesänge*, iv. Heft, opus 16, Munich, 1885 (Mbs)

Zachariae, J.F.W. *Sammlung Einiger Musikalischer Versuche*, 1–2, n.p., 1760–1

Zelter, C.F. *Sämmtliche Lieder, Balladen und Romanzen*, 4 vols, Berlin, 1811–12. (Vols 1 and 3 are in Wst; 2 and 4 in Mbs) There are various modern selections, including:

Select Bibliography

——— *Lieder, Balladen und Romanzen in Auswahl*, ed. Jöde, Nagel, 1930
——— *Fünfzig Lieder*, ed. Landshoff, Schott, 1932
Zenger, Max *Acht kleine Lieder*, opus 3, Stuttgart, *c*. 1865. (Mbs) No. 1 = 'Das verlassene Mägdlein'.
Zernial, H. *Altdeutsche Volkslieder, neu bearbeitet* . . ., Magdeburg 1885. (Bds) Skilful combination of traditional tunes and new accompaniments.
Zumsteeg, J.R. *Colma, ein Gesang Ossians* . . ., Leipzig, *c*. 1794
——— *Hagars Klage* . . ., Leipzig, 1797. Most of the short ballads and songs first appeared in various collections and were gathered together in:
——— *Kleine Balladen und Lieder*, 7 vols, 1800–5. Photorepr. Gregg, 1969.

Section 4

Altenburg, C. *Uhlands Wanderlieder* . . ., opus 3, Brunswick and Leipzig, 1900 (B)
Claudius, Otto *Neun Lieder von W. Müller*, Leipzig, 1832 (Bds) Corresponds to *Die schöne Müllerin*, nos 1–4, 9, 17–20. Hence Claudius's cycle tells the story in a somewhat truncated form.
Derège, Th. *Wanderlieder von Wilhelm Müller*, opus 2, Berlin, *c*. 1835. (Bc) 6 songs only (*Winterreise*, nos 6 and 1–5). *Wasserflut* is the best.
Dressler, F.A. *Wanderlieder von Ludwig Uhland*, opus 12, Berlin and Posen, 1877. (Bds) Nine songs: selection of texts made familiar to lovers of song in nineteenth-century Germany through Kreutzer (qv). Nos. 6–7 ('Winterreise' and 'Abreise') are the best.
Graedener, C.G.P. *Zehn Reise- und Wanderlieder von Wilhelm Müller*, opus 44, Leipzig and Winterthur, *c*. 1862. One of the composers who chooses different texts from those made famous by Schubert.
Kreutzer, Conradin *Neun Wanderlieder von Uhland*, opus 34, 2 Hefte, Augsburg, 1820 (Wgm)
Lenz, Leopold *Der Landsknecht . . . Ein Cyklus von 12 Liedern und Gesängen*, opus 38, Mainz, 1844 (Bu)
Marschner, Heinrich *Der fahrende Schüler. 6 Lieder aus dem Wanderbuche von Julius von Rodenberg*, opus 168, Hamburg, 1855. I have seen only no. 6 (single edition: Sl). To judge from that, Marschner's cycle seems more lighthearted than those listed above.

This is only a small selection from a very large number of such cycles and is intended as no more than an illustration of the point made on p. 114.

Section 5

The popularity of the guitar in the early decades of the nineteenth century led to the publication of a huge number of songs with alternative piano or guitar accompaniments. The usual layout was for the guitar part to be

Select Bibliography

printed above the vocal line with the piano below. In most cases, both versions were provided by the composer of the song(s), but occasionally it was demonstrably a second composer who supplied the guitar-accompaniment, presumably at the request of a publisher who knew the potential market. What follows is a small but representative selection. Dating is exceptionally difficult with these songs, but they nearly all belong to the first two decades of the century. A detailed study of such works would reveal much about the tastes and abilities of amateur guitarists in the period 1800–30.

Amon, J. *Sechs Lieder für's Clavier mit Begleitung einer Guitarre*, opus 36, Bonn, 1806. (Lbl) Despite the ambiguous title, these are alternatives.
—— *Sechs Lieder mit Begleitung des Klaviers oder der Guitarre*, opus 54, Offenbach, *c.* 1809 (Bu)
Anschuetz, J.A. *Trois chansons allemandes . . . pour Piano-Forté ou Guitarre*, Bonn, *c.* 1815 (Lbl)
Berger, Ludwig *Vier Gedichte von Goethe und Schiller . . .*, opus 9, Würzburg, n.d. (*c.* 1814?). (Mbs) One of several such collections by Berger.
Bornhard, J.H.K. *Lied der Freundschaft . . . für Fortepiano und Guitarre*, Hamburg, n.d. (*c.* 1815?). (Hs) The 'and' is to be taken seriously; the guitar provides an extra obbligato part in triplets against quavers in the voice and the piano.
Eberwein, M. *Trinklied. Mich ergreift, ich weiß nicht wie . . . fürs Piano-Forte oder Guitarre*, Hamburg, 1810. (Hs) The text is Goethe's and this setting became and remained deservedly popular.
Harder, A. See under Himmel. Harder supplied guitar-accompaniments to *Klavierlieder* by various composers, including Zumsteeg.
Himmel, F.H. *Zwölf alte deutsche Lieder des Knaben Wunderhorn . . .*, Leipzig, *c.* 1808. (Lbl) Originally composed with piano-accompaniment; guitar alternatives supplied by Harder.
Jusdorf, J.C. *Das Gemählde . . .*, Hamburg and Altona, n.d. (Hs) One of several such publications by Jusdorf, with alternative accompaniments in the conventional layout mentioned above.
Keller, Carl *Gesänge für Guitarre oder Pianoforte*, Hannover, n.d. (*c.* 1810?)
Lieder Kranz mit Begleitung des Pianoforte oder der Guitarre, Augsburg, *c.* 1820. Various composers represented. Some songs are well suited for the guitar; in other cases, what we see is a foolish attempt to adapt a Klavierlied to an inappropriate medium. (Bu)
Matthaei, H. *Alte und neue Zeit . . . Lied . . ., in Musik gesetzt für's Pianoforte oder Guitarre*, Hamburg, n.d. (Hs) Hints at the modest capabilities of amateur guitarists of the day; the piano version has a quite elaborate postlude which is simply omitted in the guitar arrangement.
Quandt, J.G. *Romanze (Es war ein König in Thule) von Göthe mit Guitarre- und Pianoforte-Begleitung*, n.p., *c.* 1810. (DÜk) Examination of the score, especially of the postlude, makes it perfectly clear that both instruments were expected to play together.
Reinicke, L.K. *Sechs Lieder mit Begleitung des Pianoforte oder der Guitarre*, Leipzig and Berlin, n.d. (*c.* 1815). (Mbs) Genuine alternatives, each part being equally idiomatic. The best song is no. 4 (Salis, 'Das Grab').
Seidel, F.L. *Theklas Geisterstimme . . . für Fortepiano & Guitarre*, Hamburg

Select Bibliography

and Altona, n.d. (very early nineteenth century). (Hs) Despite the title, internal evidence suggests that these are alternatives. Either would certainly be sufficient in itself. Text by Schiller.

Weber, C.M. v. Many songs, especially of the simple strophic sort, appeared originally as *Klavierlieder* and were later re-issued with guitar-accompaniment or in editions giving alternatives. These guitar-arrangements do not seem to have been by Weber himself. See F.W. Jähns, *C.M.v.W. in seinen Werken*, pp. 23ff (details in Bibliography, Section 6).

Weber, Gottfried *Vier Gesänge* . . ., opus 23, Leipzig, *c.* 1816. (Lbl) Two songs (including no. 1: 'Über allen Gipfeln') offer an alternative guitar-accompaniment.

Section 6

Abert, Hermann *Goethe und die Musik*, Stuttgart, 1922

Arnim, L.A.v. and Brentano, Clemens *Des Knaben Wunderhorn. Alte deutsche Lieder* . . ., 1806. Edition used: Leipzig, 1906.

Arnold, Friedrich *Das deutsche Volkslied*, 2 parts, 3rd edn, Prenzlau, 1912

Brentano, Clemens See under Arnim.

Bücken, Ernst *Das deutsche Lied. Probleme und Gestalten*, Hamburg, 1939

Bürger, G.A. 'Herzensausguß über Volks-Poesie', 1776, in *Sämtliche Werke*, 4 vols, Leipzig, 1902, iii, 7–12.

Büsching, J.G. and von der Hagen *Sammlung deutscher Volkslieder*, Berlin, 1807. (Tunes in a separate volume.)

Busch, Gudrun *C.Ph.E. Bach und seine Lieder (Kölner Beiträge zur Musikforschung*, xii), Regensburg, 1957

Challier, Ernst *Großer Lieder-Katalog*, Berlin, 1885. Photorepr. 1979. Plus 15 supplements, 1886–1914. An indispensable source for anyone who needs to know which composers set any given poem.

Chop, Max *August Bungert*, Berlin, 1915. A check-list of the works: pp. 349–56.

Degen, Max 'Die Lieder von Carl Maria von Weber', Diss. (Basle) 1923

Düring, W.-J. *Erlkönig–Vertonungen* . . ., Regensburg, 1972

Eckhoff, Annemarie *Dichterliebe. Heinrich Heine im Lied*, Hamburg, 1972. Check-list of Heine-settings in the Hamburg City Library. Very useful for reference.

Fallersleben, Hoffman v. *Unsere volksthümlichen Lieder*, 1856. I have seen the 3rd edn, Leipzig, 1869.

Fischer-Dieskau, Dietrich *Auf den Spuren der Schubert-Lieder*, Wiesbaden, 1971

—— *Töne sprechen, Worte klingen* . . ., Stuttgart, 1985

Forkel, J.N. *Musikalisch-kritische Bibliothek*, 1778–9. Photorepr. Hildesheim, 1964.

Friedlaender, Max *Das deutsche Lied im 18. Jahrhundert*, 1902, photorepr. Hildesheim, 1962. Indispensable for those interested in eighteenth-century song and its poetry. Vol. i, part 1 gives bibliographical details of the songs; part 2 is a representative anthology; vol. ii deals with the

Select Bibliography

poetry.

Gellert, C.F. *Geistliche Oden und Lieder,* 1757, in *Sämmtliche Werke,* Leipzig, 1769, ii, 93ff. Photorepr. Hildesheim, 1968.

Gläser, G. 'Franz von Holstein. Ein Dichterkomponist des 19. Jahrhunderts'. Diss. (Leipzig), 1930. Has a check-list of works with dates.

Goldschmidt, Hugo *Die Musikästhetik des 18. Jahrhunderts,* Zürich and Leipzig, 1915

Gottsched, J.C. *Versuch einer kritischen Dichtkunst,* first published 1730. Many editions, including a modern facsimile (Darmstadt, 1962) of the 4th (1751) edn.

Greinz, R.H. *Heinrich Heine und das deutsche Volkslied,* Neuwied and Leipzig, 1894

Hagen See Büsching.

Heinen, Clemens 'Der sprachliche und musikalische Rhythmus im Kunstlied . . .,' Diss. (Cologne), 1958

Herder, J.G. 'Über Ossian und die Lieder alter Völker', in *Von deutscher Art und Kunst,* first published 1773. Innumerable editions.

―――― *Volkslieder*: edition used = vol. xxv of the *Sämtliche Werke,* ed. Suphan, 1885, photorepr. Hildesheim, 1968. Also available in a paperback (Reclam).

Hiller, J.A. *Musikalische Nachrichten und Anmerkungen,* Leipzig, 1770

Ivey, Donald *Song. Anatomy, imagery and styles,* New York and London, 1970

Jähns, F.W. *Carl Maria von Weber in seinen Werken. Chronologisch-thematisches Verzeichnis seiner sämmtlichen Compositionen,* Berlin, 1871

Kirchner, J. *Die Zeitschriften des deutschen Sprachgebietes von den Anfängen bis 1830,* 3 vols, Stuttgart, 1969

Kistler, Cyrill *Musikalische Tagesfragen,* Eichstadt and Munich, later Bad Kissingen, 1880ff. Nationalistic view of music.

Kneisel, Jessie H. *Mörike and Music,* n.p. (= New York?), 1949

Komma, K.M. 'Probleme der Hölderlin-Vertonung', in *Hölderlin-Jahrbuch,* 1957, 201–19

Krause, C.G. *Von der musikalischen Poesie,* Berlin, 1753

Kreiser, Kurt 'Carl Gottlieb Reissiger . . .,' Diss. (Dresden) 1918. Includes a check-list of works with dates, pp. 111ff.

Kretzschmer, A. *Deutsche Volkslieder mit ihren Original-Weisen. Unter Mitwirkung . . . des Herrn von Zuccalmaglio . . .,* 2 parts, Berlin, 1840

Lämmle, A. *Friedrich Silcher. Sein Leben und seine Lieder,* Mühlacker, 1956

Landau, Anneliese *Das einstimmige Kunstlied Conradin Kreutzers . . .,* Leipzig, 1930

Lesle, Lutz *Eduard Mörike im Lied,* Hamburg, 1975. Companion volume to Eckhoff, *Dichterliebe,* and equally useful.

Lindner, A. *Max Reger. Bild seines Jugendlebens,* Stuttgart, 1923

Liszt, Franz, *Gesammelte Schriften,* Leipzig, 1880–3

Maier, Gunter *Die Lieder Johann Rudolf Zumsteegs und ihr Verhältnis zu Schubert,* Göppingen, 1971

Marpurg, F.W. *Historisch-kritische Beiträge zur Aufnahme der Musik,* Berlin, 1754ff

―――― *Kritische Briefe über die Tonkunst . . .,* 2 vols, Berlin, 1759–63. Also

Select Bibliography

contains some songs.

Mattheson, J. *Critica Musica*, Hamburg, 1722–5, photorepr. Amsterdam, 1964.

—— *Der Vernünfftler* . . ., first published 1713–14. I have seen the later edition, Hamburg, 1721. Extracts from *The Tatler* and *The Spectator* in translation.

—— *Der Vollkommene Capellmeister*, Hamburg, 1739, facs. repr. Bärenreiter, 1954.

Meier, J. *Kunstlieder im Volksmunde*, Halle, 1906

Mizler, L. *Musikalische Bibliothek*, Leipzig, 1739–54

Morik, W. 'Johannes Brahms und sein Verhältnis zum deutschen Volkslied', Diss. (Göttingen), 1953

Musikalisches Handbuch auf das Jahr 1782, 'Alethinopel' (= ?), 1782

Musikalisches Wochenblatt, Leipzig, 1870ff

Nicolai, Friedrich *Eyn feyner kleyner Almanach* . . ., 2 vols, Berlin and Stettin, 1777–9. A parody of the vogue for folksong.

Osterwald, W. *Robert Franz. Ein Lebensbild*, Leipzig, 1886

Pazdirek, F. *Universal-Handbuch der Musikliteratur*, Vienna, 1904–10. A useful check-list of composers' works, but not much help in dating.

Peake, L.E. 'Kreutzer's *Wanderlieder* . . .', in *Musical Quarterly*, lxv (1979), 83–102.

Petersen, Barbara A. *Ton und Wort. The Lieder of Richard Strauss*, Michigan, 1980

Quantz, J.J. *Versuch einer Anweisung die flute traversière zu spielen*, 1752; photorepr. of the 3rd edn (1789) by Bärenreiter (= *Documenta Musicologica*, i, 2, 1953).

Reichardt, J.F. (ed.) *Musikalisches Kunstmagazin*, 2 vols, 1782–91, facs. repr. Hildesheim, 1969.

—— (ed.) *Deutschland*, 4 vols, Berlin, 1796

—— (ed.) *Berlinische Musikalische Zeitung*, Berlin, 1805–6

—— *Vertraute Briefe geschrieben auf einer Reise nach Wien* . . ., 2 vols, Amsterdam, 1810

—— 'Die Briefe Johann Friedrich Reichardts an Goethe', edited by Max Hecker in *Jahrbuch der Goethe-Gesellschaft*, xi, Weimar, 1925, 197–252.

Rellstab, L. *Ludwig Berger* . . ., Berlin, 1846

Riehl, W.H. *Musik im Leben des Volkes*, 1858. Modern edition by J. Müller-Blattau, Cassel, 1936.

—— *Die Familie*, Stuttgart, 1861

Rosenwald, H.H. *Geschichte des deutschen Liedes zwischen Schubert und Schumann*, Berlin, 1930

Salmen, Walter (ed.) *The Social Status of the Professional Musician from the Middle Ages to the 19th Century*, translated from the German by H. Kaufman and Barbara Reisner, New York, 1983.

Sams, Eric *The Songs of Hugo Wolf*, London, 1961

—— *The Songs of Robert Schumann*, London, 1969

Sandberger, A. 'Johann Rudolf Zumsteeg und Franz Schubert', in *Ausgewählte Aufsätze zur Musikgeschichte*, first published 1921, repr. Hildesheim. 1973. 288–99.

Scheibe, J.A. *Critischer Musikus*, 1737–40. I have used the 2nd edn,

Select Bibliography

Leipzig, 1745.

Schubart, C.D.F. *Deutsche Chronik auf das Jahr 1775*, Ulm, 1775

——— *Ideen zu einer Ästhetik der Tonkunst*, 1784–5. Published posthumously, Vienna, 1806.

Schulz, J.A.P. *Briefwechsel zwischen Schulz und Voß*, ed. H. Gottwaldt and G. Hahne, Cassel, 1960

Schumann, Robert *Gesammelte Schriften über Musik und Musiker*, 4 vols, Leipzig, 1854

Schwab, H.W. *Sangbarkeit, Popularität und Kunstlied . . .*, Regensburg, 1965

Serauky, W. *Die musikalische Nachahmungsästhetik im Zeitraum von 1700 bis 1850*, Münster, 1929

Siebenkäs, D. *Ludwig Berger. Sein Leben und seine Werke*, Berlin, 1963. Gives check-list of works with dates.

Spitta, Philipp *Musikgeschichtliche Aufsätze*, Berlin, 1894

Stein, Jack M. *Poem and Music in the German Lied . . .*, Harvard UP, 1971

Stoljar, M.M. *Poetry and song in late eighteenth-century Germany . . .*, Croom Helm, 1985

Sydow, Alexander *Das Lied. Ursprung, Wesen und Wandel*, Göttingen, 1962

Tschulik, N. *Lieder aus Österreich*, Vienna, 1964. (A brief history, not an anthology).

Vogel, A.B. *Anton Rubinstein*, Leipzig, 1888

Vogel, Werner *Othmar Schoeck. Leben und Schaffen . . .*, Zürich, 1976

Volkmann, H. *Robert Volkmann. Sein Leben und seine Werke*, Leipzig, 1903. Check-list of works with dates, 195ff.

Voß, J.H. See under Schulz.

Wagner, Gunter *Franz Lachner als Liederkomponist*, Giebing über Priem, 1970. Includes check-list with dates.

Weber, C.M.v. *Sämtliche Schriften*, ed. Kaiser, Berlin and Leipzig, 1908

Wieland, C.M. 'Versuch über das deutsche Singspiel . . .,' 1775, in *Sämmtliche Werke*, Leipzig, 1840, xxxiv, 71ff

Wiora, W. (ed.) *Herder-Studien*, Würzburg, 1960. See pp. 95–108 for Walter Salmen on 'Herder und Reichardt'.

——— *Das echte Volkslied*, Heidelberg, 1962

Wirth, H. 'Max Reger und seine Dichter' in *Reger-Studien, 1. Festschrift für Ottmar Schreiber*, Wiesbaden, 1978, 47–57

Wolff, Viktor E. *Robert Schumanns Lieder in ersten und späteren Fassungen*, Leipzig, 1914

Zelter, C.F. *Darstellungen seines Lebens (Schriften der Goethe-Gessellschaft*, lxiv, Weimar, 1931)

Zuccalmaglio See under Kretzschmer.

Original Versions of Passages Quoted in Translation

p. xi (motto) Es ist kein Zweifel, daß Worte, die so nach einer geschickten Melodie gesungen werden, noch viel kräftiger in die Gemüther wirken. Was ist lyrische Poesie, die nicht gesungen wird?

p. 3 Die Melodien habe ich zu den Liedern so angemessen, wie es die Überschrift und der Inhalt mit sich gebracht haben.

p. 3 [Ich halte] es für ein unverbrüchliches Gesetz, . . . daß der Ausdruck in den Noten mit dem Ausdrucke . . . des Liedes, welches mit einer Melodie versehen werden soll, in der möglichsten Uebereinstimmung stehe.

p. 7 Ein Redner und ein Musikus haben sowohl in Ansehung der Ausarbeitung der vorzutragenden Sachen, als des Vortrages selbst, einerley Absicht zum Grunde, nämlich: sich der Herzen zu bemeistern, die Leidenschaften zu erregen oder zu stillen, und die Zuhörer bald in diesen, bald in jenen Affect zu versetzen.

p. 8 Die Musik also, als eine Sprache der Leidenschaften und Empfindungen, hat das Amt, die Gefühle und Empfindungen zu erregen, die mit den Begriffen und Vorstellungen sympathisiren, die von der Dichtkunst vorgezeichnet sind. Dadurch setzt sie den Zuhörer in eine Gemüthsfassung, die zum Eindruck einer Vorstellung schon vorbereitet, und gleichsam schon dahin gestimmt ist, wo ihn der Dichter haben will, um mit Leichtigkeit seinen Vorstellungen Eingang und Wirkung zu verschaffen.

pp. 8–9 Mein Bemühen ging . . . allzeit dahinaus, daß ich mich in das Gefühl, daß des Poeten Einbildungskraft verlangte, so viel mir möglich, zu versetzen suchte. Ich forderte meine kleine Erkenntniß in der Tonkunst auf, die Gedanken meines Dichters mit einer gefällig- und consentirenden Harmonie der Musik zu vereinigen, und hörte niemahls zu verbessern auf, bis mir der Ton der Saiten den Affect der Poesie schien auszudrücken.

p. 13 Ich habe meinen Melodien die nöthige Harmonie und Manieren beygefügt. Auf diese Art habe ich sie der Willkühr eines steifen General-Baß-Spielers nicht überlassen dürfen . . .

p. 22 Wir haben noch Volkslieder, die über hundert Jahr alt sind; aber wie ungekünstelt, wie leicht sind sie auch! Ihr Erfinder scheint die Noten aus dem Herzen gestohlen zu haben.

p. 29 Die Zeiten sind vorüber, in welchen das Blendende und Gesuchte in der Musik Beyfall fand. — Männer, die den einfachen Tönen der Natur . . . tiefer nachspürten, erkannten bald jene Fehler, und bemüheten sich, die Klippen des falschen Geschmacks zu vermeiden.

p. 29 Ueberhaupt halte ich dafür, daß das sogenannte Volkslied melodisch gesetzt seyn müsse, denn schon der Nahme Volkslied zeigt an, daß es nicht sowohl für solche, die der Musik . . . kundig sind, bestimmt sey, als vielmehr für solche, die ohne musikalische Kenntnisse doch auch gern ein Liedchen singen mögen . . .

p. 42 Diejenigen, die unter dem Schwalle wälscher und französischer

Original Versions

Gesänge, die man in allen Häusern . . . findet, oft vergebens ein deutsches Lied suchen, . . . empfangen hier . . . eine Sammlung deutscher Lieder . . .

p. 61 . . . leichte und kunstlose Gesänge . . ., womit man zuweilen, wenn man keine Opernarien von weltberühmten Tonsetzern bey der Hand hat, auch gütigst vorlieb nimmt.

p. 61 . . . ein junger Dilettant aus Schwaben, . . . der . . . seine Lieder gerade so liefert, wie die liebe Mutter Natur sie ihn auf seinem Dörfchen gelehrt hat.

p. 64 [Meine Melodien] sollten die Eigenschaft haben, daß sie ohne viele Mühe so wohl gespielet, als gesungen werden könnten.

p. 64 Iedes Lied wird sanft und leicht seyn, und auch dem Anfänger des Claviers und der Singekunst nicht schwer fallen.

p. 64 Der größte Theil [meines Publikums] bestehet aus bloßen Liebhabern, die so ein Lied gern spielen, weil es leicht ist, einen Gesang hat, der sich dem Gedächtnisse gern und bald eindrückt und sich folglich ohne Schwierigkeit singen läßt.

p. 66 Wir hätten unsere Sammlung stärker machen können, wenn wir unter diese scherzhaften Lieder die ernsthaften und erhabenen Gesänge unserer Lyrischen (*sic!*) Poeten hätten aufnehmen wollen, Gesänge, die sich mehrentheils besser deklamiren, als singen lassen.

p. 66 Selbst die Musik auf unserm Zimmer, muß uns nicht stets zur *bloßen Belustigung* dienen; und wir können auch vor unserm Klavier unsre Andacht haben, und uns mit ernsthaften Gedanken beschäftigen.

p. 79 . . . eine frappante Aehnlichkeit des musikalischen mit dem poetischen Tone des Liedes; . . . eine Melodie, . . . die, wie ein Kleid dem Körper, sich der Declamation und dem Metro der Worte anschmiegt . . .

p. 120 Die Musik schließt dem Menschen ein unbekanntes Reich auf, eine Welt, die nichts gemein hat mit der äußern Sinnenwelt, die ihn umgibt, und in der er alle *bestimmten* Gefühle zurückläßt, um sich einer unaussprechlichen Sehnsucht hinzugeben.

p. 140 Die großen Lieder-Komponisten des 19. Jahrhunderts, allen voran Franz Schubert, lösen das Lied aus dem Bereich privaten häuslichen Musizierens, erheben es zum Konzertlied . . .

Index

Christian names are given instead of initials in a few cases where confusion might otherwise arise (for instance, with very common surnames). Where definite articles figure in German titles, these come first, in order to avoid the complications that would arise where the title includes an adjective or where the definite article is a genitive. Some entries in the Bibliography offer brief comments or details which are not given in the text; entries of this kind have been indexed and are marked with an asterisk.

Abeille, L. 106–7, 203
Abert, H. 81n17
Abt, F.W.* 212
Agricola, J.F. 10
Albert, Eugen d' 150, 204
Albert, Heinrich 1
Albertsen, L.L. xii
Allgemeine Musikalische Zeitung ix, xi, 41, 93, 100, 103, 112, 114, 126n14, 138, 141n8,9,10,12, 143–6, 148, 150, 154–5, 184, 192, 202n1, 203n9,14,22
Anacreon 11, 100
Andersen, Hans 128–9, 200
André, Jean Baptiste 212
André, Johann 22, 47n3, 75, 98n17, 101n1, 211
Arion 106
Arlberg, F.* 213
Arnim, A. von 22, 166
Assmuss, J.K.G. 62
Auserlesene moralische Lieder 39

Bach, C.P.E. xi, xiii, 5, 10, 13–15, 17, 33–4, 40, 53, 60, 65n4, 70, 73, 89, 94, 100, 225
Bach, J.C.F. 74
Bach, J.E. 16, 83, 90
Bach, J.S. 16, 70, 74, 123
Bachmann, G. 94
Baehr, O. 213
Bagge, S. 143, 145
Bairstow, E.C. 126n12
Ballin, E.A. 48n10
Banck, C. xivn7, 141n12
Batteux, C. 7
Bauer, Moritz 108
Baum, C.* 213
Baumbach, F.A. 97n3

Baumgartner, W.* 213
Becher, A.J. 131
Beck, F.A. 8
Becker, A.* 214
Becker, Fritz 203n24
Beethoven, L. van 85, 91, 96–8, 106, 112, 132, 141n1, 144, 152, 187, 211
Behn, H.* 214
Bellermann, H.* 214
Benda, G.F. xi, 83, 91, 97n5
Benecken, F.B. 54, 97n5
Benkert, G.F. 164
Bennat, F. 163
Berg, A. 204–5, 209n5
Berger, Ludwig 142n14
Berger, Wilhelm 177
Berlinische Oden und Lieder see Marpurg, F.W.
Berls, J.R. 31
Bible 153
Biedermann, F. 97n7
Birke, J. 18
Bischoff, H.* 214
Blasser, G.* 214
Blech, L. 204
Blom, E. 126n13
Bode, J.J.C. 10
Bolck, O.* 214–15
Boßler, H.P. 83
Brahms, J. xiii, 101, 103, 122, 132, 135–6, 139, 151, 153–4, 156–8, 160–1, 171, 174–6
Brandl, J. 93, 96
Brauner, C.S. 178
Brecht, Bertolt 206
Brede, S.F. 9, 64, 81n5
Breitkopf, B.T.* 215
Bremer, F. 154n12

Index

Brendel, F. 147, 155n12
Brentano, C.M.W. 22, 166
Britten, B. 202n3
Bronsart, I. von* 215
Brown, M.J.E. xiii, 108
Bücken, E. 126n16, 154n12
Bülow, H. von* 215
Bürde, J.* 215
Bürger, G.A. 22, 26, 28–9, 32–3, 43–4, 49–50, 56, 58, 67, 79, 85, 87, 94, 98n17 and 20, 100, 102n2, 141n1, 151, 211, 213
Buhle, E. 18
Bungert, A. 164
Burgmüller, N. 105, 215
Burkhard, W. 209n4
Burmann, G.W. 13
Busch, G. 5, 7, 58n2

Campion, Thomas 175
Challier, E. 81n1
Chamisso, A. von 135
Chopin, F. xiv
chorale 33–6, 74, 187–8
Cläpius, W.* 215
Claudius, M. 23–4, 30, 32, 44, 68, 75, 151, 174
Clemens, C.G.* 215
Collin, M.C. von 115
Commer, F.* 215
Cornelius, P. 122, 174–5
Cox, David 42, 47n2
Craig Bell, A. 126n20
Cramer, J.A. 73
Curschmann, F. 105, 215–16

Dach, S. 1–2
Damcke, B.* 216
Danzi, F. 106
Das moderne Lied 204
Das Reich der Natur und der Sitten 57
Daumer, G. 175
Decker, C. 164
Degele, E.* 216
Deprosse, A.* 216
Der Biedermann 56
Der Patriot 56
Der redliche Deutsche 57
Der Tugendfreund 57
Des Knaben Wunderhorn 163, 166, 171n4
Dessauer, J. xivn7
Deutsch, O.E. 211
Deutsche Lieder für Jung und Alt 171n4

Dietrich, A.* 216
Dietrichstein, M. von* 216
'Dilettante aus Schwaben' 61
Dressler, E.C. 6, 33, 37n6, 64
Droste-Hülshoff, A. von 174

Eberwein, C.* 216
Eberwein, M.* 232
Egli, J.H. 39–41
Ehlers, W.* 217
Ehlert, L. xiv, 145, 179–80, 202n2
Eichendorff, J. von 153, 166, 178, 205, 227
  'Auf einer Burg' 119, 200, 227
  'Das zerbrochene Ringlein' 125n3, 166–7, 185–6, 205
  'Dein Bildnis wunderselig' 148–9, 215, 219
  'In Danzig' 207, 229
  'Intermezzo' *see* 'Dein Bildnis wunderselig'
  'Waldesgespräch' 130–1
Eicken 37n8
Eidenbenz, C.G. 90
Eisler, H. 205–6
Elvers, R. 211
Empfindsamkeit 9, 51–3, 81n2, 82
Endter, C.F. 3, 8, 11, 64
Engel, Carl 142n14
Erk, L. 161
Eschenburg, J.J. 73–4
Eunike, I.F. 106

Fallersleben, H. von 134, 164
Fesca, A. 203n20
Fesca, F.E. (father of A. Fesca) 187
Feuchtersleben, E. von 164
Fielitz, A. von* 217
figured bass xi, 1, 12–13, 40–1
Fink, C.* 217
Fink, G.W. xi, 212
Fischer-Dieskau, D. 109, 126n7, 206, 209n1
Flaschner, G.B. 29–30
Fleischer, F.G. 6, 14, 34, 71, 94
Flörke, F.J. 61, 93
Flügel, G. 158–9, 162
Foerster, E.A. 86
Forkel, J.N. 8, 35, 79
Fortner, W. 207
Fortsetzung Auserlesener moralischer Lieder 39, 41
Fouqué, F. de la Motte 187
Franz, R. 104, 122–5, 139, 159,

Index

161–2, 175, 186, 189
freemasonry 46, 62
Freystädter, F.J. 43
Friberth, K. 47n4
Friedlaender, M. xi, 48n9, 52, 65n3, 81n10 and 12, 86, 89
Fröhlich, Th. 175, 218

Gabler, C.A. 93
Gatterer, P. 100
Gellert, C.F. 34, 66, 81n11
George, S. 206
Gernsheim, F.* 218
Gerstenberg, H.W. von 81n9
Gise(c)ke, D.N. 94
Gleim, J.W.L. 14, 55, 75, 86, 224
Gluck, C.W. xi, xiii, 5, 60, 101
Glück, J.L.F. (Friedrich Glück) 125n3, 167
Görner, J.V. xi, xiii, 3, 5, 10, 15–16, 20, 68
Goethe, J.W. von viii, xii, 21, 23, 42, 43–5, 49–50, 80, 87, 93, 100–1, 115, 151, 154, 165–6, 170, 173–6, 182, 184, 215–16, 221–2, 225
 'Als ich auf dem Euphrat schiffte' 182
 'Am Fluße' 219–20, 222
 'An den Mond' 155n13, 220, 223
 'An die Türen will ich schleichen' 222
 'An Luna' 155n13
 'An Schwager Kronos' 117, 132, 183
 'Auf dem See' 42
 'Das Veilchen' 43–4
 'Der Fischer' 32, 50, 138, 165–6, 176, 184–5, 216
 'Der König in Thule' 32, 50, 101, 165–6, 170, 176, 215, 222, 232
 'Der neue Amadis' 129
 'Die Bekehrte' 133
 'Dies zu deuten' 182
 Egmont 192
 'Ein Wunder, ist der arme Mensch geboren' 183
 'Erlkönig' 50, 115, 117, 132, 165–6
 Faust 178, 215, 223–4, 229
 'Freudvoll und leidvoll' xiv, 101, 192, 222
 'Frühling übers Jahr' 136
 'Ganymed' 117
 'Gefunden' 165, 193, 201
 'Geh! gehorche meinen Winken' 135
 'Geistesgruß' 228
 'Grenzen der Menschheit' 115, 192
 'Gutmann und Gutweib' 129, 199
 'Harzreise im Winter' 101
 'Heidenröslein' 23, 32, 106, 165–6, 170, 176, 185, 192, 222, 224, 228
 'Heiß mich nicht reden' 215
 'Jägers Abendlied' 23, 165
 'Kennst du das Land' 127n21, 142n14, 193–5, 212, 214, 222
 'März' 216
 'Mailied' 23, 68, 152
 'Meine Ruh' ist hin' 224–5, 228–9
 'Mich ergreift, ich weiß nicht wie' 232
 'Mit einem gemalten Band' 45, 96
 'Neue Liebe, neues Leben' 96–7
 'Nur wer die Sehnsucht kennt' 214, 220
 'Prometheus' 117
 'Rastlose Liebe' 101
 'Schäfers Klage' 217
 'Wandrers Nachtlied, i' ('Über allen Gipfeln') 130–1, 149, 176, 193, 203n18, 221, 224, 233
 'Wandrers Nachtlied, ii' ('Der du von dem Himmel bist') 36, 101n1, 176, 188–9, 193, 216, 218, 222, 224
 'Wechsel' 216
 Werther 51–2, 82
 Westöstlicher Divan 183, 205, 216
 Wilhelm Meisters Lehrjahre xiv, 46, 117, 176, 192, 194
Göttinger Hainbund 37n1, 50–1, 80, 115
Göttinger Musenalmanach xi, 23, 28, 35, 68, 80, 100
Göttsching, R. 153
Goetz, H.* 218
Goldschmidt, A. von 175
Goldschmidt, Hugo 18
Gottsched, J.G. xi, 4, 81n16

Index

Gräfe, J.G. viii, 81n5, 88
Graener, P.* 219
Gräser, T.C.G. 98n11
Graun, C.H. 10, 14
Greith, C.* 219
Grell, A.E. 143
Grönland, P.* 219
Grosheim, G.C. 106
Groth, K. 175
Gruber, G.W. 87, 93, 97n6
Grünwald, J.J. 43, 47n4, 93
Grund, F.W. 106
Günther, J.C. 2
guitar-songs 231-3
Gumbert, F. 178

Hackel, J.C. 47n4, 93
Härtel, A. 151
Häßler, J.W. 12, 83
Häußler, E. 41, 84, 142n14, 203n22
Hagedorn, F. von xii, 11, 20, 35, 51
Halm, F. 175
Hammerstein, R. 37n4
Hartmann, L. 131, 141n7
Hasse, G. 163
Hauptmann, Moritz 154n8, 194-5
Hausius, C.G. 33
Hausmusik 150-3, 157, 160, 163, 173, 204, 214
Haydn, J. 42, 44, 60, 97n2
Heine, Heinrich xii, 105, 115, 118, 121, 124-5, 126n6, 128, 139, 154, 161, 167-8, 170, 173-4, 176-80, 184, 196-8, 216, 219-20, 225
  'Allnächtlich im Traume' 125
  'Am fernen Horizonte' 221
  'Am Kreuzweg wird begraben' 129, 180, 214, 225
  'Am leuchtenden Sommermorgen' 121, 125
  'An die blaue Himmelsdecke' 189
  'An die bretterne Schiffswand' 124
  'Auf Flügeln des Gesanges' 177
  Buch der Lieder 121, 168, 176
  'Da droben auf jenem Berge' 171n7
  'Das Fischermädchen' 224
  'Der deutsche Professor' 179
  'Der Doppelgänger' 117, 129, 180, 200
  Dichterliebe 120, 125, 198
  'Die alten, bösen Lieder' 120-1
  'Die Jahre kommen und gehen' 179
  'Die Rose, die Lilie . . .' 125
  'Du bist wie eine Blume' 177, 196-7
  'Ein Fichtenbaum steht einsam' 214, 217, 222
  'Ein Jüngling liebt ein Mädchen' 178
  'Es war ein alter König' 168
  'Gekommen ist der Maie' 171n7, 186-7
  'Hör ich das Liedchen klingen' 125, 220
  'Ich stand gelehnet an den Mast' 215
  'Ich steh auf des Berges Spitze' 171n7
  'Ich will meine Seele tauchen' 131, 177
  'Im Rhein, im heiligen Strome' 125
  'Im wunderschönen Monat Mai' 125, 185
  'Ja, du bist elend' 124
  'Lehn deine Wang' 197-8
  'Leise zieht durch mein Gemüt' 177
  'Lieb' Liebchen, leg's Händchen . . .' 133-4, 180, 227
  'Lorelei' 149, 170, 185, 215, 230
  'Mein Wagen rollet langsam' 203n25
  'Mit schwarzen Segeln' 124, 216, 229
  'Philister in Sonntagsröcklein' 179-80
  'Sie liebten sich beide' 180
  Tragödie 227
  'Und wüßten's die Blumen' 198
  'Weltlauf' 204
  'Wenn ich auf dem Lager liege' 212
  'Wenn ich in deine Augen seh' 177, 216
  'Wenn zwei voneinander scheiden' 171n7, 221
Helms, S. 171n1
Hemmleb, R. 153
Herbing, A.B.V. 11, 84

Index

Herder, J.G. 20–3, 29, 33, 43, 50, 78, 164–6
Hermes, J.T. 45–7, 52–3, 57–8, 67, 82, 86
Hertel, J.W. 12
Hertz, H. 155n14
Herzog, S. 142n14
Herzogenberg, H. von* 220
Hesse, J.H. 83, 85
Hessenberg, K. 207
Hetsch, L. 203n20
Heubner, K. 142n14
Heuchemer, J. 152
Hille, C.F. 175
Hiller, Ferdinand* 220
Hiller, J.A. 31, 63, 79, 225
Hillmer, G.F. 53
Himmel, F.H. 141n6
Hinrichs, F.* 221
Hitzelberg, M.J. 54
Hobein, J.F.* 221
Hölderlin, J.C.F. 151, 174, 202n3, 205
Hölty, L.C.H. xiv, 23–4, 32, 37, 44, 50–1, 62, 69, 90, 174
Hoffmann, E.T.A. 119, 121
Hoffmann, H.A.* 221
Hofmann, L. 47n4
Hofmeister, A. 210
Holländer, A. 185, 201
Holstein, F. von 192
Holzer, J. 43, 47n4, 93
Horace 11, 51
Hortschansky, K. 125n4
'Hoven, J.' *see* Püttlingen
Huber, J.* 221
Hübner, O.R. 153
Hummel, Ferdinand 142n14
Hummel, J.B. 98n9
Hurka, F.F. 97n5
Hutchings, A. xiii

Ivey, D.W. 127n26

Jäger, Daniel 45–7
Jansen, G.* 222
Jensen, Adolf 141n12, 197–8
Jensen, W.G.M. 90
Joseph II (of Austria) 46
Just, K.J. 126n20

Kahn, R.* 222
Kalbeck, M. 171n1
Kallenbach, G.E.C. 31

Kauffmann, E.F.* 222
Kayser, P.C. 101n1
Keller, G. (Swiss author) 104, 153, 174, 230
Keller, J.G. (composer) 32
Kempe, F. 149
Kienzl, W. 141n13
Kilpinen, Y. 206
Kindscher, L. 144
Kinkel, J. 145, 149
Kirchner, Th. 142n16, 144
Kirnberger, J.P. 10, 22, 70, 100–1
Kirsten, F.* 234
Kistler, C. 151
Kittl, J.F. 174
Klein, B. 187, 223–4
Klenau, P. von 204
Klitsch, E. 148
Klopstock, F.G. xii, 35, 38, 42, 43–4, 50–1, 60, 75–6, 102n1, 115, 174, 202n2, 209n7, 217
Knab, A. 207
Kneisel, J.H. 171n11
Konzertlied 133, 138–40, 141n12
Kosegarten, L.T. 77, 115
Koßmaly, C. 144
Kraus, Joseph 53
Krause, C.G. viii, 3, 8, 11, 66–7, 71–2, 94
Krazeisen, C. 175
Krebs, J.L. 35–6
Krenek, E. 114, 175, 205, 207, 209n7
Kreutzer, C. xiii–xiv, 105, 113, 126n17
Kriegel, C.F.W. 102n1
Kuntzen, A.C. 10
Kunzen, F.L.A. 29, 32, 98n9, 100, 211

Lammers, J. 159, 162
Landau, A. xiii
Lang, E.J.B. 85
Lange, O.H. 157–8
Lavater, J.C. 38
Lecerf, J.A.* 223
Leibniz, G.W. 11
Leitner, K.G. von 115, 117
Lemacher, H. 153
Lenau, N. 123, 128, 134, 150, 174, 220–2, 230
Lenz, Leopold 140
Lessing, G.E. 74
Leyding, J.D. xi

243

Index

Lieder, mit neuen Melodien 16
Liederspiel 126n17
Lieder Tempel 106, 212
Liedparodie 2–3
Lind, Jenny 141n13
Lindner, A. 202n5
Liszt, Franz 122, 139, 142n14 and 16, 145, 148, 185, 192, 208, 213–14
Loewe, Carl 47n3, 96, 117–18, 132, 136, 139, 142n14, 155n14, 184, 199–200, 203n16, 227
Löwen, J.F. 5
Lorenz, O. 154n3, 203n8
Louis, R. 175–6, 202n5
Lührss, C. 142n16, 224

Machts, C. 163
Mahler, G. 122, 153, 163–4, 174–5
Mann, Thomas 25, 110
Marpurg, F.W. 5, 10–11, 14, 22, 43, 59n7, 81n6,11 and 15, 100–1, 102n1
Marschner, H.A. (Heinrich) 105–6
Mathieux, *see* Kinkel, J.
Mattheson, J. 6–7, 57, 58n2, 67
Matthison, F. von 101
Mayrhofer, J. 101
Mendelssohn-Bartholdy, F. 106, 122, 139, 152, 160, 164, 177, 212
Methfessel, A. 106
Metz, K. 154n10
Metzner, L. 209n6
Meyer, C.F. 174
Mikuli, C. 188
Miller, J.M. 50–1, 90
Mizler, L. 7, 18n7
Möbius, P. 151
Mörike, E. xii, xiv, 153, 168–70, 173–4, 176, 180–2, 189–92, 195, 205, 209n6, 220–2, 230
  'Auf einer Wanderung' 138
  'Das verlassene Mägdlein' xiv, 169, 181, 189–90, 203n20, 217–18, 220, 226
  'Denk es, o Seele!' 189–91, 216
  'Die Geister am Mummelsee' 129, 181
  'Ein Stündlein wohl vor Tag' 123, 169–70, 189–91, 203n20, 216
  'Frage und Antwort' 181–2, 192
  'In der Frühe' 182

  'Nixe Binsefuß' 136
  'Seufzer' 182
  'Um Mitternacht' 220
moral weeklies 4–5, 12, 39, 57
Morgenstern, C. 204, 206, 209n4, 219
Morik, W. 171
Moritz, C.T.* 224–5
Moses, J.G. 83
Mottl, F.* 225
Mozart, W.A. xiii, 41–2, 44–7, 60, 62, 96, 212
Muck, F. 36
Müller, Wilhelm 116, 166–7, 175, 215–16
  Die schöne Müllerin 110, 112–13, 115–16, 216–17, 229, 231
  Winterreise 109–11, 112–13, 116, 163, 196, 200, 231
Müller-Blattau, J. 155n15
Müthel, J.G. 8, 69, 91
Musikalische Gartenlaube 106, 212
Musikalisches Handbuch 5–6
Musikalisches Wochenblatt 148
Musikalisch-wöchentliche Belustigungen 39

Nägeli, H.G. 35, 41–2, 141n10, 145
Nauert, G.E. 97n5
Naumann, J.G. 29, 62
Neefe, C.G. 65n4, 83, 97n4, 100, 225
Nessler, V.E.* 225
Neubauer, F.C. 47n3, 96, 97n3
Neue Musik-Zeitung 150
Neue Zeitschrift für Musik ix, 141n9, 145, 147–8, 154n3 and 6, 155n12, 177
Nevin, E.* 225
Nicolai, F. 157
Niederrheinische Musik-Zeitung ix, 143–4, 146, 154n5 and 7, 203n12
Nietzsche, F. 153, 174
Niggli, F.* 225
Novalis 117, 187

Orpheon 106, 212
Ossian 37n1, 95
Otto, W. 147
Overbeck, C.A. 77

'P., C.J.' 86
Paradis, M.T. 43, 47n4, 79

Index

Paulsen, C.F.F. 68
Peake, L.E. 126n17
Pepping, E. 153, 207
Perfall, K.* 226
Pfeffel, G.K. 31
Pfitzner, H. 122, 207, 229
Pilz, K.P.E.* 226
Platen, A. von 174
   'Der Pilgrim vor St Just' 227
Pohl, Richard 154n11
Pohl, W. 47n4, 97n2 and 4
Porter, E.G. 109
Preu, F. 37n8, 97n3
Preuß, C. 75-6, 78
Püttlingen, J.V. von 105, 178-9, 196
Purcell, H. xii

Quantz, J.J. 7-10, 34, 60
Queck, J.C. 98n17

Ramler, C.W. viii, 11, 18n9, 66, 72, 79, 94
Redlich, H. 209n5
Reger, M. 122, 129, 140, 163, 175, 193, 204
Reichardt, J.F. viii, xi, xiii, 9, 18n10, 29, 37n12, 40, 44, 47n3, 54, 60, 62, 69, 83-4, 98n8 and 9, 100-1, 102n1, 106, 151-2, 157, 192, 211, 225
Reichardt, L.* 226
Reinecke, C.* 226
Reissiger, C.G. 178
Reiter, Josef* 227
Reitzenstein, J.H. von 51-2
Rellstab, L. 154n1
Répertoire international des sources musicales (RISM) 210
Rheineck, C. 33, 61, 93
Richter, Jean Paul 120
Riehl, W.H. 150-1, 155n16, 164, 175
Ries, Franz* 227
Rilke, R.M. 209n2
Ritter, Alex 175
Rochlitz, F. 145
Romberg, A. 32, 36, 98n19
Rosenbaum, C.E. 16
Roth, W.A.T. 59n7, 91
Rousseau, J.-J. 7, 21
Rubinstein, Anton xiv
Rückert, F. 121, 153, 174
Ruprecht, M. 43, 47n4

Rust, F.W. 84, 98n9, 225

Sahr, H. von* 227
Salis, J.G. von (Salis-Seewis, J.G. von) 67, 90, 202n1, 232
Salmen, W. 125n2
Sammons, J.L. 176
Scharwenka, X. 105
Scheibe, J.A. 7, 70, 89-90
Schellenberg, E.L. 155n17
Scherzer, O. 191
Schiller, F. von 95-6, 98n8, 106, 115, 117, 151, 174, 213, 225, 233
Schilling, G. 147
Schlechta, F.X. von 115, 117
Schleinitz, A. von 203n18
Schmidlin, J. 38-40
Schmügel, J.G. 74-5, 86-7
Schnell, H. 202n2
Schnyder von Wartensee, X.* 228
Schoeck, O. 207, 209n4
Schönberg, A. 126n12, 204
Scholz, B. 152
Scholze, J.S. *see* 'Sperontes'
Schröter, C. 33
Schubart, C.F.D. 22, 26, 29-31, 85, 98n11
Schubert, F. xiii, 5, 32, 36, 47n3, 71-2, 78, 81n13, 91, 94, 98n12, 100-1, 103-4, 106-11, 112-18, 120, 123, 129-33, 136, 138-40, 141n2, 146, 149, 151-2, 174-5, 180, 183-4, 187, 192-3, 195, 200-1, 212-13, 221, 231
Schuberth, J. xiv
Schulz, J.A.P. xiii, 1, 20, 22-7, 28-32, 37n1 and 12, 40-2, 47n3, 49, 71, 73-4, 79, 100-1, 102n1, 133, 151-2, 161, 163, 186, 219, 221, 224
Schumann, Clara 154
Schumann, Robert xiii, 5, 103-6, 117-23, 125, 128, 130-5, 139, 144-5, 151, 154n12, 175, 178, 180, 183, 187, 196-8, 200-1, 203n25
Schwab, H.W. 37n10, 141n13, 142n15
Schwalm, R. 186-7
Seckendorff, S. von* 228
Seidel, F.L. 115
'sensibility' *see Empfindsamkeit*
Serauky, W. 18

245

Index

Shakespeare, W. 108, 115, 153
   Hamlet 204
Siebmann, F. 130-1, 148
Siering, M. 203n18
Silcher, F. 147, 185
Singspiel viii, 5, 42, 140
song-cycle 112-14, 231
Spectator 4, 57
Speidel, W. 190-1
'Sperontes' xi, 2-3, 9, 14-15
Spitta, P. 114, 126n18
Spohr, L.* 229
Stade, W. 158, 171n3
Stange, M. 141n6, 229
Staudigl, J. 140, 141n13
Steffan, J.A. 42-4
Stein, Jack 194
Stier, A. 204
Stifter, A. 104
Stockhausen, Julius 141n13
Stolberg, F.L. von xi, 23-5, 28, 30,
   41-2, 44, 50-1, 73, 86
Stoljar, M.M. 141n1, 142n15
Stoppe, D. 55
Storm, Th. 104, 170, 174, 205,
   209n5
Strauss, Richard 122, 129, 140,
   150, 163, 193, 203n15 and 25
Streben, E. 161-2
Sturm, C.C. 34, 50, 73
Sturm und Drang 22, 50

Tag, C.G. 37n8, 98n9
Tatler 4, 57
Taubert, W. 106, 134, 164
Telemann, G.P. xiii, 14-15, 35-6,
   55, 60, 70
Teumer, C.F. 89
Thomas, Richard Hinton 18
Thonus, P.J. von 98n11
Tiehsen, O. 178
Tiessen, H. 204
Tomasek, W.J. xii, 142n16, 211
Tovey, D. 111, 126n12
Truhn, F.H. 126n17
Tschulik, N. 43
Türck, D.G. 74, 84, 90, 93

Uhland, L. 113, 136, 152, 166,
   218, 222, 231
Urspruch, A. 142n14, 202n2
Uz, J.P. 37n12

Veit, W.H. 198
Vetter, W. 18
Volkmann, R. 141n6
Voß, J.H. xii, 23-4, 26, 30, 32,
   44, 50, 101, 174

Wagner, Richard 148, 150, 208
Walder, J.J. 41, 216
Walter, Gustav 141n13
Walther von der Vogelweide 153,
   192, 225
Warneke, G.H. 36
Weber, C.M. von 161, 233
Webern, A. von 205-6, 209n2
Weinmann, A. 211
Weis, F.W. xi, 100, 102n1 and 2
Weisinger, C.F. 57
Weiß, F.X. 97n4
Weiße, C.F. 48n11, 91, 97n2
Werner, H. 106
Whistling, C.F. 210
Widemann, P. 134
Wiedebein, J.M. 75, 98n17
Wieland, C.M. xi, 66-7, 202n2
Winterberger, A. 142n14
Wiora, W. 55
Witthauer, J.G. 32
Wöhler, G.* 230
Wöß, J. *see Das moderne Lied*
Wolf, Hugo xiii, 104, 122, 129,
   135-6, 138-9, 150, 175-6,
   180-2, 189-92, 194-5, 199,
   201, 207
Wolff, C.M. 92, 97n5
Wolff, E.J. 204
Wolfrum, P. 188

Young, Edward (*Night Thoughts*) 82

Zachariae, J.F.W. von 16-17, 66
Zeitung für die elegante Welt 126n5
Zelter, C.F. viii, xiii, 44, 60-1,
   100-1, 102n1, 106, 151-2, 211,
   225
Zenger, M. 203n20
Zernial, H.* 231
Zuccalmaglio, A.W.F. von 157,
   159, 171n5
Zumsteeg, J.R. xiii, 41, 44, 60, 71,
   77-8, 83, 91, 94-6, 100-1,
   102n1, 106-7, 115, 117-18,
   211, 225, 232

For Product Safety Concerns and Information please contact our EU
representative GPSR@taylorandfrancis.com
Taylor & Francis Verlag GmbH, Kaufingerstraße 24, 80331 München, Germany

www.ingramcontent.com/pod-product-compliance
Lightning Source LLC
Chambersburg PA
CBHW071820300426
44116CB00009B/1376